Illicit Drugs

Illicit drugs and their use are a dominant concern of politicians, policy-makers and the general public. As such, this second edition of the popular *Illicit Drugs: use and control* provides a timely, up-to-date discussion of the key issues raised in the first edition, whilst also providing new chapters that address:

- class, gender and race;
- the geo-politics of illicit drug production and distribution;
- Britain's drug use within a global context.

Drawing information from wide-ranging sources, Adrian Barton illuminates the complex nature and broad impact illicit drug use carries in its wake and provides an overview of the contemporary state of the drug 'scene'.

This accessible book, with its inclusion of new pedagogical features, will be essential reading for students and researchers working in the area of drugs and society.

Adrian Barton is Associate Professor of Criminal Justice at Plymouth Law School, University of Plymouth. His research focuses on illicit drug use, child abuse and child protection, and organisational behaviour, and his recent publications include *Trust in New Labour* (Edward Mellen Press, 2009), *Illicit Drugs: Use and Control*, First Edition (Routledge, 2003), and *Managing Fragmentation* (Ashgate, 2002).

Illicit Drugs

Use and control

Second edition

Adrian Barton

Routledge

Taylor & Francis Group

LONDON AND NEW YORK

First published 2011
by Routledge
2 Park Square, Milton Park, Abingdon, Oxon, OX14 4RN

Simultaneously published in the USA and Canada
by Routledge
711 Third Avenue, New York, NY 10017

Routledge is an imprint of the Taylor & Francis Group, an informa business

British Library Cataloguing-in-Publication Data
A catalogue record for this book is available from the British Library

Library of Congress Cataloging in Publication Data
Barton, Adrian.
Illicit drugs : use and control / by Adrian Barton. -- 2nd ed.
p. cm.
1. Drug abuse- -Great Britain. 2. Drug traffic- -Great Britain. 3. Drug
control- -Great Britain. I. Title.
[DNLM: 1. Street Drugs- -Great Britain. 2. Substance-Related Disorders- -Great
Britain. 3. Drug and Narcotic Control- -Great Britain. 4. Public Policy- -Great
Britain.]
HV5840.G7B34 2011
362.290941- -dc22
2010043373

ISBN13: 978-0-415-49233-1 (hbk)
ISBN13: 978-0-415-49237-9 (pbk)
ISBN13: 978-0-203-87991-7 (ebk)

Typeset in Garamond
by Integra Software Services Pvt. Ltd, Pondicherry, India

Printed and bound in Great Britain by
CPI Antony Rowe, Chippenham, Wiltshire

Contents

Preface and acknowledgements

It has been about seven years since the publication of the first edition of this work. In that time we have seen some change and some continuity in the field of illicit drug policy and attempts to control illicit drug use and supply: the content of the work reflects this – some chapters remain broadly the same whilst others are new in order to update and reflect current thinking in the area.

Illicit drug 'problems' fall into a number of discrete but connected areas. For example, organisationally, is illicit drug use a medical or law and order problem? Philosophically, how can we prohibit some mind-altering substances yet openly promote others, and even use them as an integral part of some Christian ceremonies? Strategically, should we seek to stop illicit drugs at the point of production, point of entry into the country, at the point of distribution or the point of consumption? Economically, are we prepared to subsidise replacement crops in developing nations in order to prevent production of opium or coca? Educationally, do we aim for zero use or promote a harm minimisation approach? Tactically, do we fight a 'war on drugs' or negotiate an 'honourable peace'? So it goes on.

What we are dealing with is a subject area that encompasses a range of academic disciplines and thus provides myriad opportunities to analyse quite specific aspects of the illicit drug scene. For instance, illicit drugs can, and have, been examined using the disciplines of history, sociology, criminology, economics, medicine, politics and geo-politics, philosophy, and policy studies. There are also elements of geography and anthropology evident in some works. It is even possible to use literary criticism to analyse illicit drug use! The result can be a bewildering amalgam of facts and directions, each with an important part to play, but somewhat confusing when viewed as separate entities.

The aim of this book remains the same as its predecessor; that is, draw together some of those disparate threads and provide the reader with a broad overview of the history, development and contemporary state of the British 'drug scene'. Inevitably, such an approach to a subject area occasionally sacrifices detail at the expense of inclusion. The contention here is that specific detail surrounding, say, the link between drugs and crime can be found in specialist publications. It is the aim of this book to locate specific aspects of illicit drug use, such as drugs and crime, within a broad framework of inter-related events and circumstances, allowing the reader to gauge the complexities involved in defining and solving the 'drug problem'.

The remainder of this book will be divided into three separate but inter-related areas. The first section is concerned with introducing and con-textualising drug misuse and policy responses in the UK. This includes a historical review of drug misuse; the development of what South (1997) calls the 'British System' for dealing with drug misuse; an examination of the nature and extent of drug misuse within contemporary Britain, concentrating on the limitations of measurement tools; and a brief introduction to legal and policy responses to drug misuse.

The second section traces the 'life' of some of the illicit drugs available in Britain, moving from cultivation and synthesis, through market based exchanges, the sources and problems of funding drug markets create for users and the state, to a review of the consequences of drug misuse. There is a new chapter in this section that examines drug use in terms of race, gender and class, and the manner in which the media reports differential usage.

The third section begins with an examination of the current polices adop-ted by Britain in attempting to combat drug misuse. It then expands this debate by asking questions of the current approach and comparing the development of policies in Britain with those adopted elsewhere, specifically the Netherlands and New Zealand. Here, the link between socio-economic, cultural and political systems and drug control strategies are explored. This section also sees the inclusion of two new chapters, one of which examines the results of the changes in geo-politics: as the nature of global conflict has changed, illicit drug production and smuggling have become entwined with terrorism.

The overall aim of the book is to draw together current information on illicit drug use, thus providing readers with a broad overview of the history, development and contemporary state of the British drug 'scene', and locate this in a global context. This is important, not least because the diversity of interest in illicit drugs creates a situation where students often have to draw from a number of sources – sociological, criminological, economic, policy studies, geographical, medical and, increasingly, from international relations – in order to become aware of the complex nature and wide-ranging impact illicit drug misuse carries in its wake.

Looking at each chapter in detail, Chapter 1 provides a historical overview of drug misuse in Britain. It encourages the reader to view drug misuse through a variety of lenses in order to better understand the social, political and economic impact on the creation of the 'drug problem'. It begins by outlining the nature of drug use prior to the 1800s and notes that drugs were used for a variety of reasons, including 'hedonistic' or what we would now term 'recreational' purposes. It then moves into the post 1800s and charts the move from Britain's determination to defend the opium trade, and opiate based products being freely available, to the moral and medical driven social construction of the drug problem during the latter part of the nineteenth century and the early part of the twentieth century. It moves the reader across time to review the findings of the Rolleston Committee (1926) and the impact that body had on the creation of the British system, especially the division of labour between the medical and criminal justice model. It then notes the period of relative inactivity that characterised the inter-war period and the 1950s.

The latter part of the chapter examines the growth and changing nature of drug misuse that has occurred since the 1960s, making links with the growth of youth culture, improved communication routes, and changing public attitudes. It also reviews the state's response to these rapid and wide-ranging changes, and the fluctuations between increased legislation, abstinence policies and the growth in harm reduction.

Chapter 2 builds on the conclusion of the previous chapter, namely the apparent rise in the misuse of illicit drugs. It takes as its core the problems we have in measuring drug misuse. It compares and contrasts two types of measurement: official statistics compiled by treatment providers and the criminal justice system, with self-report data compiled by non-practice organisations and academics. It then reviews the methodological weaknesses of each approach, and highlights the difficulties in measuring a hidden population such as drug users. The chapter concludes by employing the available data to draw a picture of contemporary drug misuse in Britain and to locate it within an international context. It notes the division between heavy-end users who are most likely to come to the attention of the state system, and the low risk 'recreational' users who represent the majority of drug misusers within Britain.

Chapter 3 begins to explore the official responses to drug misuse in Britain. It examines the two parts of the British system, the medico-socio treatment model and the criminal justice based punishment model. It begins by arguing that policing in the context of drug misusers is based around notions of control. This control can be through the medical or criminal justice systems. It reviews the content of the Misuse of Drugs Act 1971 and then moves toward an outline of the legal position in relation to various aspects of the misuse of illicit drugs. The second part of the chapter looks at the manner in which the medical profession polices drug misusers through treatment regimes and prescription policies. The chapter concludes with a discussion on the nature of drug misuse, as outlined in the previous chapter, and the dual nature of the British system's approach to policing the same problem.

Chapter 4 is a new chapter that begins by outlining the normalisation thesis. Following the manner in which illicit drug use is spread somewhat unevenly across society, it asks questions about the possible reasons for this. From there, it offers a more in-depth look at the use of illicit drugs in terms of gender, social class and race and ethnicity in order to explore the effects of social and cultural pressures on different social groups. The chapter concludes with an examination of the manner in which the media reports on illicit drug use in relation to gender, class and race and will argue that the media's 'horror-distortion' techniques often provide a false impression regarding the extent and nature of drug use.

Chapter 5 marks a watershed in the work. Up to this point drug misuse has been discussed in a somewhat narrow and parochial manner with only a few references to the international dimensions of illicit drug use. The purpose of this chapter is to alert students to the fact that drug misuse in Britain is, in fact, part of a much wider global phenomenon. This is the starting point for the chapter. Following this, the chapter provides a geographical breakdown of the main drug-growing nations and their outputs. The chapter then focuses on the impact the growth and production of drugs has for the economies of some of the drug-producing nations. It will focus on Afghanistan in parti-cular. Following this, the chapter moves on to explore the production of synthetic drugs in Europe, noting that the bulk of these types of drugs are either produced in Britain, or are imported from very near neighbours. The chapter concludes with a discussion of the problems posed for Western nations by the economic aspect of drug production in developing nations.

Chapter 6 is another new chapter that explores in detail the geo-politics of illicit drug production and distribution. It begins by examining the US led 'war on drugs' in central America, the manner in which it was partly informed by concerns about the growth of communism in the region and the way in which this has impacted on the politics and crime of the Andean region. From there, it moves to discuss developments in Afghanistan, the effect on opium production of the Afghan war and the links between opium production, distribution and global terrorism. It concludes by arguing that the size of the global drug industry, when taken in tandem with the eco-nomic importance of drug production to most producing nations, means that in some cases, organised crime and organised politics merge, which has major implications for geo-politics.

Chapter 7 builds upon the foundation laid above. It suggests that given the economic impact of drug production it is perhaps necessary to view illicit drugs as tradable commodities over and above all else. To support this view, the chapter begins by reviewing some basic economic theory concerning the relationship between supply and demand and their combined effect on prices. It moves away from economic theory and outlines the nature of the drug market in Britain, identifying key 'players' and their roles in each stage of the retailing of illicit drugs. The chapter concludes with a review of the applica-tion of economic theory as a potential controlling mechanism for dealing with drug misuse.

Chapter 8 turns its attention towards the problems drug misuse poses for the user and society, in terms of paying for the goods and of health and social welfare related costs. The chapter begins with a new section that synthesises our current knowledge and response to the crime/drug links. It then produces a typology of drug criminals and identifies and discusses three distinct, but not mutually exclusive, groups. It then broadens the definition of 'cost' and asks the reader to view costs, not solely in economic terms but also in terms of health and social welfare. Moreover, the chapter suggests that 'cost' in this context can be both individual and societal, and concludes by discussing and outlining both aspects of cost.

Chapter 9 begins with a review of anti-drug polices in the 1980s, noting the abstinence messages of this period and the impact of the US drug policy on British policy-makers. It comments that official policy was removed from street level interventions. The chapter then moves to locate developments in drug policy with wider developments elsewhere in social policy, namely the growth of the partnership approach. This is used to explain the growth in the concept of harm reduction, and comment is made on the transition of harm reduction being based around individual need to its more recent application, which encompasses individual and societal harm.

The chapter then reviews key legislative and policy developments since 1990, in particular *Tackling Drugs Together* (1995) and *Tackling Drugs to Build a Better Britain* (1998) and the 2002 updated drug strategy. It concludes with a discussion of the merging of the medical and criminal justice wings of the British system, and the impact this is having on illicit drug use in Britain.

Chapter 10 is another new chapter that compares Britain's drug policy with that of two other developed nations. It begins by outlining the usefulness of comparative work but also seeks to alert students of the need to consider a number of socio-cultural, political and economic factors when making comparisons. It looks at the Netherlands as the Netherlands has a well known policy of tolerance, but again the socio-cultural influence is noted as a key to the Dutch approach. It then looks at New Zealand's approach to illicit drugs. The work concludes by offering a review of the impact the British state and society has had on our own approach to drug misuse.

Just before moving on to the first substantive part of the book it is important to clarify one point. Throughout the book, the terms 'drug', 'illicit drug' and 'substance' will be used interchangeably, although the preferred option is 'illicit drug'. These terms relate to all substances covered under the 1971 Misuse of Drugs Act and nothing else, except where specifically stated. The work does not, nor is it meant to, cover licit substances used by persons under the legal age of consumption, neither does it refer to the misuse of substances such as aerosols, lighter fluid, correction fluids and the like. Equally it does not refer to the misuse, either through zealous or uncontrolled prescription, or misappropriation, of prescription drugs. This is not to say that I do not recognise the potential harm these substance hold, it is simply that this book takes as its focus drugs that are outlawed for all and sundry.

Finally, before commencing with the main part of this work, it is important to mention that although I am the sole author of this book and take full responsibility for its content, work such as this always involves other people. That being the case there is a number of people that need to be mentioned and thanked. First, the editorial staff at Routledge have shown incredible patience in waiting for the final version of this book and I am grateful for that. Second, Nick Johns, my colleague at the University of Plymouth, has always been on hand to offer advice about any queries I may have had and has been a great support for me. Finally, although they were probably unaware of it at the time, I would like to thank those students who have sat through my drug course in the past four years, as they have allowed me the space and time to try out some of the new material featured in this book. Their responses have to a large extent shaped what you are about to read and I am grateful for their unknowing but important contribution.

1   British society and illicit drug use

Historical perspectives

Introduction

It is only relatively recently that we have come to conceive of 'drugs' as either licit or illicit and 'good' or 'bad'. For example, paracetamol can and does kill humans if too much is ingested, but it is a legal, freely available and socially sanctioned drug that is seen as 'good' inasmuch that it acts as a pain relief. Conversely, opium, which historically has been used as an analgesic in much the same way as paracetamol is today, is proscribed and those who do use opium for 'recreational' purposes are often stigmatised and criminalised, making opium a 'bad' drug. The purpose of this chapter is to examine how we have arrived at this situation. It will begin by offering a very selective overview of drug use from pre-history up to the beginnings of the 1800s. From there it will provide a more detailed look at the manner in which drugs were used, supplied and controlled from around 1800 up until the end of the 1970s. Drug use and control since the 1970s will be integral to much of the content of subsequent chapters.

A further organising principle, which will run throughout the whole of this chapter, is the use of a basic typology to ascertain the nature of drug control throughout history. Holloway (1995: 77) provides a useful analytical tool where he states that 'three distinct models of regulation can be constructed (around drug control): consumer sovereignty, occupational control and bureaucratic legislation'. However, the same author goes on to note that this typology is a 'rough and ready' sorting device. Nevertheless, the above typology enables us to make some sense of the growth of the control of substances from pre-history to the present day, but it needs some words of explanation.

In this work, consumer sovereignty will be taken to mean unfettered access to all manner of substances, with the only barriers to use being either the inability to pay for the substance or the inability to harvest and synthesise the plant. Thus, in pre-history for example, individuals were free to collect and use plant-based substances at will, free from any form of physical or moral control, making access to and use and trade of substances entirely at the discretion of the consumer. Occupational control can be taken to mean the control of the access, sale and use of substances by trades or professional groups, such as the case of the guild system in the Middle Ages. Here, the guilds used the need to be a guild member to limit the extent of trade. Bureaucratic control relates to control exercised over the use, sale and access to drugs by the local or central state and would most closely fit today's approach to the control of substances.

This opening section looks briefly and selectively at drug use from pre-historic times up until the start of the 1800s. For brevity's sake I have divided this opening section into three eras: pre-history, Greco-Roman societies and the Middle Ages. The purpose of this historical journey is not to give a definitive historical guide to drug use and control, rather to allow students to realise that alongside many other aspects of social life, the origins of the manner in which we both use and control substances can be found in our history. It is also useful as it allows us to recognise early on in the book that the manner in which societies have thought about, used and controlled what we now see as 'drugs' is fluid and is as much dependent on social mores as it is on the pharmacological effects of substances.

Drug use and control: pre-history

Due to a lack of a written language no one can say exactly when people started to use plants for purposes other than to eat and sustain life, just as in the same way no one can be sure about what, if any, restrictions were placed on the use of these substances. However, based on the work of both archaeology and anthropology there is every reason to believe that our pre-historic ancestors would recognise the properties and the uses of plants that that we now understand to be 'drugs': that is they would understand that a 'drug' can be defined as a substance that instead of being assimilated by the body has the ability, often when taken in very small amounts compared to other substances, to make significant organic and/or mood changes. Evidence supplied by both archaeologists and anthropologists suggests that our ancient ancestors understood this and used state-altering substances in their everyday life for both sacred and profane reasons. Initially, these substances were plant-based and would have been gathered alongside other herbs and plants.

Thus, we can speculate that via a process of trial and error Neolithic hunter gatherer tribes began to understand that certain plants, taken either alone or in tandem with others, could heal their bodies. We can equally speculate that they realised plants could also alter their consciousness and began to be used for either relaxation or spiritual purposes. Based on this, we can begin our journey into the history of drug use with a dilemma that still haunts us today: plurality of use. In short, even in pre-history some substances were used for medicinal purposes whilst some substances were used to alter consciousness for religious or recreational ends. How, when and by whom those mind and body altering substances were used was as much a problem historically as it is today.

What types of drugs were hunter gathers and emergent societies using? According to Escohotado (1999: 6–11), our ancestors would be familiar with many of the plant-based substances that are now outlawed. For example, there is reference to poppy heads in Sumerian texts from the BCE third millennium. Egyptian hieroglyphs make mention of the juice extracted from poppy heads – opium – and provide tips on the healing properties of opium, including the use of opium to prevent babies from screaming too loudly. Homer, in *Odyssey*, refers to opium, again noting its analgesic properties. Most of the poppies that were used in this period were grown in Greece, the South of Spain and North Africa. Given the degree of trade between early Phoenician traders and part of South West England from 1200 to 800 BCE it is probable that poppies or opium found their way to parts of England as early as 1200 BCE.

Archaeological evidence suggests hemp, and by association, cannabis, was cultivated in China from around 4000 BCE. Hemp production and use in India can be traced back to at least the ninth century BCE, where there is evidence it was used to treat fevers and dysentery. Hemp production and use was also entrenched in Western Europe, evidenced by examples of pipes found from the Celtic era, indicating that the Celts were aware of its use as a drug. Similarly, plant-based hallucinogens such as henbane and belladonna have a long history of use in Western Europe and have established associations with religious festivals, sorcery and witchcraft.

It is clear then that our early ancestors had a sophisticated and coherent working knowledge concerning the properties and effects of certain substances and were also aware of a plurality of use. The next key question is if and how access to these plant-based drugs was controlled and managed. Because of a lack of written history it is difficult to be certain about control of use in prehistoric societies. However, anthropologists working in remote and relatively unexplored regions of the globe note that use of drugs for mind-altering events, such as inducing visions, are often controlled by shaman and we can suppose that the same degree of control existed in some prehistoric societies, especially as they developed over time (Parry 2008).

Therefore we can speculate that in certain instances the use and trade of plant-based substances resembled the consumer sovereignty model, as prehistoric people would be free to collect and use plants at their will. Evidence from anthropology (Parry 2008) does however point to a state of affairs where shamen or similar religious leaders could control the timing of access to certain mind-altering substances when used in sacred rituals.

Drug use and control: Greco-Roman societies

Once a written language exists we are able to be more precise about social customs and the manner in which they were controlled, including substance use. By examining evidence left by two of the three most well known ancient civilizations, the Greeks and Romans, we begin to see that the use of substances for medicinal, recreational and religious purposes was common-place throughout every layer of those societies. What is equally instructive is the degree and sophistication of Greco-Roman knowledge about the use substances. Scarborough (1995: 4) notes that 'Greco-Roman medicine and pharmacology incorporated a very succinct knowledge and command of the dangers and benefits in the use of the opium poppy, and actions of drugs were widely understood'. The same author goes on to note that there appeared to be a sophisticated and nuanced use system in place in ancient Greco-Roman society, which included a widespread practice of assisted suicide using opium.

For example, according to the works of Dioscorides (CE 70), there were at least two types of opium available: that which was prescribed and dispensed by the physician-pharmacist or the numerous druggists that flourished in both societies, and that which could be cultivated at home. Scarborough (1995: 7) notes that the garden variety would have been less potent and used for ' ... bread and as a plant with a nourishing oil, as well as some limited use as a narcotic'. In this way, it would appear that families in the Greco-Roman period used opium in the same way we use medicines such as paracetemol. However, just as in contemporary society it would appear that advice and guidance from those with knowledge of illness and drugs was sought for the more serious complaints again, it would appear that opium was a staple drug of the physicians. Indeed, opium use was so widespread in Roman society that its price was fixed by the state.

Moreover, it would appear that there was little concern about what we would now refer to as addiction: Escohotado (1999: 20) notes there is no Latin phrase for 'opium addict' but there were at least six that refer to alcohol addiction. Thus, we could argue that in Greco-Roman society there existed a hybrid of control that incorporated the consumer sovereignty model that was inherited from pre-historic society, working in tandem with the beginnings of an occupational control model emanating from the emerging druggist trade.

However, the widespread approval of substance use – the consumer sovereignty model – is dependent on a social and cultural acceptance of self-medication and diagnosis, as well as a belief system that does not stigmatise or condemn inebriation, as well as a separation of law and morality. All of these flourished in Greek society and in Roman society during its pre-Christian era, but as Escohotado (1999: 24) notes, the conditions that supported the consumer sovereignty model 'underwent a collapse when the Roman Empire became Christianised (*sic*)'. Escohotado (1999) argues that whilst early Christian groups such as the Coptic sect were often involved in heavy drinking and feasting as part of the Eucharistic celebrations, later branches of the religion condemned all forms of inebriation including heavy drinking and the use of plant-based substances; as a result many Christians became abstemious.

Over a short period of time, feasting associated with the Eucharist became largely symbolic with the use of bread and wine restricted to the priest. Equally, the use of plant-based substances as an aid in religious ceremonies became the subject of moral condemnation and curbed the influence of priests from outside the Christian religion. As well as restricting the use of opium for religious and recreational purposes, the Christian religion attacked and proscribed one of its key historical uses – as a method of suicide – on religious grounds. Under the Christian doctrine suicide is a mortal sin and thus the subject of moral, social and religious sanction, owing to the belief that one's life belongs to God and only God can choose to end life.

Another important change was the fact that prior to the establishment of Christianity various religions and sects had existed side by side. However, very soon all non-Christian forms of worship and belief were seen as associations with 'false prophets' and in some cases associations with the devil, and any accompanying form of inebriation was seen as morally lax. Interestingly, in the Greco-Roman world, law and morality had been kept separate. Thus, whereas prior to the rise of Christianity there had been tolerance of inebriation for religious and relaxation purposes, the world, post-Christian expansion, became a different place.

There are numerous examples of recourse to law and prohibition to support this. For example, in around CE 388 the Roman Emperor Valentinian decreed the death penalty for participation in 'nocturnal ceremonies'; in CE 391 Bishop Theophilus incited the burning of the library in Alexandria destroying some 120,000 texts, many of which contained pharmacological knowledge and information passed down from early Greco-Roman scholars; Charlemagne declared that opium was the work of Satan. Therefore, the expansion of Christianity saw a shift in the method of control of access, use and trade in substances. The consumer sovereignty model was superseded by a mixture of occupational control and the beginning of bureaucratic control as the nascent state intervened in the use of mind-altering substances. By the time we reach the Middle Ages the state and the Church had become as one and we see a very different approach to the use of drugs.

Drug use and control: Middle Ages to the 1800s

It is instructive to note that the early Middle Ages are also sometimes referred to as 'the Dark Ages'. This is taken to mean that the type of social structures and cultural and literary achievements promoted by the Greek and Roman civilisations collapsed, and in their wake came a time of uncertainty. Plagues and pestilence were common, as were wars and invasions. In Britain we can see that the period from around CE 400 to the early 1500s was one of huge social, political and religious change, and all three conspired to impact the manner in which certain substances were used and controlled.

The civic and social upheavals of the time led to something of a purge on the use of substances designed either to heal or alter consciousness, due, in the main, to rising concerns about heresy against the Christian church and the impact magic, particularly that performed by witches, had on the condition of the environment and the morality of the population. Specifically, there were concerns about women and women's sexual activity in relation to substance use. Bailey (2003: 1) notes that in the mid-1430s, an unknown cleric described a nocturnal gathering in which the devil appeared to his followers in order to welcome a new convert. Whilst the mainstay of the cleric's description revolves around sex and cannibalism it is instructive for our purposes to note that once the carnal pleasures had been sated, the devil instructed his disciples in 'magical arts and would give them certain magic potions, poisons and unguents', which could then be used to harm or corrupt other members of society. Chief protagonists in these types of activities were 'witches' who were particularly persecuted for their ability to use 'potions' and cast 'spells', all of which were unholy activities and represented a potential corrupting presence to Christian society.

Integral to this is the concept of the 'flying witch' and her broomstick. Whilst popular mythology and children's' fairy tales would have us believe that female witches actually 'flew' the reality is grounded in sexual activity. Both Bailey (2003) and Escohotado (1999) note that according to the Christian inquisitor's records many of the women burnt for witchcraft admitted to using wooden dildos anointed with ointments to produce sexual satisfaction. However, the inquisitors were unable to detail these sexually explicit confessions so engaged in the use of metaphors in their reports. Thus, 'flying' became a metaphor for the erotic dreams and images leading to the female orgasm and 'broomstick' became a metaphor for a dildo. The fact that these women either prepared the ointments themselves or obtained them from other female 'witches' led to their persecution, arrest and punishment. Thus, arguably for the first time we see the state begin to wage war not only on 'drugs', because of the impact certain substances had on the morality of populations, but also on 'drug dealers' for being the ones that supplied the substances.

And what a war it was: Bailey (2003) tells us that from the fifteenth to the seventeenth century over 200,000 people were burnt as witches and the state confiscated the property of millions more. Interestingly, whilst the witch hunts could be seen to be a form of control by the criminal justice agencies of the use and distribution of some drugs, there was also a form of control of the supply and use of drugs by professional and trade organisations aided and abetted by the local state.

Holloway (1995) reports that in late medieval Europe craft guilds were formed with the express intention of overseeing and regulating the activities of people practising a certain craft or trade. Dyer (2002: 223) goes further and argues that 'often regulation was used ... [by guilds] to secure control of commodities and exclude competition', and this regulation was endorsed and backed by the town officials. This is an important development because it means that for the first time there was an organised and active professional attempt to control ownership, and by association the lawful supply, of certain substances, backed by the emerging local state. Certainly the supply of substances by pharmacists and apocatharies seemed to be a profitable enterprise for the expanding merchant class. Holloway (1995: 78–79) informs that 'organized commerce in the supply of drugs in the principal urban areas of England was [visible] from at least the fourteenth century'.

So, by the time that we leave the Middle Ages and begin to enter the 1600s and 1700s, we can see a system of control where any attempt at consumer sovereignty was proscribed either by religion or by law. That is not to say self-diagnosis and recourse to folk remedies did not exist – they clearly did. However, especially in the increasingly urbanising towns and cities, the scope for finding plants on which to base remedies began to constrict, meaning that more and more people had to purchase plants and patent medicines from guild-based apothecaries.

According to Pomeranz and Topik (2006), it was the development of a free market form of commerce and trade around the 1600s and certainly into the 1700s that began to shift the use, supply and purchase of substances into a form that would be more familiar to us today. As Pomeranz and Topik (2006) go on to describe, around the end of the 1600s and the beginning of the 1700s the concept and practice of free trade began to take hold, due in some measure to the influence of thinkers such as Adam Smith and Jeremy Bentham. Coupled with this intellectual revolution, developments in transport and navigation began to drive an expansion in trade and the importation of more exotic goods.

As a result, the restrictive practices of the guilds were questioned and ultimately disappeared, leaving in their wake an expanding merchant class and the emergence of a consumer society by the time we reach the beginnings of the 1800s. For our purposes it is instructive to note that Holloway (1995: 86) writes that 'by 1780 sales of medication in England stood at £187,500 per annum' (which translates to around £12 million in today's prices). Returning to our analytical framework we can see that the reduction in consumer sovereignty visible in the late Middle Ages was under threat, as free market techniques and philosophies led to an avowedly *laissez faire* approach to the use, supply and sale of substances.

From this point the work moves to discuss developments in the use and control of substances from 1800 up until the end of the 1960s. This period can be said to cover the origins and development of contemporary British society and therefore deserves a more detailed examination. As a result, the chapter will be broken down into six specific eras. Nevertheless, the typology of control outlined above will still be used as an analytical tool designed to allow us to understand how and by who control developed over the use and supply of certain substances.

1800 to 1850 drug use and control: the resurgence of consumer sovereignty

One of the immediate features of the period between 1800 and 1850 is the relative lack of worry exhibited by society over substances that today cause us considerable concern. In our contemporary language, substance use in the early 1800s was 'normalised', and for the majority of the nineteenth century supply was unrestricted (Berridge 1989). Indeed, whilst most histories of Britain acknowledge that alcohol has always had a widespread appeal and usage (Stearn 1975), few give space to the fact that 'Opium has been consumed wholesale, largely with equanimity, in Britain for centuries' (Harding 1998: 1). It was not only opium: morphine, cannabis and latterly cocaine were all freely available and unrestricted; although it appears that opium was by far the most used by the general public. (Berridge 1989; Mott and Bean 1998).

As an indication of normalisation of opium use, Berridge (1989: 23) cites an inquest held in Hull during 1854 where the coroner noted that a baby was poisoned due to an overdose of laudanum (a liquid opiate consisting of raw opium, distilled water and alcohol). The child was given the laudanum as a result of it being mistaken for syrup of rhubarb. She further remarks that the original sale was to a child messenger of six or seven years old. It appears that the grocer kept opium-based products on a shelf alongside 'other bottles of the same shape and size'. Why, then, was there so little concern over the use of what are now seen as dangerous drugs?

There are two significant sets of reasons. First, at the beginning of the eighteenth century the medical profession was only just starting to capitalise on the advances set in train by both the Enlightenment movement (Gamble 1981) and the industrial revolution (Hobsbawm 1969). As a result, medicine was often far from 'scientific' and often not trusted: doctors were not always well trained, held in high esteem or easily accessible for large sections of the population (Coleman 1985). Thus, at the start of the 1800s the medical profession was only just beginning to establish itself in the form we know today, and certainly did not have the professional or political power, or widespread public support to 'own' the control of opium or other drugs.

As a consequence, the locus of medical attention was the family. Treatment and cures were often dependent upon folk remedies and recourse to tried and tested methods. The lack of trust, accessibility and affordability of doctors experienced by large tracts of the population meant that self-medication was widespread and often the only option. Within this framework, opium and opium derivatives had a long-established position as a cure-all. This is apparent in the literature of the time: Thomas Hardy (1880), in *The Trumpet Major*, depicts Bob Loveday falling into a state of unconsciousness due to the over-use of poppy head tea; a point endorsed by London *et al.* (1990) who note the prevalence of poppy head tea drinking during this period. Moreover, the absence of a professional body to oversee the dispensing of substances such as opium meant there were a variety of outlets. As we have seen, grocers and hawkers vied with pharmacists in the supply of all manner of substances (Berridge 1978: 438).

The key point to recognise here is that opium use, especially amongst the working classes, was restricted to a 'culturally sanctioned practice restricted largely to self-medication' (Harding 1998: 3). That is not to say there was a lack of recreational use of opiates. DeQuincey (1822) charted its non-medical use in *Confessions of an Opium Eater*, but as Berridge (1989) remarks, public reaction was muted, never rising far above mild curiosity. Moreover, as Robson (1994: 127) notes, recreational use was seen to be the domain of 'creative types' such as authors like Barrett-Browning, Coleridge, Collins and Dickens. Similarly, there were some fears expressed over the recreational use of opium by Chinese in and around London's docklands, but it is arguable this had more to do with issues of race, especially 'otherness' and concern over 'foreigners', than worries around opium use (Berridge and Edwards 1981; Robson 1994).

Therefore, one of the primary reasons that opiate use was seen as unproblematic at the beginning of the nineteenth century was widespread social acceptance of opiates. The fact that there was an absence of a professional body able to claim either expertise, or establish the power to exercise control over the use and supply of opium and other substances needs also to be taken into consideration.

The second set of reasons why opiate use was not conceived of as problematic during this period lies in the position of the British government, especially in relation to the global trade in opium, and more specifically, the smuggling of opium, grown in British colonial India, into China. At its most extreme, Hooker (1996: 56) argues that:

> By the 1830s, the English had become the major drug-trafficking criminal organization in the world; very few drug cartels of the twentieth century can even touch the England of the early nineteenth century in sheer size of criminality. This trade [in opium] had produced, quite literally, a country filled with drug addicts, as opium parlours proliferated all throughout China in the early part of the nineteenth century ...

Certainly, Britain was heavily involved with the illegal importation of opium into China. Chesneaux *et al.* (1976: 54) chart the growth of the trade during the period from 1820 to 1835. They state that in 1820 the number of crates of opium being smuggled into China stood at 9,708, which rose to 35,445 crates by 1835 (these figures are approximations but each crate weighed around 60 to 72 kgs). The effect of this trade was devastating to Chinese society. Chesneaux *et al.* (1976: 55) note that:

> Around 1835, senior officials and generals assumed that 90 per cent of their staff were opium smokers. Estimates of the total number in the population were various and imprecise: Lin Ze-xu reckoned that there were 4 million opium smokers in China, while a British doctor in Canton set the figure at 12 million. Because of opium, business slowed down, the standard of living fell, and public services no longer worked smoothly.

The motives behind the British state's entry into drug smuggling are complex, and a detailed examination is beyond the remit and scope of this work. However, it is important to point out that the move was a calculated one, which was designed to balance British trade with China, who at the time had a closed-door policy to foreign goods. A desire to force China to accept imports from Britain and British colonial India, coupled with an unwillingness by the British state to continue to pay for Chinese goods in silver, led directly to the British government sanctioning the breaking of Chinese laws relating to the use of opium. Some would add that it was a contrived move to destabilise China and force a conflict in order to 'improve' trading relations between the nations.

This happened in 1839 when Britain declared war on China following a series of arrests and confiscation of opium in and around the Canton area of China. The ensuing conflict afforded a comfortable victory for the British, and led to the signing of the Treaty of Nanking in 1842, which opened up parts of China to Western merchants (Chesneaux *et al.* 1976: Chapter 3).

Thus, the second set of reasons behind the relaxed attitude to opium in the first half of the 1800s can be seen to revolve around the role of the British state. Clearly, it would have been difficult for a nation to go to war to protect the trade in opium whilst at the same time striving for control or prohibition at home. So, turning again to our typology of use and control what we see is a return to consumer sovereignty with little or no restrictions being placed on either the use, trade or supply of any substances. However, this period marks the end of consumer sovereignty as the dominant model and sees the start of a period of increasing control.

1850–1900 drug use and control: the rise of occupational control and moral condemnation

Two social groups were instrumental in the development and growth of this change of attitude toward substances: the medical and pharmaceutical professions who were keen to cement their newly-found public acclaim triggered by improvements in public health (South 1997) and the increasingly influential, religion-inspired moral philanthropists (Thane 1996). In many respects, the concerns of these two groups were intertwined, and across the last part of the nineteenth century their respective claims against the consumer sovereignty model became mutually reinforcing. In turn, their growing confidence, alongside increasing public support, enabled pressure to be exerted upon the British government to tighten the controls governing domestic use of substances, and to desist from participating in the global opium trade.

Although the widespread use of opiates continued unabated post-1850, there were increasing public concerns about its use, especially in relation to the use of opium-based products as a 'quietener' for infants, and the rising number of accidental poisonings this practice generated (Edwards 1981). This coincided with more specific worries about the state of children, generated by public shock over the issue of 'baby-farming' and the systematic infanticide of young children who were fostered to unscrupulous professional child minders (Burke 1996). Moreover, as medical knowledge developed in the 1800s there was a re-evaluation of opium and its long-term effects on those users who had developed habitual use.

Harding (1998) argues that prior to around 1850, habitual use of opium was recognised, but seen as an effect of the drug itself or as result of the social condition of the user. Hence, at that time, there was an absence of moral condemnation, due to the fact that the addictive properties of opium were seen as the problem and not any moral laxity on the part of the user. However, by the middle of the 1800s there was a growing chorus of voices linking opium use to morality: Harding (1998: 3) cites a Dr Thompson, writing in 1840, who suggested that opium use by women 'affected all that was good and virtuous'.

Equally, the developing medical profession was keen to establish control over the use and supply of opium. Self-medication and widespread availability ran counter to their increasing professionalisation of practice and knowledge (Duin and Sutcliffe 1992). Added to this, the medical professions were beginning to gain some form of public recognition and, as Lawrence (1994) notes, were keen to cement the advances they had made in public confidence following their work in the cholera epidemics of 1853–54. Lawrence (1994: 29) also points to the impact of one other factor contributing to the growth of confidence in the medical profession: the use of medicine as a form of social policing. This, according to Harding (1998), led to an increasing concern over the actions of the working class by the medical profession. This was especially the case in their use and abuse of certain substances, with very real concern being voiced over the use of opium as a cheap alternative to alcohol, itself seen as a corrupting influence on the 'deserving poor' (Midwinter 1994).

By 1850, the medical profession had gained confidence, a degree of public and political support and an acknowledged scientific knowledge base from which to begin to make inroads into all manners of social practices, as well as starting to take control and ownership of previously unregulated activities. An example of this can be seen in the 1868 Pharmacy Act, which Berridge (1978) sees as a confluence of a number of factors, including increasing medical concern over the effects of opium, the general concerns over the need to control poisons and worries over the morality of the working class. The 1868 Act started to control the sale of opium, allowing only registered pharmacists to trade in it. Interestingly, however, patent medicines, many of which were opium-based, were exempted from the restrictions of the Act, thus allowing the general sale of opium-based products to continue.

Another manifestation of this growth in medical power was a re-formulation of the habitual use of opium. This saw a moving away from seeing addiction as a property of the drug, and toward a view that the addict was an 'irresponsible individual wilfully adopting a course of self-destruction' (Harding 1998: 4). Thus addicts could be blamed for their addiction and then visited upon with moral indignation and medical treatment. It is at this stage where the growing power and influence of the medical profession became intertwined with the burgeoning late-Victorian, religion-inspired moral philanthropic movement, and particularly in the case of opium, the Society for the Suppression of the Opium Trade (SSOT).

This organisation was formed in 1874 and quickly became 'the most prominent organisation in the Victorian anti-opium movement' (Harding 1998: 5). The SSOT was part of a general moral crusade undertaken by members of the religious group, the Society of Friends, or Quakers as they are more commonly known. It was the Quaker movement's approach to life that enabled Quaker-inspired groups such as the SSOT to exert such a profound influence on British society.

First, Quakers have a unique view on the influence of the corporeal world on the soul. Essentially, the path to righteousness needs a combination of prayer and a dynamic pursuit of activities that feed the soul's morality, as well as an avoidance of factors that adversely affect the soul. Thus, pride, extravagance, self-indulgence, extreme behaviour and luxurious living are to be avoided. Harding (1998: 7) suggests that Quakers were able to implicate the non-medical use of opium as damaging to morality. In addition, the Quakers possessed a formidable organisational structure that spawned some of the most influential philanthropic reformist movements of the Victorian period, including the National Temperance Society and the Anti-Slave Society.

These organisations provided a knowledge base derived from hands-on information gathered by Quakers working within poor communities. This information was then spread across the whole Quaker organisation via regular 'business meetings' where data on the physical and moral condition of Britain's poor was disseminated and discussed. Harding (1998: 7) notes that 'The Quakers' organisational structure functioned as an apparatus for surveillance of society's moral order'. In this way, the Quaker movement gained social prestige and a reputation for providing the 'truth', in terms of social commentaries.

Alongside the SSOT's moralistic crusade on substance use by the poor came the growth of concerns within the medical profession about substance misuse generally, and inebriation specifically. This led to the foundation of the Society for the Study of Inebriety in 1884, headed by Dr Kerr. Kerr, and like-minded medics on both sides of the Atlantic, began to reformulate notions and definitions of addiction to the point where:

> What emerged by the end of the [nineteenth] century was the hybrid 'disease of the will' concept, in which the eugenic bias of scientific thinking emphasised the importance of race and constitutional inheritance in predisposition to addiction. It [drug dependence] was a form of 'moral insanity' or 'moral bankruptcy'.
>
> (Berridge 1978: 458)

This allowed the moral imperative of the SSOT to be intertwined with the growing professionalisation of the medics and their desire to own and control the right to control the use and supply of substances (and, some would argue, act as moral police to the working classes [Doyal and Pennell 1979]). Berridge (1978: 459) expands this point, where she argues that there was significant cross-fertilisation between both groups. The powerful combination of medical 'expertise' and moral high ground influenced 'educated public opinion', and began to transform opium use into a deviant activity, in need of increased control. This can be witnessed in the growth of legislation aimed at controlling the negative effects of opium use. For example, the medical profession attempted, but failed, to include opium addiction into the 1888 Inebriates Act, which allowed for the voluntary detention of habitual drunkards. Undaunted, medical professionals were able to utilise their diagnostic powers to control opium addicts two years later following the passing of the 1890 Lunacy Act.

The British state still maintained and supported the opium trade, fighting a second opium war with China between 1856 and 1860 (Chesneaux *et al.* 1976). Nevertheless, at the very end of the century the government responded to growing public concern over the opium trade by setting up a Royal Commission on Opium. However, the report, published in 1895, is generally seen as a 'whitewash', finding in favour of a continuation of the trade. Moreover, the British state seemed uninterested in the problems of addiction, and was reluctant to make it part of government policy (Berridge 1978). Importantly, however, a number of authors point out that the opium trade was diminishing in its economic importance by the end of the 1800s (Edwards 1981; South 1997; Mott and Bean 1998), as was the domestic consumption of opiate-based products. Equally, there was growing international concern about the use of opium and other substances.

By the end of the 1800s opium use in British society still remained 'something quite normal … everyone has laudanum at home' (Robertson 1975 in Berridge 1978), but the dawning of a new century would see a sustained and successful challenge to this situation. As the new century dawned, an occupational control model, driven by a combination of the medical professions and religious condemnation of inebriation, was rapidly replacing the consumer sovereignty model.

1900–1926 drug use and control: toward bureaucratic domination

This period represents the era where substance use was defined by the state as a serious social, political and economic problem. It is important to note that, as Berridge (1978: 461) remarks, 'the attitudes which underlay control … were already formed. Developments in the 1900s brought into play the complex motivations which had marked responses to opiate use in the nineteenth century'. Those attitudes can be best understood as a continuum where substance misuse is seen as a medical problem in need of treatment at one pole, and substance misuse as a vice in need of control via law and order at the other extreme.

Initially, the British state was reluctant to become involved in any policy surrounding the use and control of substances, beyond a general concern over poisons. This can be evidenced in the Poisons and Pharmacy Act 1908, which amended the 1868 Pharmacy Act but made no changes to the controls put in place in 1868. However, the 17 years from 1909 to 1926 witnessed a massive shift from a consumer sovereignty model to a situation where there were stringent controls of a number of substances. Essentially, there are two significant forces of change: first, the advent of international concern forcing Britain to take action on controlling certain substances, and second the development of moral panics concerning the use of substances, especially during the First World War.

Once again, Britain's involvement in supplying opium to China plays an important role. Mott and Bean (1998: 32) refer to the fact that in order for the United States to control the opium problem in the newly acquired Philippines, the US decided to gradually prohibit the sale of opium over a three-year period starting in 1904. This would have proven difficult if the flow of opium into China from European nations remained constant. To this end, the US arranged an international convention, inviting major European trading nations, as well as representatives from the producing nations of Turkey and Persia, to attend.

At first Britain saw little point in the process due to the fact that in 1907 Britain had negotiated the Anglo-Chinese agreement with China to reduce shipments of opium by 10 per cent per year, up until 1916 when the trade would cease, thus marking the end of the economic importance of the opium trade. Eventually Britain became one of 13 attendees at the 1909 Shanghai Commission. The findings of the commission were, at the request of Britain and the Netherlands, only recommendations with no binding force on the signatories. Nevertheless, the Shanghai Commission marked the starting point for the international control of substances.

Three years later, again following agitation from the US, the Hague Convention was signed and circulated for ratification as international law. The 1912 Hague Convention had four main provisions, which were:

1. the production and distribution, including import and export, of raw opium to be controlled by national legislation;
2. opium smoking to be gradually and effectively repressed;
3. the manufacture, sale and consumption of morphine and cocaine and their salts to be limited by national legislation to medical and legitimate purposes, and to be controlled by a system of licensing;
4. statistics relating to the drug trade, and information about national laws and administrative arrangements, to be exchanged through the Netherlands government.

Following a further two conferences at The Hague in 1913 and 1914, Britain, reluctantly, ratified the Convention in 1914. Robson (1994: 131) cites Britain's continued economic interest in the drug trade as a reason for this tardiness, arguing that Britain's role as the major morphine producer was a significant barrier to ratification. Interestingly, and demonstrating a lack of state concern over substance misuse up to this point, there was no government department responsible for substance control, and none willing to assume the mantle. Subsequently, early British substance misuse control became the responsibility of the Privy Council Office (Mott and Bean 1998).

Such a reluctance to take on new work may be seen as understandable at a time when Britain and the rest of the world was plunged into a war that was to wreak havoc across mainland Europe. In a more parochial vein, the First World War was also to have an influence on the control of substances in Britain, and it is to this the chapter now turns.

Central here is the Defence of the Realm Act (DORA). Thurlow (1994: 48) provides a clear description of DORA, stating that 'DORA, and its attendant regulations for the period 1914–20, meant that a watered down form of martial law was superimposed on the workings of the common law and civil jurisdiction'. Citing DORA allowed wartime leaders to intervene in all manner of areas of state and social life. How did such far-reaching powers, clearly central to Britain winning the war, come to be applied to substance use? Mott and Bean (1998) suggest that DORA's gaze turned to substances following a series of moral panics over the use of cocaine by British and Canadian troops, allied to wider concerns about substance consumption by munitions workers hampering their ability to work at full capacity. It appears that troops were in the habit of visiting prostitutes and taking all manner of substances, possibly as a reaction to being sent into the trenches where 'Kitchener's army found its graveyard' (Taylor 1992: 61).

Under the initial DORA legislation the sale or gift of intoxicants to a member of the armed forces with the intent to make him drunk or incapable was an offence. However, Robson (1994: 131) comments that legislation pre-1916 was weak and that there was a 'roaring' black market in cocaine and other drugs as soldiers were 'keen to get hold of drugs which might make life in the trenches a bit more acceptable'. He notes that it was possible to buy morphine and cocaine kits, complete with syringe and spare needles in Harrods. These kits were labelled 'A Useful Present for Friends at the Front'.

In May 1916 the non-medical sale or supply of cocaine to armed forces personnel was banned. This had very little impact amongst the troops, leading, in July 1916, to DORA 40B coming into force. It is here, as a result of moral panics over the use of substances by troops, that the British state made its first big inroad into defining and controlling 'harmful' substances. DORA 40B restricted those who could possess cocaine to authorised persons, including doctors and retail pharmacists. Transactions in cocaine were to be recorded in order that the Secretary of State could inspect them. These regulations were amended in December 1916 when licences were issued for the manufacture of cocaine, making it an offence to issue a prescription for cocaine other than in accordance with the legislation. Importantly, the ability to check records on the use and supply of cocaine was extended to police officers of inspector rank and above (Mott and Bean 1998).

Thus, 'a significant step had been taken', because unauthorised supply and all unauthorised possession had been criminalised. In turn, this moved the Home Office to the centre stage in terms of government's substance control policy. At this point it might be worthwhile to note the absence of a Ministry for Health; such a Ministry did not emerge until 1919. Thus, even if it had wanted to, the wartime government may have felt uneasy entrusting the policing of substances to a medical service whose 'administration ... had been found inadequate' (Leathard 2000: 12). Further domestic legislation followed renewed international pressure at the end of the First World War. The Treaty of Versailles contained a clause that required all signatories to introduce domestic legislation to deal with their respective drug 'problems' as a condition of accession (Lowes 1966; Bruun *et al.* 1975). In Britain this led to the Dangerous Drugs Act 1920.

Edwards (1981) suggests the passing of this legislation marked the birth of our contemporary system. It could also be added that the 1920 Act set in train a still unresolved issue as to which arm of the state should 'own' the drug problem: in short is illicit drug use a medical or criminal justice issue? This will be explored in depth in a later chapter. For now, it is important to note that from 1920 onwards possession of all opiate- and cocaine-based products without the necessary authorisation or medical prescription became proscribed, with heavy legal penalties and social disapproval for those infringing the regulations.

It will be of little surprise, considering the state department with responsibility was the Home Office, that the state response to the 1920 Dangerous Drugs Act was decidedly penal in nature (Berridge 1989). There are two points worthy of consideration here. First, and this point will be discussed in more detail below, the Home Office was particularly keen to emulate developments in the US, where the passing of the Harrison Act in 1914 had practically outlawed the medical prescribing of opiates and thus created a very minor role for the medical profession in the 'ownership' of the drug problem. Thus, non-medical use, possession and supply became perceived as a criminal matter.

Second, and due in some measure to the above point, the public's reaction to drug use had shifted considerably in the century between its 'mild interest' in DeQuincey's revelations of opium eating in 1820 and the death of actress Billie Carleton in 1919 and dance instructor Freda Kempton in 1922. There was a high degree of concern over drug use, and, again paralleling developments in the previous century, the media emphasised the involvement of 'outsiders' and 'foreigners' in the supply of these newly dangerous substances. Mott and Bean (1998: 40), for example, point to extensive media coverage of the trials of Edgar Manning, a Jamaican, and Brilliant Chang, a Chinese, for their involvement in trafficking cocaine.

Such levels of public unrest had an impact upon the government, and 1923 saw the Dangerous Drug Amendment Act enter the statute books. Berridge (1989) notes that this new Act provided a significant impetus for the penal approach to substance control. Although this initial raft of substance control legislation gravitated toward a punitive and legal approach, it should not be thought that the medical profession, which was instrumental during the previous century in bringing substance misuse to the public's attention, was ready to relinquish its claim of ownership of substance policy.

Kidd and Sykes (1999: 17) draw on the content of the Act to note that doctors were allowed to dispense opiates but only 'so far as may be necessary for the exercise of his profession'. This clause of the Act, they argue, provided doctors wishing to prescribe opiates with a vagueness that allowed the medical profession a great deal of leeway. The problem at this time was a lack of clarity and the ever-present threat of prosecution, which led to some pharmacists and physicians refusing even to prescribe or dispense cocaine or opiates. As a result, the newly formed Ministry of Health set up a committee to investigate opiate prescribing and to clarify what constituted legitimate prescribing. The committee, headed by Sir Humphrey Rolleston, published its report in 1926.

Unsurprisingly for a committee comprised entirely of delegates holding medical qualifications, Rolleston found in favour of the retention of significant medical input into the 'problem' of substance misuse. Key amongst their findings was the argument that the prescribing of opiates should be seen as a legitimate medical treatment and therefore remove the threat of prosecution from doctors prescribing maintenance doses. By acknowledging the right to prescribe, Rolleston established that addiction and substance misuse became a medical problem, able to be addressed by doctors and not police officers.

Rolleston defended this stance by claiming that:

> There are two groups of persons suffering from addiction to which the administration of morphine or heroin may be regarded as legitimate medical treatment, namely:
>
> (a) those who are undergoing treatment for cure of the addiction by the gradual withdrawal method;
> (b) persons for whom, after every effort has been made for the cure of addiction, the drug cannot be completely withdrawn.

Rolleston created a 'British system' whereby drug-dependent users who were prepared to play the 'sick role' were able to receive a regular supply of heroin or morphine in order to maintain or gradually reduce their use. Doctors were able to diagnose and prescribe with immunity from prosecution, creating a situation diametrically opposite from that in the US.

There are a number of reasons for this. First, the medical profession was keen to defend their position in relation to the state. As Berridge (1989) notes issues such as the ownership of the definition of addiction were seen as direct challenges to the autonomy of doctors, and the medical profession was prepared to go to great lengths to resist such challenges. Second, the use of opiates was declining even as the Rolleston Committee sat. Rolleston estimated that there were only in the region of 500 addicts in the whole of Britain and they were to be pitied not persecuted. Moreover, there was a distinct class element to Rolleston's deliberations: he saw opiate addicts as middle aged, middle class and mostly drawn from the medical profession (South 1997).

The legacy of Rolleston was to create a dual approach to substance use and misuse. On the one hand the police retained the power to prosecute unauthorised use, supply and possession, thus criminalising drug users not authorised by the medical profession. On the other hand, the medical profession retained the right to diagnose, define and treat addiction. In this way a dual approach developed with substance misusers being able to be defined criminal or sick depending on which arm of the British system they came into contact with. This legacy is still with us today. If we return once more to our typology of use and control we can see that by the time we reach the mid 1920s consumer sovereignty is dead, and we see a battle for control between the occupational and bureaucratic control models.

1926–1964 drug use and control: inactivity and apathy

Edwards (1981: 9) encapsulates the period when he claims that 'Britain's drug problem was of interest exactly and only because of its trivial size'. Due to enforcement and a shift in the moral and social base of the country substance use generally was in decline. Most addicts were elderly and, because of the British system, were able to receive maintenance doses from their doctor. It appears that recreational use elsewhere was small and restricted to the 'fast set'. Kohn (1992) claims that there was still the occasional lurid media reporting of drug misuse, but overall illicit substance use had all but disappeared.

As an example, the first Brain Committee, an interdepartmental group set up in 1961 to investigate the use of illicit drugs, stated that the British drug problem was of little concern. In 1958 there were only 58 known addicts, with none under the age of 20. Britain's only involvement in substance policy during this period was ratifying international treaties. Initially, following the Hague Convention of 1912, the League of Nations was the international body with responsibility for drug policy. From there, the United Nations took over responsibility as from 1964. Britain's substance control legislation from 1923 to 1964 was implemented as a response to international treaties, not domestic problems. They were:

- the 1925 Dangerous Drugs Act, as a response to the Geneva Convention;
- the 1932 Dangerous Drug Act in response to the 1931 Limitation Convention;

- the 1964 Dangerous Drugs Act, in response to the 1961 Single Convention.

Key developments in these Acts were the extended control of alkaloids of opium and cocaine as well as the creation of offences in relation to cannabis. In terms of our typology bureaucratic and occupational control dominated what was a very small number of users.

This was the situation at the beginning of the 1960s, a decade seen by many as the catalyst for a number of society's current problems (James and Raine 1998). The inactivity, complacency and apathy regarding Britain's drug problem shown by the first Brain Committee in 1961 was about to disappear, as a combination of changing culture, expansion of travel and communication routes and increasing wealth brought a rapid return to the 'luxurious' use of substances.

1964–1979 drug use and control: rising use and reactive control

By the time the second Brain Committee sat in 1965 the pattern and prevalence of substance misuse in Britain was undergoing a significant change. For example, the number of known addicts stood at 470 in 1961; by 1965 this figure had almost doubled to 927. Equally the demographics of addicts were changing; in 1961 the 'non-therapeutic' total was 153; in 1965 it stood at 580. Addicts were also getting younger. In 1961 addicts aged 50 plus comprised the largest group; by 1965 addicts aged from 15 to 34 had become the largest group. This increase in substance misuse related workloads was not restricted to the medical profession; the number of prosecutions/convictions under the Dangerous Drugs Acts also rose in the period 1961–65, from 365 in the former year to 767 in the latter. Socially, substance misusers were also changing. As Bean (1994: 105) notes, by the mid 1960s users were: 'the antithesis of their pre-war counterparts'; in short substance misuse was becoming increasingly a pastime of working and middle class youth.

The rise in 'problematic' drug use among younger people from the working class was mirrored by rises in 'recreational' substance use. Shapiro (1999: 20–23) notes that during the 1960s, as a result of a burgeoning 'youth culture', substance use became more prevalent amongst musicians and their fans. Initially, the substance of choice for 'recreational' use was amphetamine, but increased use of LSD, and a more wide-ranging use of cannabis rapidly followed. The growth in recreational use was restricted mainly to 'the young ... relatively few being over thirty five' (South and Teeman 1999: 73). The reasons behind this phenomenon will be explored in another chapter; the concern here is to chart the state's response to the growth in substance misuse.

What we witness in Britain during the 1960s and 1970s is not only the growth of 'recreational' use of prohibited substances amongst young people, but also a growth in the variety of substances being used. In terms of policy, this created a number of problems as the old control regimes struggled to come to terms with the rapid developments in substance use, culture and practice. As a result, the period from 1964 until the present can be seen as one where the state has been forced to constantly reassess both the policy and practice of controlling substance use. What is interesting in the period from 1964 to 1979 is that there were two distinct sets of problems taxing policy-makers: old problems and new developments.

Looking first at the old problems – addiction to opiates, opiate derivatives and cocaine – at one level the 'British system' was seemingly struggling to cope with the rapid increase in use. Much of this seems to centre round the ability of doctors to prescribe 'maintenance doses' with impunity. There was clearly over-prescribing taking place, leading to pharmaceutical heroin being diverted onto the illegal market. Evidence for this can be seen in a number of instances. For example, Leech (1991: 35–36) reports that one doctor prescribed six kilos of heroin in 1962 alone. Much of this began to filter out into the 'street' market. Stimson (1987: 39–40) states that up until the start of the 1970s there was little or no smuggled heroin in Britain: almost all illegally used heroin was diverted from medical sources. Customs and Excise did not make their first major seizure until 1971.

At the same time, new problems were emerging: young people were using other substances, hitherto seen as unproblematic, for 'luxurious' purposes. Shapiro (1999) points out that most of the amphetamine used by 'Mods' in the 1960s was diverted from licit sources. LSD was increasingly being used by young people, and, up until 1966 use, supply and possession of LSD were not against the law. Cannabis, initially seen by the state as a problem restricted to the (*sic*) 'coloured population' (Bean 1994), was beginning to find its way into aspects of white youth culture.

As a result, the government reconvened the Brain Committee that issued its second report in 1965. What followed was a 'battery of legislation' (Kidd and Sykes 1999: 19). It is important to recognise that the dichotomy between 'treatment' and 'punishment' introduced by the Rolleston Committee in 1926 was not compromised or indeed challenged by the Brain Committee. The resulting legislation still contained the essential paradox in the British system; namely the use of criminal law to achieve public health gains (Pearson 1999: 16), with its inherent tensions between the needs of health and law and order.

The first piece of post-Brain legislation was the Dangerous Drugs Act 1967. This allowed prescriptions to continue but with more stringent controls on general practitioners and a requirement to notify the Home Office of new addicts. Moreover, specialist Drug Dependence Units were opened in 1968, mainly around the London area, where 'experts' in addiction monopolised the ability to prescribe heroin and cocaine. The 1967 Act was quickly followed by the 1971 Misuse of Drugs Act.

This Act introduced the standing Advisory Council on the Misuse of Drugs (ACMD), a committee whose remit is to continually monitor and review the misuse of drugs within the UK. Other features of this Act were the distinction between possession offences and supply offences as well as the introduction of a dichotomy between 'soft' and 'hard' drugs. This was achieved by introducing the controlled status to the manufacture, supply and use of drugs. Substances were divided into classes A, B and C, with sanctions and penalties graded according to its harmfulness if the substances were misused (Kidd and Sykes 1999). The next piece of legislation was the Misuse of Drugs (Notification and Supply to Addicts) Regulations (1973). This required doctors treating a patient they believed to be addicted to drugs to notify the Chief Medical Officer; it also further restricted the ability of GPs to prescribe substitute substances such as diamorphine and dipipanone.

Stimpson (1987: 37) sees much of the thrust of this legislation as an attempt by the state to 'make the major task [of the medical profession] the social control of drug distribution' in order to 'keep the Mafia out'. If indeed this was the intention of policy in the period 1964 to 1979 it failed somewhat spectacularly. By all available measures problematic substance misuse kept on rising: levels of addiction, levels of recreational use, levels of prosecutions and levels of seizures (Bean 1994; Pearson 1999; Stimpson 1987). The drug 'problem' had reached a level beyond which the Brain Committee (1965) inspired legislation could cope. By the end of the 1970s society was changing just as rapidly as it had in the early 1960s. Old certainties were being questioned and a 'new social order' was developing (Gladstone 1995). Thus, by the time we reach the beginnings of the 1980s the use and supply of substances is clearly in the grip of bureaucratic control with central government taking the lead.

Conclusion

Clearly, the manner in which substances are used and supplied has changed out of recognition in the last 200 years. It has become, arguably, one of the three major social problems in contemporary Britain and receives considerable state and public attention. Advances in medical science and shifts in morality have been significant contributors in the move from the consumer sovereignty model of use visible in the 1800s to today's bureaucratic dominated control system. However, do we really know the extent of drug use in Britain today? Often, some of the statements made are based on nothing more than supposition and personal opinion. Does the actual prevalence of drug use in contemporary Britain match the level of investment in policing it? These questions form the basis of the next chapter, which examines the extent of drug use in modern Britain, and the problems we have in measuring use.

Suggested further reading

Bailey, M.D. (2003) *Battling Demons: Witchcraft, heresy and reform in the late Middle Ages*, University Park, PA: Pennsylvania State University Press.

Courtwright, D. T. (2002) *Forces of Habit: drugs and the making of the modern world*, Cambridge, MA: Harvard University Press.

Dyer, C. (2002) *Making a living in the Middle Ages: the people of Britain 850–1520*, New Haven, CT: Yale University Press.

Escohotado, E. (1999) *A Brief History of Drugs: from the stone age to the stoned age*, Rochester: Park Street Press.

McLeod, I. (1999) *Legal Theory*, London: Macmillan (especially Chapter 11).

Pomeranz, K., and Topik, S (2006) *World That Trade Created: Society, Culture, and the World Economy, 1400 to the Present*, New York: M.E. Sharpe.

Porter, R., and Teich, M. (eds) (1995) *Drugs and Narcotics in History*, Cambridge: Cambridge University Press.

Some questions and areas for reflection

1. To what extent have concerns about the morality of young people, but especially young women, been at the forefront of society's responses to substance use?
2. Why are some mind-altering substances socially sanctioned whilst others are not?
3. It would appear that the human race has a desire to take mind-altering substances. Why do you think this is?

2 Measuring the 'problem'

Drug use in contemporary Britain

Introduction

In the Preface it was stated that to fully understand the nature of the 'drug problem' in contemporary Britain, it was necessary to draw from a number of academic disciplines. Chapter 1 used history as its base to provide a broad overview of the manner in which the use of substances has changed over the millennia, especially in terms of societies' and states' responses to drug use. This chapter employs social science research methods as its foundation, questioning as it does the capacity to generate accurate figures on the extent of illicit drug use in Britain.

The ability to provide detailed and exact measurement of illicit drug use is important, not least because the apparent increase in the use and misuse of drugs over the past two and a half decades has generated a great deal of public and state concern. Accordingly, successive governments have had to respond to clarion calls by the media, by opposition politicians, by community leaders, by contemporary moral entrepreneurs, and by the Church for 'something to be done', leading to a whole raft of initiatives and policy documents. However, in order to 'do something' in an effective manner, there is a need to be clear as to the extent of the problem – in short, in order to produce and implement effective policy, it needs to be known exactly, or as exactly as possible, how many; who; what; where; when; how; and, if possible, why people take drugs. Although this may appear axiomatic, the practice of supplying such information is fraught with difficulties. As the Institute for Study of Drug Dependency (ISDD 1995: 7) noted: 'Estimating just how many people use illicit drugs in Britain is like trying to do a jigsaw puzzle with many of the pieces missing'.

This chapter will not, and cannot, for reasons that will become clearer as the work progresses, complete that jigsaw. Instead, it takes as its core the problems we have in measuring drug misuse. It begins with a review of the methodological weaknesses of each approach to measuring drug misuse and highlights the difficulties of measuring a hidden population, such as drug users. It then compares and contrasts two types of measurement: official statistics compiled by treatment providers and law enforcement agencies, with self-report studies compiled by government agencies and academics. It then moves to discuss a method that is gaining popularity in research areas where measurement is difficult – the 'capture-recapture' approach. This chapter, by employing the available data, draws a rough sketch of drug use in contemporary Britain, noting the division between 'heavy-end' drug users, who are most likely to come to the attention of the state system, and recreational users who do not, yet it is this group that appears to represent the majority of drug users in Britain. It ends by briefly discussing developments in measuring drug use since the first edition of the work was published in 2003.

Before moving on to those points, it is perhaps germane to close this section with a brief explanation as to why accurate measurement is important. To start, the Home Office recognises that 'an understanding of the extent of drug use and its impact on ... society is key to the development of appropriate polices ... ' (Singleton *et al.* 2006: 1), yet the same authors note that 'traditional approaches to estimating the extent [of illicit drug use are] inappropriate' (Singleton *et al.* 2006: 1).

At present, the lack of a definitive figure, based on solid research, allows any number of assertions about the prevalence of drug misuse in Britain. For example, David Davis MP speaking in the House of Commons in May 2008 noted that 'the UK has the worst level of overall drug use in the European Union' (Hansard 2008)'. The media often take up this message: for example Tim Hollis writing in *The Times* suggests that 'the fact that we have Europe's highest proportion of problem drug users within the adult population and you have a very depressing picture indeed' (Hollis 2008). Yet although those figures can be quoted, their accuracy cannot be definitively proven.

Several authors (Sutton and Maynard 1993; Hay 1998) question the veracity of such statements and raise issues about the data on which they are based. Indeed, Sutton and Maynard (1993: 455) argue that statements like those above are 'unquantified assertions based on opinion rather than measurement'. Such imprecision should, in theory, make it difficult for policy-makers to: (a) allocate funds, (b) target policy and (c) measure outcomes. However, that is patently not the case as central government spends ever-increasing sums of money tackling the 'drug problem'; a problem whose true nature and extent is largely hidden, making its actual prevalence unknown. Sutton and Maynard's work is more than a decade old now and part of the role of this chapter is to assess how far we have come in measuring illicit drug use since they made the claim that:

> ... policy design and execution in this area is conducted in an almost data free environment where, because of ignorance, it is impossible to set sensible policy targets, let alone measure the success of spending hundreds of millions of pounds across the Whitehall Departments. One wonders, for example, how targets for drug use, such as those for alcohol and tobacco in the *Health of the Nation* can be set and monitored.
>
> (Sutton and Maynard 1993: 456)

For now, it is important to remember that failure to accurately measure the prevalence of substance misuse creates problems in terms of deciding what to input, where and when to make that input and how to measure 'success'. Accurate figures that provide information on all aspects of substance misuse are important, but difficult to provide. The next section of the chapter turns its attention to the methodological weaknesses of our current measurement instruments.

Measuring drug use: conflicting messages

It is important to be clear from the outset that although this chapter will offer a critique of a variety of organisations and the manner in which they measure illicit drug use, none of the agencies claim the capacity to provide the definitive picture of drug use in Britain. Instead, what each offers are very varied pictures of drug use, each related to their particular field of interest, be that organisational or academic. In short, each measurement sector produces data relative to its own concerns and based on the contacts it has with drug users in that particular organisational context.

Historically, there have always been some voices that show concern as to the veracity of our measurements and the sources these come from. For example, in 1993 Sutton and Maynard (1993: 455) identified four sources of information relating to illicit drug use in Britain: 'indirect measures provided by the seizure and intelligence arms of enforcement agencies, surveys of drug use attitudes, knowledge and experience, surveys of known users and surveys of hidden users'. The ISDD (1995: 9) narrowed this down and suggested that there are two forms of data available:

> ... regularly collected official statistics on drugs or drug misusers who are known to the authorities, which have the benefit of a degree of continuity; and (usually one-off) surveys conducted according to no standard methodology and therefore difficult to use as trend or national indicators.

For our purposes, we can classify these two as official statistics, which relates to data collected by state agencies in the course of their work, and general household surveys, which relate to data derived from self-report questionnaires. Recognition is given to the fact that other forms of data collection may take place, but these two methods are most instrumental in informing official policy, thus fit the general concerns of this work. With that caveat in mind, the next section of the chapter reviews each of these methodological approaches, searching for weaknesses that may impact on the validity of the data, thus reducing the capacity to accurately measure the extent of substance misuse in Britain.

Data collection and the problem of hidden populations

Most people who use illicit drugs do not want to be identified to the state and therefore are part of a hidden population that is not readily available for accurate measurement. Conversely, many of those whose drug use has become a problem are known to a number of different agencies, which can also make accurate measurement difficult, because there is the chance they will be double counted, thus increasing the number of estimated drug users. Everyone working within the substance misuse field recognises this as the key weakness in methods designed to measure the 'drug problem'. For example, the ACMD (1995: 32) are clear about the nature of the methodological problems faced by research and practice:

> ... it can be difficult to define adequately cases or categories of use. The illicit nature of drug taking makes the task of establishing its prevalence very complicated. Self-report data can be unreliable. There are sampling difficulties ... [this] should be borne in mind when trying to draw conclusions from questionnaire research.

The concerns about measurement that tasked the ACMD in 1995 remain true today with Hay *et al.* (2006: 3 emphasis added) noting that, in the case of illicit drug users 'direct enumeration is not possible', and our only recourse is to use 'indirect techniques [which] can provide *estimates*'.

Essentially, much of our data relating to drug misuse is derived from two basic forms of data collection: that which is collected from official sources and that which emanates from general population surveys, where randomly selected members of households and/or schools are asked to complete self-report questionnaires. Whilst each has its strengths, each has a corresponding degree of weakness and it is to these the chapter now turns its attention. Before starting, it should be made clear that no attempt is being made here to comprehensively review the technological pros and cons of each approach. More accurately, the intent is to provide a broad overview of the general problems and pitfalls of each methodology.

Official statistics

May (1997: 65) provides a succinct working definition of official statistics as being 'data collected by the state and its agencies', making drug-related data derived from medical and criminal justice sources part of a whole range of information collected and disseminated by the state. However, just because these 'facts' are released by the state does not automatically mean they should be accepted at face value and taken as some form of 'ultimate truth'. Rather, as a number of social scientists have noted (Cicourel 1964; Turk 1969), official statistics need to be seen as a 'social construction', whereby they do not reflect any social reality but merely 'actions of persons in the social system which define, record and classify certain behaviour ... ' (Cicourel and Kitsuse 1963). Thus, official statistics can be seen to reflect the concerns, working practices and interests of the compiling organisation, as opposed to any definitive measurement.

In more detail, and focusing on the construction of crime statistics, it is possible to see that far from being accurate indicators of 'crime', these figures simply represent the criminal justice system's ability to detect, define and process certain, but not all, criminal actions. May (1997: Ch. 4) provides an informative review of this process. Essentially, May argues that it is important to remember, as Quinney (1970: 104) reminds us, that 'Full enforcement of the criminal law ... is not a realistic expectation'. Wasik *et al.* (1999) expand this point and argue that police discretion as to which laws to enforce, and when to enforce them, is a key determinant of 'policing' any crime.

For example, the case of the Tetra Pak heir Han Rausing, and his wife Eva, demonstrates that although being caught in possession of 5.6 g of crack, 2.9 g of heroin and 52 g of cocaine (amounts that are large enough to incur possession with intent to supply charges), plus being caught attempting to smuggle crack and heroin into the American embassy in London, the couple were given nothing more than a caution (*Daily Telegraph*, 29 August 2008). Although that example is extreme, it demonstrates that the processes between the act of breaking the law, even when the crime is as serious as the above example, and being convicted, then sentenced for that act, is highly complex and dependent upon the discretion of a number of officials, and the manner in which those officials define the actions and demeanour of the offender.

Equally important is the fact that the public, in their guise as either victim or offender, may choose not to report the crime to the police. For the offender, the motivation not to report is self-evident. However, victims often choose not to report for a variety of reasons, including fear of the offender, thinking the police will dismiss the crime as insignificant or a general mistrust of the police. This leads to the creation of a 'dark figure of crime'. Barclay *et al.* (1995) suggest that incomplete recording by the police and reporting by the public mean that only somewhere between 27 to 39 per cent of crimes end up as 'official statistics'. As Mayhew (2000: 104) notes, drug possession is a classic exemplar of the type of crime that is very often not reported to the police.

The crime being detected or reported and a suspect being identified and subsequently arrested is simply the start of the process. Following arrest and charge, the police pass details of the case to the Crown Prosecution Service, who then make a decision as to whether to prosecute based on the joint criteria of evidential sufficiency and public interest (Ashworth 1998: 176–88). Finally, the prosecution need to prove satisfactorily to a magistrate or jury that the accused is guilty, prior to punishment being meted out. Thus, instead of being a measure of all illicit activity related to drug use, Home Office and Revenue and Customs figures can be seen to simply represent those crimes the criminal justice system knows about, and importantly, decides to act upon. Moreover, changes in policy or policing agency practice can lead to alterations in rates and patterns of recorded crime, a point noted by Corkery (2001) in relation to the impact the Lawrence Inquiry seems to have had on stop and searches in London, with a concomitant effect on drug-related offences.

A similar critique can be made of medical data. Not all those presenting to doctors and specialist drug agencies will be automatically classified as in need of help, or registered as 'addicted'. Indeed, some academics argue that many patients, including heavy-end drug users, who present to doctors, will not receive the treatment they may need due to their reluctance to comply with the 'sick role' (Navarro 1979). Bean (1994: 91) provides evidence of this, citing the *British Medical Journal* 'any questions?' section as an indicator that if heavy-end drug users are co-operative they will be treated, if not they run the risk of being labelled 'difficult' and may not receive the treatment they need.

Equally, just as in the crime statistics, there is a large unreported 'dark figure' of medical problems. Jones (1994: 11–12) cautions against assuming that medical data provide an accurate indicator of the health of the nation. Rather, Jones (1994: 11) suggests medical statistics are seen as unreliable indicators of illness because: (a) some people do not present to the doctor for treatment and thus go un-recorded, and (b) not all those who present across the country to different doctors will be treated or recorded in the same way. In this manner, far from being definitive figures, official medical records, and official classification of illness, are 'influenced by individual circumstances and the different methods of recording and reporting sickness across the country'.

Self-report data

Clearly, therefore, many drug users remain hidden from the gaze of official statistics. In order to combat the recognised discrepancy between 'actual' figures and 'official' figures in areas such as crime and ill health, many researchers have turned to self-report surveys, issued to households identified either from the Electoral Register (ER) or Small Users Post Code Address File (PAF) (Mayhew 2000). A prime example of this type of work is the British Crime Survey (BCS), which looks at people's experience of being victims of crime, and, since 1992, has included questions on illicit drug use. The BCS uses a sample of 10,000 people aged 16–59 from England and Wales selected at random via the ER or PAF. Scotland has its own version of the BCS.

The BCS only provides data on adults and thus fails to provide data on younger children. Some surveys work exclusively with school children aged 11–15, such as that conducted for the Office of National Statistics (Goddard and Higgins 1999a and b). Work of this type provides, amongst other things, an indication of drug use amongst school children. The sample size here was 5,000 English children and 3,500 Scottish children. Other notable surveys of this type include the work of Balding (1999).

There are, however, problems with this methodological approach. This is articulated by Mayhew (2000: 104–5) who has comprehensive experience of this type of work, being a key figure in previous BCS research. Commenting directly on the BCS she notes five problem areas, which can be broadened to cover all self-report, general household surveys.

Mayhew suggests that: (i) household surveys of this type do not measure each and every incident for a variety of reasons; (ii) no matter what sampling frame is used, surveys of this type will not be representative of the population. Hard-to-reach groups such as the homeless, those living in non-household environments, such as prisons, and others with chaotic lifestyles will not be included. Ironically, being a victim of crime and being involved in illicit drug use is often highest amongst these hard to reach groups; (iii) there are sampling errors that may be imported. For example, Mayhew notes that for rare crimes, even a survey as large as the BCS fails to adequately sample. The same may be said of drug addiction, itself a relatively rare occurrence amongst the general population; (iv) respondents often undercount incidents for a variety of reasons; (v) people have trouble in remembering and locating incidents within a time-frame. For example, Mayhew (2000) claims that people are prone to pulling serious events forward in time and not remembering repetitive incidents. This point is further endorsed specifically in relation to drug users by Hay *et al.* (2006: 7), where they note that 'large household surveys such as the British Crime Survey tend to underestimate those individuals whose drug use is problematic'.

Clearly, each of the primary measuring instruments has its flaws and is unable to adequately reach the hidden population of drug users. That being the case, data derived from official statistics and general household surveys should be treated with caution. However, that is not to say that they are lacking merit: they are, and, taken together, can begin to provide a tentative overview of the extent of illicit drug use in Britain, as well as giving us an indication of trends over time.

New approaches – capture-recapture as a method for estimating prevalence

The capture-recapture method has a long history in measuring livestock populations, especially in fish biology. In essence, the method involves capturing a sample of animals, marking all of them and then releasing them. A second sample is then captured. The proportion of marked animals in the second sample is assumed to be equivalent to the proportion of animals captured in the original sample. For example, if 100 fish were caught, marked and then released in the first sample, and following the capture of the second sample, 10 per cent were found to be marked, the 100 fish in the first sample is the equivalent of 10 per cent of the population, making the population 1,000.

Hay *et al.* (2006) who used the capture-recapture method to examine the prevelance of drug use in Drug Action team areas in the UK note that when using the method to assess drug use the two samples are replaced with a list of sources drawn from a number of available data sources such as treatment services, police data and so on. The number of individuals in each data source equates to the numbers of fish, and the number appearing in both sources equates to the number of marked recaptured fish in sample two (Hay *et al.* 2008: 11).

Remembering the caveat that each set of figures is compiled for particular reasons, and not with the purpose of providing a definitive picture of drug misuse in Britain, comparisons of the different findings offer a fascinating picture of the manner in which the sectors of the British system define and deal with the 'drug problem'.

Medical data: patients and clients

The first set of figures to be examined originates from within the medical sector. This data is derived from the National Drug Treatment Monitoring System (NDTMS), which replaced the Regional Drug Misuse Database (RDMD). These are relatively recent measurement tools, which were set up in 1989 following recommendations from ACMD (Department of Health 2000). Prior to 1989, medical-based figures were collected in a significantly different form, and by an agency not readily associated with the medical profession: the Home Office. It is interesting to trace the development of this situation, which reflects the inherent tensions between the health and law arms of the British system.

Mott (1994) provides a comprehensive account of this train of events. She notes that the Brain Committee (1965), echoing a consideration (subsequently omitted from the final report) of the Rolleston Committee (1926), recommended that doctors notify a central authority about the addicts they were treating. This move was justified by Brain with reference to various public health Acts. Under these acts, doctors have a duty to notify a central authority about patients 'who are suffering from an infectious disease' (Mott 1994: 272). Brain argued that drug addiction is an infectious disease, thus ensuring the medical profession retained 'epidemiological assessment and control' of the drug problem. In a move further designed to protect doctors, the Brain Committee suggested that any medic failing to notify should be dealt with by the General Medical Council, and not the criminal courts.

The Chief Medical Officer at the Home Office was subsequently named as the central authority to be informed by doctors, placing the central authority within the Home Office. This provoked reactions from medics, again reflecting the ongoing struggle for 'ownership' of the drug problem. Mott (1994: 273) points to an article that appeared in the *British Medical Journal* (1965), which was supportive of the idea of notification on the grounds it would allow the creation of treatment centres for addicts. However, Mott (1994) further reports that in the same year another author, contributing to the *Lancet*, made the point that:

> On the one hand the Home Office has done well for a long time overseeing this exceedingly difficult problem; on the other, it does use policemen for the purpose.

The requirement to notify addicts first came into force under the Dangerous Drugs Act 1967. This was subsequently modified under the Misuse of Drugs Act 1971 and the (Notification of and Supply to Addicts) Regulations of 1973. Under these regulations doctors were required to notify the Home Office of the name, age, sex, address, national health service number, date of attendance and type of drug used of all people addicted to one or more of 14 Class A drugs, including heroin and cocaine. Absent from the list of notifiable substances were amphetamines, barbiturates and benzodiazepines. Data from notifications was published annually by the Home Office as the *Home Office Statistical Bulletin: Statistics of drug addicts notified to the Home Office, United Kingdom* series.

However, the information produced by the addicts index was limited and did not provide the type of detailed information required by the DoH, which was trying to respond to changing patterns of drug use. In 1982 the ACMD called for local drug teams to be set up to collect more detailed information on the patterns and methods of use, as well as types of drugs used (it is worth remembering this was around the time of serious worries as to the effects of HIV and AIDS, and thus can be seen to reflect wider social and medical concerns). This subsequently happened, and by 1989 all Regional Health Authorities (RHAs) had in place a regional monitoring system. The Department of Health (DoH) funded the (then) Regional Health Authorities (RHAs) to create anonymous databases relating to drug misusers who were attending specialist services. The RDMDs returned data to the DoH on a six-monthly basis, and findings from the RDMDs were used to inform medical policy and responses to the 'drug problem'.

This was modified again in 1996 and from 1 April 1996 health regions had to submit data on 'people presenting to services with problem drug misuse for the first time, or for the first time in six months or more' (DoH 2000). This data included information on the following: 'age, sex, and other personal information; details of up to five drugs misused, information regarding injecting/sharing equipment behaviour, treatment profiles, together with the type of agency attended and the Health Authority (HA) of treatment' (DoH 2000). It is important to also note that the scope and range of substances recorded broadened considerably, and included 'any drug of misuse, including solvents and tranquillisers but excluding tobacco'; there was also a provision to include alcohol, but only as a subsidiary drug (DoH 2000).

Clearly, RDMDs provided a fuller picture of those people who turned to the medical profession for help with their drug problems than did the old Home Office Index. However, the government further developed this system and launched the National Drug Treatment Monitoring System (NDTMS). The NDTMS is a treatment surveillance system centred on data collection carried out by regional centres. This regional data is then coordinated and collated by the National Treatment Agency. In terms of types of data, the

NDTMS gathers demographic information and data on up to three different types of drugs being used by each client. At the time of writing the NDTMS figures (up to 31 March 2008) show that:

- 202,666 people were in contact with drug treatment agencies in the year 2007/08 which marks a rise on the previous year;
- the main drug of use by adult clients was heroin – 65 per cent – but adjunctive use of crack was common;
- the main drugs of use by clients aged under 18 years was cannabis – 78 per cent;
- 72 per cent of clients were male;
- 88 per cent of clients were white;
- the number of under-25s treated has fallen as has the number of under-18s.

Thus, it is possible to argue that for today's medical profession, drug misuse is a serious and growing problem, but one that involves a relatively small number of patients. Moreover, one drug – heroin – is clearly the most problematic. If, however, this data is flawed inasmuch that it cannot provide an accurate picture of current levels of use, does it have any value to the policy community? The answer lies in its ability to allow us to compare trends over time.

Comparison of data over the last 30 years demonstrates that Britain has witnessed a paradigmatic shift in the characteristics and numbers of those presenting to health agencies, yet the drug of problem for the medical profession has remained the same. Even given the methodological problems in using different sets of data, it is possible to see that heavy-end substance use has increased, and that users have become younger, with a recognisable growth in the under-20s presenting for treatment. In the 12 months up to March 2008, of the 202,666 people presenting to health agencies in England and Wales, 21,074 were aged 20 or below (DoH 2009). This can be compared (tentatively) with the 1964 figures, where, from a total of 753 known addicts on the Home Office Index, only 40 were aged 20 or below (Bean 1994: 98, Tables VI & VII). However, the drug that creates most problems for addicts, heroin, has remained the main problem drug across all age ranges in both 2008 (DoH 2009), and 1964 (Bean 1994: 99, Table VIII).

Criminal justice data: offenders and offences

There are three main sources from which this data is derived: HM Revenue and Customs, the Serious Organised Crime Agency (SOCA) and from the various police forces across Britain (Smith 2008: 2). Seizures and arrests made by the first two agencies generally 'reflect levels or drugs types at, or soon after, the point of importation' (Corkery 2001: 2), whereas police seizures may give an indication of the distribution patterns for 'home produced' drugs or those diverted from medical sources. The police, SOCA and Revenue and Customs deal with offences that contravene the 1971 Misuse of Drugs Act and the Drug Trafficking Act 1994. The data relating to this is available from the Home Office and is published in the *Home Office Statistical Bulletin* series.

Based on the most recent figures at the time of writing (for 2006/07), it is possible to examine the extent of drug misuse as recorded by the law and order arm of the British system. All the following figures, except if specified, come from Smith 2008. The Home Office provides data relating to drug seizures and drug offenders (Smith 2008). Turning attention to the former, the number of drug seizures reported to the Home Office in 2006/07 stood at a record 186,028, a 15 per cent increase on the previous year's figure. However, this increase may be partially due to the increase in cannabis seizures following changes in the legislation in 2004. This raw data can be broken down into its component parts in order to provide a picture of which agencies seized what drug, as well as the types of drugs being seized.

As will be seen in the next chapter, 'policing' drugs by the law and order arm of the British system has a distinct division of labour, which is visible in seizure figures. Essentially HM Revenue and Customs and SOCA tend to make fewer seizures, but of larger amounts, than their police force counterparts. For example, in 2006/07:

Table 2.1 Drug seizures by HM Revenue and Customs and UK Police Forces 2006–07.

Class of drug and organisation seized by	Number of seizures
Class A drugs	
HM Revenue and Customs	1,456
Police Forces including Transport Police	40,885
Class B drugs	
HM Revenue and Customs	128
Police Forces including Transport Police	8,668
Class C drugs	
HM Revenue and Customs	5,058
Police Forces including Transport Police	135,319
All drugs	
HM Revenue and Customs	5,209
Police Forces including Transport Police	126,985

Source: Smith 2008.

However, when this is compared to numbers and quantity of drugs seized it becomes clear that Revenue and Customs seize larger amounts. Thus, for the sake of illustration, only concentrating on the cannabis and heroin seizures that took place in 1999:

Table 2.2 Heroin and Cannabis seizures by HM Revenue and Customs and UK Police Forces 1999.

Organisation	Type of drug	% of all seizures	Weight in kgs.
HM Revenue and Customs	Heroin	53	530
Police	Heroin	47	473
HM Revenue and Customs	*Cannabis	88	40,364
Police	*Cannabis	12	5.036

Source: (Smith 2008).

* These figures are aggregated to include herbal and resin and exclude plants.

What of the general picture concerning drug seizures? Based on the Home Office data it is possible to see that in 2006/07:

- Cocaine was the most commonly seized Class A drug, with 16,079 seizures netting 3,191 kg.
- Heroin was the next most seized Class A drug with 13,205 seizures netting 1,003 kg.
- There were 7,752 seizures of ecstasy type drugs netting 6,584,000 doses.
- There were 137,127 cannabis seizures providing 45,400 kgs.

Drug offending data can be obtained via the Home Office British Crime Survey. Figures for the year 2007/08 saw 229,000 cases recorded by the police, which marks an 18 per cent rise on previous years. In detail: 158,086 (69 per cent of all drug offences) were for cannabis possession; 41,933 (18 per cent of all drug offences) were for possession of drugs other than cannabis; and 28,130 (12 per cent of all drug offences) were for drug trafficking (Home Office 2008b: 3).

Finally, in this section, the focus falls on the action taken against offenders. Sentencing information is available on the Ministry of Justice website. There are essentially two options: a non-custodial penalty (probation or community sentence order, a fine, a caution) or immediate custody. In total 44,500 people were sentenced with drug offences in 2007. Of those, 8,186 received an immediate sentence (making custody the option for 18.4 per cent of drug-related offences) with a further 2,678 receiving suspended sentences with the average custody length being 32.4 months. The most common form of sentence was the fine with 14,190 people being fined and a further 10,296 receiving community sentences (Ministry of Justice 2008: 10).

At this stage we can begin to construct some tentative comparisons. Clearly, the law and order arm of the British system deals with more people than the medical arm. It also has a different main 'problem' drug, inasmuch that, as Runciman (1999) forcefully comments, 'cannabis is the drug most likely to bring people into contact with the criminal justice system'. Evidence for this is provided by the manner in which people charged with cannabis offences dominate the prosecution figures and also in the way cannabis features heavily in seizure statistics.

However, a close inspection of the medical and legal data can beg the question: does somewhere in the region of 200,000 people, known by the state agencies to be involved in the use and/or supply of illicit drugs, out of a total population of about 60 million people, really constitute the 'serious problem' claimed by politicians and the media? If we add in the fact that some of those receiving medical help for their drug problem will have been simultaneously processed by the criminal justice system, the actual 'official' number of 'problem' users can seem insignificant and sets up questions relating to the millions of pounds being spent on substance misuse programmes. The final set of figures paint a somewhat different picture, and perhaps offers a rationale for our current concerns over substance use.

Self-report data: the bigger picture?

Thus far, concentration has been on those people who, for one reason or another, have come to the attention of the state agencies in relation to drug use. One way to conceive of this group is to see them as 'problematic drug users', either by virtue of the extent and nature of their use, making them a medical problem, or the social danger their drug use poses in terms of law and order, making them a criminal justice problem.

However, this problematic group remains relatively small, even allowing for under-counting: so small in fact that they cannot possibly be representative of the true extent of drug use. Arguably, this becomes clearer if greater attention is paid to the level of drug seizures. Stimpson (1987: 50) claims that, 'no law enforcement agency anywhere in the world credibly claims more than a ten per cent interception rate'. Thus, even if the law enforcement agencies were achieving that maximum target, it can be estimated that at least 23,420 kilos of heroin, or in excess of 60 million doses of ecstasy-type drugs were circulating in Britain during 1999. There are two conclusions that can be drawn from these figures: (a) either the known drug users are consuming vast quantities of drugs, or (b) there is a substantial 'hidden population', who, for the most part, use drugs unproblematically.

The next data sets examined by this chapter seem to indicate that the latter scenario is a more accurate picture, pointing to a very large 'hidden population' of drug users. Data that attempts to gauge this is derived from self-report questionnaires, many of which are part of larger government sponsored project such as the British Crime Survey (BCS), which has included questions on personal drug use since the 1992 survey (Mott and Mirrlees-Black 1993). Others emanate from agencies such as the Health Education Authority (Heuston *et al.* 1996) and the Schools Health Education Unit (Balding 1999). There is a remarkable similarity across all of these surveys, and collectively they paint a picture very different from the two previous sources of information.

Space precludes a detailed examination of each and every survey, so the intention in this section is to combine sets of data to provide a broad picture of the results. Essentially, the concern of academic researchers and government departments over the past ten years seems to be: (a) to examine the extent of use; (b) to search for differential patterns of use across time and age groups; (c) to identify 'drugs of preference'; and, latterly, (d) to gauge public attitudes toward different types of drugs.

Extent of use

The concern here is to try to gauge how many people use illicit drugs and whether there have been any changes over time. It would appear that there is a rise in use across the 1990s. For example, Mott and Mirlees-Black (1993) working with data from the 1992 BCS, found that 17 per cent of their sample admitted to taking an illicit drug. This rose in subsequent BCS findings, from 28 per cent in 1994 (Ramsay and Percy 1996), to 29 per cent in 1996 (Ramsay and Spiller 1997) to nearly 32 per cent in 1998 (Ramsay and Partridge 1999), and in 2006/07 an estimated 35.5 per cent of 16–59 year olds admit to using a drug at least once in their lifetime.

Goddard and Higgins (1999a,b) found that overall 13 per cent of English and 18 per cent of Scottish children aged between 11–16 reported ever having taken drugs. However, both sets of figures represent lifetime use and are guilty of aggregating data from very broad age ranges. They do not tell us very much about current use or differential patterns of use between age groups.

Differential patterns of use across time and age groups

Once the time and age variables are factored into the findings, the bold data, outlined above, begins to assume a different pattern and paint a clearer picture of where drug use is most commonly located in contemporary society. Concentrating first on school children, it is possible to view significant differences in use both across time and age groups. For example, working in Glasgow and Newcastle, McKeganey *et al.* (2003) found that about 6.5 per cent of 10–12 year olds admitted to having tried cannabis and a further 31 per cent had been exposed to some type of illicit drug. In a different survey Goddard and Higgins (1999) found that 13 per cent and 19 per cent of 13–14 year olds in England and Scotland had used some type of illicit drug. It was amongst the older children (15 years old) where prevalence of use was highest, with 31 per cent of English children and 39 per cent of Scottish children admitting to ever having used a drug (Goddard and Higgins 1999a and b). What is equally interesting, and in contrast to the medical and criminal justice figures, is that although boys admit to using substances more than girls, the difference is slight, with only a 2 per cent difference across all age ranges (DoH 2000).

This pattern of age difference in illicit drug use is repeated across the adult population: in 2006/07, 35.5 per cent of those aged 16–59 admitted to having ever used a drug, compared to 28 per cent in 1994 (Home Office 2008). However, if that wide age band is broken down into sub-groups, it appears that drug use is more prevalent amongst younger people:

- 44.7 per cent of 16–24 year olds admit to ever having tried a drug.
- 50.7 per cent of the 20–24 year old age range admit to ever having used a drug.
- Again, although across all age groups, males were likely to have used drugs more than females, the difference does not reflect the medical or criminal justice data.
- For example, in terms of lifetime use, 41.9 per cent of males and 29.3 per cent of females aged 16–59 admitted to using a drug and 49.3 per cent of males and 40.1 per cent of females aged 16–24 admitted lifetime use.

However, whilst this information can tell us about lifetime use (that is, ever having used an illicit drug) as DrugScope (2000: 57) remark, 'lifetime use does not accurately reflect the proportion currently using drugs on an occasional or regular basis'. In order to do that it is necessary to examine more recent use. According to the findings from the 2006/07 BCS (Home Office 2008a):

- Just under 24.1 per cent of those aged 16–24 used illicit drugs in the last year, with this falling to just under 14.3 per cent claiming usage in the last month.

This can be compared with other age groups:

- 8 per cent of those aged 25–34 admitting to using drugs in the last month;
- 3 per cent of those aged 35–44 admitting to using drugs in the last month;
- 2 per cent of those aged 45–54 admitting to using drugs in the last month;
- 1 per cent of those aged 55–59.

Drug of preference

Most of this information stems from the BCS data. Cannabis is the most widely used drug in both the adult and child populations. (Home Office 2008a) state that 8.2 per cent of people aged 16–59 admitted to using cannabis in the last month. The other most commonly reported drugs used in the last year by BCS respondents were cocaine (2.6 per cent of the population admitting last year use), ecstasy (1.8 per cent admitting last year use), amyl nitrite (1.4 per cent admitting last year use), amphetamines (1.3 per cent admitting last year use) and 0.7 per cent admitting last year use of hallucinogens. Again, the pattern established with cannabis use repeats itself, with use amongst the younger groups being more prevalent than those in the older age group. Heroin use fell well behind the others with 0.2 per cent of the population admitting heroin use in the last year.

Public attitudes toward illicit drugs

Information for this section comes from the work of Leitner *et al.* (1993) and an ICM poll commissioned by the *Observer*. Much of this is covered in the Runciman Report (1999, Chapter 2). In summary, Runciman suggests that:

- across all ages, heroin, cocaine, ecstasy and amphetamines are judged as harmful or very harmful by 90 per cent of the population;
- 32 per cent of the population feel drug laws are too liberal;
- across all ages, only one-third (33 per cent) judged cannabis to be harmful or very harmful;
- across all ages, 66 per cent of adults wanted strong and effective drug laws;
- support for decriminalising certain drugs now stands at 27 per cent of the population.

Finally, before concluding this chapter, it is time to return to the capture-recapture method outlined above. Hay *et al.*'s (2006) study examined data from 2004. Based on the capture-recapture method Hay estimates that there are 327,466 problematic drug users in England, with 281,320 being opiate users and 137,141 injecting, all of which are slightly higher than the figures relating to users in treatment. However, the other trends noted about age and gender remain constant in both sets of data.

The changing nature of drug use in Britain

It is hoped that by now it should be clear that it is beyond the scope of this study, or any other study for that matter, to be able to make definitive claims as to the true extent of illicit drug misuse in Britain at the beginning of the twenty-first century. That explains why any text, when discussing numbers or figures in any way related to drug misuse, is littered with caveats:

> *Best guess* at nos. of problem users who need treatment ...
>
> (Edmunds *et al.* 1998, emphasis added)

> Because of the absence of reliable prevalence data ... questions relating to prevalence of drug misuse in the adult population *cannot be answered with certainty*.
>
> (Welsh Drug and Alcohol Unit 1998: 11, emphasis added)

Anyone working with use and misuse of drugs issues is immediately confronted with the difficulty of obtaining good information.

(Davidson and Sturgeon-Adams 1997)

However, it is possible to offer some tentative conclusions based on the available data. We can say, with some certainty that:

- somewhere in the region of 11 million people – more than one-third of the adult population – have used an illicit drug at least once;
- close to half of all people aged 16–24 have used an illicit drug at least once;
- over one million people aged 16–24 have used an illicit drug this month;
- cannabis is overwhelmingly the most popular drug, with the 'hard' drugs of heroin and cocaine falling a long way behind;
- the use and likelihood of use of an illicit drug diminishes with age;
- there are somewhere in the region of 250,000 problematic illicit drug users in England and Wales with around 160,000 of those in some form of treatment;
- the majority of illicit drug users do so recreationally or experimentally.

We can also begin to look at the socio-demographics of illicit drug users in order to build our picture. Users are overwhelmingly male with a ratio of male to female users approaching four to one. They are also likely to be single, unemployed, have an income between £5,000 and £10,000 per annum, live in a privately rented flat and be educated to A level standard. Where employed they have either skilled or semi-skilled occupations. They are more likely to visit clubs and pubs than their peers who do not use illicit drugs. This pattern is summarised by the Home Office:

> ... being young ... being male, visiting nightclubs, not being married ... frequenting a pub or wine bar three times a week or more, living in a flat/maisonette or terraced house and living in a household with no children or being a single adult with children.

(Chivite *et al.* 2005: 59)

Official statistics drawn from medical and legal data shows that for some people using illicit drugs creates problems. These problems can be medical, social or legal, and a problematic user can experience all of these problems simultaneously. Medical and legal data also shows that drug use is mainly the preserve of the young, with few people aged over 30 coming to the state's attention. Where there are problems, especially medical problems, the drug that causes most concern seems to be heroin. Over the last 30 years there have been marked rises in the numbers of people coming to the attention of both the medical and legal arms of the British system. Equally, we know through seizure data that there are relatively large amounts of illicit drugs circulating in Britain. Care needs to be taken in basing conclusions on these figures alone as there are serious methodological weaknesses with this data, and it is generally recognised that official statistics do not cover all aspects of drug use, be that 'problematic' or 'recreational'.

Household surveys provide a fuller picture, although, again, the data they produce is self-acknowledged as lacking accuracy. Based on work such as the BCS, it is possible to suggest that recreational or experimental drug use has risen in Britain across the 1990s and has begun to peak in recent years. At present, a significant minority, somewhere in the region of one-third of the British population, have used an illicit drug at some time in their life. Mostly, this use is sporadic and/or experimental, and seems to be confined to those in their teens and early 20s, with use reducing considerably by middle age. Equally, those who use drugs recreationally or experimentally seem to favour one in particular – cannabis. Arguably, the widespread use of cannabis across the population has led to a situation where it is not seen as a problem in the way in which drugs such as heroin or cocaine are, creating a situation where public attitudes to that particular drug are at odds with those of the state. Where the public and state do seem to agree is on the problems posed by 'harder' drugs such as heroin and cocaine.

However, although our measurement techniques are improving, no one can say for sure that this amalgam of data provides the definitive picture. Social scientists, government researchers and those working for state agencies dealing with illicit drug use have yet to devise a method that counts and measures hidden populations with any degree of accuracy. The most any camp can do is to offer 'best-guess' figures, and it is on these, plus anecdotal evidence, plus the 'knowledge' of those working in the 'drug scene', that much policy is based. It is a measure of the seriousness with which the British state treats the 'drug problem' that sums of money as large as £6 billion are spent, especially based on such flimsy evidence. The next chapter focuses on two aspects of state reactions to drug use by examining the manner in which the use of illicit drugs is 'policed' by both arms of the British system.

Suggested further reading

Any of the government's publications that deal with statistics relating to drug use. For example, the most current edition of *Drugs Misuse Declared* is always a good starting point.

Also, most of the methodological problems discussed above are covered in the myriad of research methods texts that are available in all university libraries.

Singleton, N., Murray, R., Tinsley, L. (eds) 'Measuring different aspects of problem drug use: methodological developments' (2nd edition) *Home Office online report 16/06*, London: Home Office. Available www.homeoffice.gov.uk/rds/pdfs06/rdsolr1606.pdf (accessed 12 January 2009).

Some questions and areas for reflection

1. Above, much is made of the importance of being able to accurately measure illicit drug use. Is it really that important to have accurate data in this policy area?

2. The 'lifetime use' figures (that is ever having used an illicit drug even if it was only once) are often used to evidence high levels of illicit drug use. Should we really be concerned with 'one off' usage or should we discount these when estimating illicit drug use?

3. Based on the figures presented above, is illicit drug use a social, medical or criminal justice problem?

3 The British state's legal and medical responses to illicit drug use

Introduction

One of the recurring themes throughout this work is the fact that much of the data surrounding illicit drugs lacks certainty and as a result the illicit drug field is one where policy is based on 'best guess' figures. Nevertheless, the British state exhibits concern about the damage illicit drugs do to both individuals and society: witness the opening statement of the most recent policy document:

> Drug misuse wastes lives, destroys families and damages communities. It costs taxpayers millions to deal with the health problems caused by drugs and to tackle the crimes such as burglary, car theft, mugging and robbery which are committed by some users to fund their habit. The drug trade is linked to serious organised crime including prostitution and the trafficking of people and firearms. Drugs remain a serious and complex problem that we – along with all modern societies – must face.
>
> (Smith 2008: 4)

In many respects, this reflects the position outlined above, which noted that the British response has been characterised by a mix of criminal justice, medical and paternalistic concerns and it is to the manner in which those concerns are turned into policy and action this chapter now turns.

In order to achieve this, the chapter will provide an overview of the broad policy approaches and the main statutory instruments that dictate the responses of the criminal justice agencies and the medical profession. These two bodies, both collectively and independently from each other, but increasingly in a joint approach alongside other socio-welfarist agencies, 'police' drug use in Britain. The rationale in including this chapter is to establish the parameters of 'policing' and alert the reader to the *general* direction of British drug policy.

No specific policy initiatives will be explored at this stage in the book, contemporary policy developments being covered, in detail, in Chapters 9 and 10. Rather, this chapter will demonstrate the British state's policing of drugs is based on controlling certain types of drugs, via the manner in which, and by whom, they are supplied and used, or ensuring that drug use is carried out safely within socio-medically defined parameters. Additionally, the chapter will emphasise the importance of realising that 'policing' drug use can be exerted either through the law or socio-medical models of control, or, in many cases, combinations of both.

The chapter begins with a brief discussion on the meaning of 'policing' as employed in the context of this work. From there, it continues by outlining the international context from which most of Britain's drug laws emerge and are based. This mixture of internal political pressure to 'do something' in relation to drugs, coupled with external requirements to ratify international treaties, gave rise to the 1971 Misuse of Drugs Act (hereafter MDA) which at present is the key British legal control relating to drugs. From this base, the chapter moves to review the content of the MDA.

Following this, the chapter turns its attention to the other main form of policing, the control of drugs by the medical profession. It outlines the importance the concept of prevention holds for the medical profession, before moving to review *Drug Misuse and Dependence: UK Guidelines on Clinical Management* (DoH 2007). In particular, it notes the manner in which the DoH suggests that problematic drug users are policed via a mixture of prescription, increased compliance, withdrawal and dependence management. By way of conclusion, the chapter ends with a brief discussion of the general nature of drug policy, noting the tension between the manners in which the arms of the British system 'deal with' what is, essentially, the same problem.

'Policing' drugs: a broad definition

For a number of readers, a discussion around a definition of 'policing' may seem slightly superfluous: policing is surely what the police do. Policing revolves around the images television programmes like *The Bill* provide on an almost daily basis. For those of that persuasion, the notion that the medical profession can be engaged in 'policing' may be seen as (a) a novel idea, or (b) stupid. However, neither is the case: consider this quote from Reiner (2000: 1):

> It is important to distinguish between the ideas of 'police' and 'policing'. 'Police' refers to a particular form of social institution, while 'policing' implies a set of processes with specific social functions.

He continues, noting importantly that 'policing' is, in fact, *a set of activities that attempt to maintain a particular form of social order.* That order may result from a society-wide consensus, or it may be the result of latent conflict between differently placed social groups. Whatever the case, the function of 'policing' is to ensure that a particular form of social order is encouraged, maintained and upheld. And, as Chapter 1 informed one area of contention around social order is the place of mind-altering substances in a 'good society'.

In turn, social order is dependent upon two related concepts: that of creating and encouraging conformity and also of maintaining control over populations. However, as Reiner (2000: 2–3) points out, there is a problem in linking 'policing' to general social control. Policing is, according to Reiner, a specific aspect of the overall social control process. Policing excludes concepts such as punishment, socialisation, family structure and religious beliefs, all of which have different functions within the totality that has become known as 'social control'. Policing is one of many 'sub-sets' in the whole social control process. Reiner provides a definition that neatly summarises the approach to 'policing' taken in this book. For our purposes then, 'policing' should be seen as:

> ... systems of surveillance coupled with the threat of sanctions for dis-
> covered deviance – either immediately or in terms of the initiation of
> penal processes or both.
>
> (Reiner 2000: 3)

As will be argued below, this definition can encompass the work of not only the police and the other law enforcement agencies such as Revenue and Customs, but can also be seen to cover much of the work of what are defined as 'welfarist' agencies, such as social work, and, of course, the medical profession. Using this definition allows us to conceive of 'policing' as being on a continuum. At the 'hard-end' of the continuum are the law and order agencies, employing legislation, which is often a blunt instrument, to achieve control and conformity. At the other 'soft-end' comes the 'social' agencies, which often employ less overt, more subtle means, but nevertheless use the twin tools of surveillance and threat of sanctions as a means of controlling populations, allowing these agencies to be seen by some of a radical persuasion as being 'iron fists in velvet gloves' (George and Wilding 1992).

This is a key concept to grasp. Whilst the manner in which the law enforcement agencies operate within our particular definition of policing may be axiomatic, the involvement of the medical profession in policing may need to be further explained. Viewing medicine as a sub-set of social control may go some way to endorsing a few of the points made in Chapter 1, concerning the medical profession's early interest in, and links with, late Victorian moral philanthropists. It also allows us to look beyond medical involvement with problematic drug users from the simplistic 'treatment model' perspective, and ask questions about the social, moral and political functions performed by doctors in 'treating' (perhaps policing?) drug-dependent users. This becomes important because control of the work of both the hard-end and soft-end agencies emanate from the state, and as previously stated it is a contention of this book that the 'drug problem' in Britain is at least partially a political construct often revolving around the perceived paternalistic need to control the actions of young people – to 'save them from themselves'.

In that respect 'policing' the drug problem by hard- and soft-end agencies clearly has functions beyond arresting and/or treating drug users; it also becomes part of wider social control by promoting and cementing conformity to a certain set of practices. That said, the chapter moves on to its main task; that of exploring and examining the central documents that shape Britain's general policy approach to 'policing' drugs. The immediate section will provide a brief contextual overview of the genesis of the key British legal policy document, the 1971 Misuse of Drugs Act.

The 1971 Misuse of Drugs Act: a brief contextual note

As Chapter 1 explained, the genesis of much British drug policy lies in various international treaties. By creating laws such as the MDA, Britain is able to meet its international obligations, although as Runciman (1999) notes, the MDA goes beyond the scope of many of the United Nations (UN) Conventions. The MDA is able to do so because, although the United Nations conventions oblige signatories to meet certain broad demands, including the creation of criminal offences for contravening the conventions, the day-to-day minutiae of law enforcement is left to the discretion of the individual nation. This explains why drug laws often exhibit significant variations from country to country.

Since the beginning of the 1960s, when the UN replaced the League of Nations as the main body with responsibility for the international control of drugs, there have been three key UN treaties that have had a direct and significant impact on British drug laws. The first was the Single Convention on Narcotic Drugs 1961. This convention attempts to standardise the control of narcotics across nations so that certain drugs are only used for scientific, medical and in some cases, industrial purposes. The 1961 Convention arranges drugs into schedules that determine the nature of the controls over any given drug. Any activity that contravenes the Convention must be a punishable offence, with a custodial term for serious breaches. Crucially, such a requirement almost invariably makes certain aspects of drug use a criminal offence within signatory states.

The second key international convention is the UN Convention on Psychotropic Drugs 1971. This is concerned with, amongst other drugs, hallucinogens, stimulants and sedatives. Again, the aim here is to limit drug use to scientific or medical purposes. The important point in this Convention is that it severely restricts the use of certain drugs to such an extent that many cannot be used, even on prescription. This accounts for the fact that some cannabis-type drugs (for example, cannabinol) cannot, at the time of writing, be prescribed freely in Britain. In line with the 1961 Convention, actions that contravene the 1971 treaty must be punishable up to, and including, prison sentences for serious breaches.

Somewhat problematically, it appears that the wording of both the 1961 and 1971 UN Conventions lacked clarity in relation to the offence of possession, purchase and cultivation in relation to personal use, thereby creating a loophole in the law. The UN recognised this and used the United Nations Convention against Illicit Traffic in Narcotic Drugs and Psychotropic

Substances 1988 (known as the Vienna Convention) to close this gap. The 1988 Convention specifies that breaches in the conventions must be seen as criminal offences under each signatory state's domestic law. Greater care in wording the Vienna Convention was taken to ensure there is greater clarification of 'criminal' activity, in a concerted effort to create a loophole-free document. Both illuminating and recognising the evolving nature of the illicit drug industry, there are sections on the control of precursor chemicals, used in the manufacture of illicit substances, and money laundering by drug dealers. As with the previous two conventions, the detailed implementation is left to the discretion of the signatory state.

However, and again highlighting the size and scale of the international drug trade, in September 2003 the UN Convention against Transnational Organized Crime and in December 2005 the UN Convention against Corruption came into force. Both conventions broaden the scope of money-laundering offences by stating that money laundering should cover the proceeds of all serious crimes including drug trafficking. Each convention urges states to create all-encompassing domestic supervisory and regulatory processes for banks and other financial institutions and call for the establishment of Financial Intelligence Units (FIUs) to police this.

In addition, the International Convention for the Suppression of the Financing of Terrorism came into force in April 2002. This requires member states to protect their financial systems from being misused by persons planning or engaged in terrorist activities. This occurred as a direct result of 11 September 2001, because member states recognised the links between terrorism, transnational organized crime, the international drug trade and money-laundering, and cemented international concerns about the links between terrorism and the international drug trade.

British drug law, including the MDA, must therefore be seen in this wider international context. In many respects, the UN conventions set the broad parameters of drug legislation, but the details are left to the individual states to interpret within their own political, social and cultural frameworks. Thus, it could be argued that the best way to view the legal side of British drug policy (as with many other nation states' legal response to drug use) is as a hybrid of international law and uniquely domestic concerns and worries. With those thoughts in mind, the chapter now reviews the content of the 1971 MDA.

The 1971 Misuse of Drugs Act

This section of the chapter will outline some of the main sections of the 1971 MDA so the reader is able to better understand the main points of British law relating to substances controlled under the MDA. The intention here is to provide a broad-brush overview of the law and not to enter into a discussion of the fine details of the legislation (for a fuller resume of the 1971 MDA, see Runciman 1999, Chapters 1 and 3).

The MDA 1971 replaced the three principal drug control acts of the 1960s: the Drugs (Prevention of Misuse) Act 1964, and the Dangerous Drugs Acts of 1965 and 1967. In this way, the British state was able to bring together all the hitherto disparate controls and use the 1971 MDA to act as the statutory framework in the control of drugs. That framework included: a system of licensing for doctors to prescribe heroin and cocaine; the requirement of all doctors to notify addicts to the Home Office; the introduction of national stop and search powers for the police; and the introduction of regulations on the safe custody of drugs. The MDA was also responsible for establishing Britain's first statutory advisory group on illicit drugs, the Advisory Council on the Misuse of Drugs (ACMD). Importantly, as far as the law is concerned, the MDA introduced a number of new approaches that are clearly important today.

First, it instigated a strict classification of drugs. Following the passing of the MDA, drugs were placed in one of three categories: A, B or C. The category each particular drug is placed in is determined by the extent of harm misuse inflicts. For example, heroin and cocaine are class A drugs, recognising the serious effects of prolonged misuse, whereas cannabis is a class B drug, and substances such as benzodiazepines (tranquillisers) are class C drugs. The penalties issued by the courts for any contravention of the MDA are concomitant to the class of drug involved in the cases, with class A drugs attracting the most severe legal responses. Equally important is the dichotomy of the offence of unlawful possession, with a distinction being made between possession and possession with intent to supply, the latter being seen as more serious.

Running briefly through the sections of the MDA, Section 1 established the ACMD and codified its duty as being the standing body charged to advise the government on the prevention of the misuse of drugs, and how to deal with the social problems linked to drug misuse. This is still the case some 40 years later. Section 2 identified which drugs were to be controlled by the MDA, and ordered them into their respective classes. Sections 3 to 6 identified those activities that became criminal offences under the MDA. These offences include; import and export, possession, supply, possession with intent to supply and the cultivation of the cannabis plant. Sections 8 and 9 made it an offence for the occupier or manager of any premises to knowingly allow those premises to be used for the smoking of opium or cannabis, the production or supply of controlled drugs, and the preparing and taking of controlled drugs. Section 9 concentrates specifically on the supply of materials or articles that can be used in the unlawful administration of drugs.

Vital for the medical profession's ability to prescribe for and treat drug users who experience problems, Section 7 lists exemptions from the MDA, thus allowing the medical profession, including dentists, pharmacists and scientific researchers, the ability to carry on their work free from the fear of prosecution. Sections 10 and 11 of the MDA provide power to the Secretary of State to make regulations governing most aspects of drug management and administration, including transport, storing, destruction, labelling, record keeping and prescribing. Section 11 concentrates on providing directions to the occupier of any premises where controlled drugs are to be kept. Sections 12 to 16 provide the power to the Secretary of State to withdraw the ability to prescribe, administer or manufacture controlled drugs from any member of the medical, pharmaceutical or veterinary profession.

Sections 23 and 24 outline police powers of stop and search, the searching of premises and arrest. These have subsequently been superseded in England and Wales by the 1984 Police and Criminal Evidence Act, but still apply in Scotland. Sections 25 and 26 provide for maximum penalties, and it is important to note that following the Crime (Sentences) Act 1997, a third consecutive trafficking offence involving a class A drug receives a minimum seven-year prison sentence. Section 28 is an interesting addition to the MDA as it allows for any defendant the ability to prove lack of knowledge as to the nature of the substance they are charged with mis-using and thus be acquitted. However, Runciman (1999) notes in reality, as a defence, Section 28 'is a high hurdle for a defendant to overcome'.

It is important to reiterate the point made at the start of this part of the chapter that the above is merely a brief overview of the MDA. It is equally important to be aware that over time certain parts of the MDA have been replaced by other legislation, as in the case of police stop and search powers with the Police and Criminal Evidence Act 1984 or mandatory sentences under the 1997 Crime (Sentences) Act. It is also necessary to be aware of other related legislation such as the Criminal Justice (International Co-operation) Act 1990, which enabled the UK to comply with parts of the Vienna Convention 1988 and is primarily concerned with the supply of precursor drugs used in the manufacture of many illicit substances. Other important Acts for consideration would include The Drug Trafficking Act 1994, which created offences in relation to money laundering and handling the proceeds of drug trafficking. It also introduced measures to confiscate the proceeds of drug trafficking.

Given the benefit of hindsight, the 1971 MDA can be seen as a product of its time, and was drafted as a response to the situation during that period. The ever-changing nature of the illicit drug 'industry' has required various other Acts to be implemented over time. For example, when the MDA was drafted there was very little importation of heroin: as Chapter 1 notes, HM Customs and Excise only made their first major seizure of heroin in 1971. The contemporary growth and constantly changing nature of international drug trafficking has subsequently required a review of policy responses, both domestically and internationally. World wide, this gave rise to the Vienna Convention in 1988. As a result, Britain responded to the Vienna Convention by passing the Drug Trafficking Act 1994, demonstrating the impact changes in both international law and domestic events have had upon British law in relation to drugs.

Essentially, what the MDA tried to achieve was a codification of, and organising framework for, the British state's legal response to the use and supply of certain drugs. Simplistically, this involves the prohibition and pro-scription of all aspects of use and supply of substances controlled under the auspices of the MDA. Only in extremely limited scenarios are the general public allowed to use drugs controlled under the MDA without medical approval, and, for example, as with the case of Section 28, once knowledge has been confirmed, use must cease. The state's legally based reaction to drug use, as enshrined in the MDA, can be seen to be draconian with little or no leeway given. In short, the strict letter of the law prohibits the use and supply of certain substances and any transgressions that are detected will result in punishment.

Quite clearly, the MDA provides a framework within which the law enforcement agencies are able to undertake the policing of drug use. There is ample scope within the MDA for surveillance operations by criminal justice agencies and there is an ever-present danger for those illicit users, identified and arrested by the criminal justice agencies, of invoking legal sanctions. For the British legal system, the MDA is both a codification of the state's legal response to illicit drug use and the social control tool with which to promote and ensure conformity with a drug-free lifestyle. The next section of the chapter moves away from the British state's legal response and examines the approach to drug use championed and directed by the DoH to the other 'police officers' of drug use: the (broadly defined) medical profession.

The medical profession: policing via prevention and prescription

The response of the state's criminal justice arm has been to control and define the type of legally acceptable drugs via prohibition and proscription. The ultimate response of the medical arm has been to attempt to control the type and amount of drugs used by the power of treatment and prescription, via the use of doctors. Before going on to review the key role played by doctors in policing drug users, it is important to point out that many other statutory and voluntary bodies, which come under the broad rubric of 'socio-medical' agencies, also work with drug users and the wider population in preventing, reducing or altering drug-taking behaviour. This represents an important part of the overall strategy and it is to these that the next section turns.

As McDermott (1998: 93) confirms, 'there have been two primary strategies ... to deal with the drug problem ... interdiction and demand reduction'. Essentially, interdiction is within the realm of the law enforcement agencies, and has been covered above, whereas aspects of demand reduction fall into the remit of socio-medical agencies. In itself, this type of demand reduction can take two forms: (i) general messages aimed at preventing people from starting to take drugs and/or to encourage those taking drugs to either cease, or reduce the harm they are doing, or (ii) to use drugs issued on prescription by doctors, often supplemented by counselling or other treatments, to control the demand for illicit drugs. As already noted, the control of problematic drug users by prescription will be explored later in this chapter. The immediate concern is to review those general preventative techniques which are aimed at reducing demand for drugs amongst the wider population.

Policing via prevention

Ham (1992) argues that health promotion has had a long-term impact on improving the quality of health in Britain, but only relatively recently has it become a specialism in its own right. He points to the 1976 DHSS document *Prevention and Health: Everybody's Business* as a watershed point, inasmuch that it gave recognition to the importance of health promotion via preventative campaigns. In the world of drug use, the importance of prevention messages was writ large during the AIDS scare of the 1980s, which ran alongside other campaigns aimed at reducing AIDS-related drug use, such as the *Heroin Screws You Up* promotions of the mid to late 1980s.

The rationale behind the majority of most health promotion campaigns is to prevent the general population from damaging their health due to the manner in which they live their lives, be this related to heart disease, tooth decay or illicit drug use. Prevention campaigns generally operate on one of three levels: primary, secondary and tertiary. Primary campaigns are usually highly generalised and quite often the message is simplistic, mainly because it is aimed at the widest possible audience. This type of prevention was, for a long time, at the forefront of British drug prevention initiatives (McDermott 1998). However, the effectiveness of such a strategy has been questioned because it does:

> ... little more than confirm the beliefs of those people who were never at risk of using in the first place, while having little or no impact whatsoever on those people who were going to use drugs.
>
> (McDermott 1998: 93)

Thus, the 'just say no' or 'heroin screws you up' prevention campaigns ran counter to the experiences of many young users, but at the same time perhaps reinforced some of their elders' views on drug use. The effect was to devalue information in the eyes of those sections of society perhaps most 'at risk' of drug-related problems, whilst at the same time cementing stereotypical, uni-dimensional views of a complex social phenomenon in social groups that had little first-hand knowledge or experience of drug use.

A gradual realisation of the futility of this situation led to an increase in secondary prevention campaigns. Promotions of this kind are far more specific and are aimed at groups thought to be 'at risk' of currently using, on the verge of using, or being exposed to, controlled drugs. The driving principle of this approach is that of 'harm reduction' or 'harm minimisation', itself a primary influence in both contemporary and historical British medical drug policy. The overall impact of harm reduction on British drug policy will be explored further in Chapters 7 and 8, for now however, it is important to grasp the three guiding principles of modern harm reduction approaches, in order to better understand the nature of secondary and tertiary prevention campaigns. These are:

1. excessive behaviours occur along a continuum of risk, ranging from minimal to extreme;
2. changing addictive behaviour is a stepwise process, complete abstinence being the final step;
3. sobriety simply isn't for everybody.

(Westermeyer 1998: 1)

Secondary prevention campaigns can take several guises. For example, there are a number of school-based initiatives aimed at both pupils and their parents (Barton 2001), where teachers and outside specialists make their audiences aware of the dangers of drug use, as well as the importance of using safely once the decision to use drugs has been taken. Likewise, and often used in support of such campaigns, the Health Education Authority (HEA) publishes a number of guides. These are often magazine-style booklets that promote a zero-use approach but also contain sections on safe use and first aid, as well as detailing the properties and effects of different drugs. In a similar vein, again with the intent of targeting a highly specific audience, drug projects such as *Lifeline* in Manchester have published a series of cartoon-based pamphlets. From a completely personal perspective, my favourites are those serialising the drug-related misfortunes and adventures of characters such as *Peanut Pete* and *Claire and Jose*, which are aimed at ensuring safe use, whilst highlighting the possible dangers associated with drug taking.

Arguably, it is from this realist base that the government's own drug prevention/education website has emerged. The *Frank* site (www.talktofrank.com) was launched by the British government in 2003 and has the following stated aims:

> FRANK aims to ensure that:
>
> - young people understand the risks and dangers of drugs and their use
> - young people know where to go for advice or help
> - parents have the confidence and knowledge to talk to their children about drugs
> - professionals who work with young people, especially vulnerable groups, are supported
>
> (Home Office 2009)

Any look at the *Frank* site, or a perusal of the campaigns it runs makes it clear that the government has recognised that illicit drug use is part and parcel of the everyday experience of Britons in the early part of this century and that abstinence campaigns may be misplaced: rather the emphasis ought to be on ensuring that those who take drugs do so in a safe manner and are supported and informed if things begin to go wrong. In short, there is very little point in a general anti-drug message when statistics demonstrate that as many as one-third of the population aged between 16 and 64 have at least tried an illicit substance (Home Office 2009).

Rather, and of special importance to the success of any prevention campaign, the tone and content of the prevention message needs to correspond and resonate with the target audience's lived experience. The result is the beginning of a secondary prevention regime that has credibility and thus commands the respect of its intended audience by virtue of promoting a realistic and non-patronising message. However, the central elements of policing are still visible. Surveillance of the drug-taking behaviour of the population takes the form of general household surveys that, despite being imprecise, nevertheless provide tangible target populations. In this example, sanctions refer to the implications that excessive drug taking will lead to ill health and/ or criminal convictions. Primary and secondary prevention campaigns thus attempt to promote and ensure conformity to the drug-free lifestyle.

The final form of prevention is tertiary. This is also targeted, and is aimed directly at those people whose drug use has moved toward the problematic area of the continuum of risk. It is here that the full weight of the 'hard-end' of socio-medical policing enters the 'fight against drugs', along with its 'ultimate weapon': the right to prescribe.

Policing via prescription: a brief contextual note

As Chapter two noted, for many years following the findings of the Rolleston Committee in 1926, British doctors could prescribe all manner of substances to those addicted to drugs with virtual impunity. Indeed, the first controls on the prescribing behaviour of doctors only came into being during the 1960s due, in the main, to the over-prescription of heroin, leading to large quantities of licit drugs being diverted into the illicit drug market. Whilst this legislation may have curbed the autonomy of some doctors, it was not a serious problem for the majority, due to the fact that during the 1960s and into the early 1970s the numbers of problematic drug users were relatively small, and those being treated were often referred to specialist services. This meant that the vast majority of doctors, especially General Practitioners (GPs), rarely, if ever, saw a drug addict. The outcome of this was that the issue of how, when and why to prescribe for drug addicts never became a pressing question for the majority of doctors.

However, as has been documented (Gerada and Farrell 1998: 330–31), the number of problematic drug users 'surged' during the late 1970s and into the 1980s, leading to the then DHSS encouraging GPs to become more involved with problematic drug users. Clearly, this placed GPs in a predicament, as many of them had never been asked to deal with a group that some see as 'problem patients' and, perhaps crucially, at that time too few medical undergraduates had received even basic education in treating problematic drug users (BMA 1997: 121). As a result, many GPs were left isolated and lacking advice or direction. Those that would accept drug addicts as patients were sometimes inundated with addicts all demanding treatment. Some GPs quickly became disillusioned; many made injudicious prescribing policies, many more simply retreated behind long-held prejudices (Hutchinson 2001).

Given the rise in 'recreational' drug culture and a concomitant growth in problematic use, this situation could not be allowed to continue. This was recognised in the DHSS (1982) report *Treatment and Rehabilitation*. In turn, two years later the DHSS published *Guidelines of Good Clinical Practice in the Treatment of Drug Misuse* (DHSS 1984). These were updated and re-named in 1991, appearing as *Drug Misuse and Dependence: Guidelines on Clinical Management* (DoH *et al.* 1991) and were again updated in 1999, with the latest revision taking place in 2007 and being re-named *Drug misuse and dependence: UK guidelines on clinical management* (DoH *et al.* 2007). Before moving to examine the 2007 revisions it is germane to this chapter to briefly look at the impact the 1999 revision had.

The DoH guidelines on managing drug misuse

Robertson (2000: 325) emphasises the importance of the 1999 revisions and notes their timeliness, claiming that there was a real and pressing need for the 1999 review owing to the fact that:

> The demise of the British Addict Index and the revocation of the statutory requirement for British doctors to notify the Chief Medical Officer of cases of addiction, many national and international events seem to threaten and confuse clinicians and policy-makers ... These Guidelines, therefore, are opportune and bear a considerable responsibility ... There should be no doubt, therefore, that they are ... heavy weight ... and are likely to give rise to substantial changes in clinical practice in the UK ...

At a very basic level, the importance vested in the 1999 document can be seen in its size in comparison with its predecessors: it runs to some 138 pages compared to the 57 the 1991 guidelines contained. Obviously, the authors intended it to be a comprehensive and authoritative tome, able to be used as a source of reference for all manner of drug-related information. The same can be said for the 2007 revision running as it does to 128 pages and it is to this the chapter now turns.

Running through its content, the 2007 document begins with an introductory chapter that has the role of affirming that 'Drug treatment is effective' (DoH *et al.* 2007: 3). It then moves to outline clinical governance, essential elements in treatment provision, the psychosocial components of treatment, pharmacological interventions, health considerations and specific treatment situations and populations (DoH *et al.* 2007).

However, what has become clear is that in the eight years between the two documents the socio-medical treatment landscape has altered due to changes in the NHS, a growing importance of joined-up working and more nuanced and informed understanding of the needs and lives of problematic drug users. Thus, the treatment landscape has changed from one where:

> A single 'shared care' model – described in the 1999 clinical guidelines as partnerships between primary, secondary and specialist providers – has, in practice, developed into a range of different models, often driven by local circumstances and including a wider range of providers.
>
> (DoH *et al.* 2007: 13)

As a result, much greater emphasis is placed on the need for a response that is tailored to local needs and conditions. Equally, the monopoly that doctors once held over the ability to prescribe is breaking down with 'new opportunities for non-medical prescribers, and an increasing number of pharmacists and nurses have acquired the training necessary to prescribe for their patients' (DoH *et al.* 2007: 14), and a recognition that 'joint working across health and social care is therefore a key feature of effective treatment. It is seldom the case that one clinician will be able to meet these needs in isolation' (DoH *et al.* 2007: 14).

In the previous edition of this book, I stated that 'the DoH Guidelines encourage doctors to "police" problematic drug use by employing a mixture of four approaches: managing and treating withdrawal; agreeing to and servicing a maintenance regime; cultivating and maintaining the compliance of the patient; retaining the power to prescribe'. Due to the changes noted above this is not now the case. However, this does not mean that drug users are not policed by socio-medical professionals: they are, but in a different, and arguably a more informed, holistic and enlightened way, which can be seen in the fact that the DoH *et al.* recognise that treating problematic drug users has become a multi-agency task, and involves much more than simply prescribing substitute drugs. It needs an holistic approach, designed to help the problematic drug user navigate their way to a safer, sometimes drug-free life. This recognition marks a significant change in approach by the medical profession.

Nevertheless, doctors will still play a major part in the life of a drug user once they enter treatment. Patients with problematic drug use can present to the doctor for a broad range of reasons, but generally share the common desire for treatment designed to improve their health. This is recognised by the DoH *et al.* (2007:11) who categorically state that the 'focus for the clinician treating a drug misuse is on the patient themselves'. However, and marking a shift of emphasis from previous guidelines, the same section goes on to note that 'the impact of their drug misuse on other individuals – especially dependent children – and on communities should be taken into consideration'. The first task for the medic is to assess the nature and extent of drug-related problems, to establish patterns of use, determine the patient's motivation to change and then to determine the need for substitute medication. The DoH *et al.* guidelines also stress the need to assess the patient's expectation of treatment.

For the patient, once the decision has been made to cease or reduce drug use, one of the first effects will be the onset of withdrawal symptoms, the nature, intensity and speed at which these symptoms occur being heavily dependent upon the type of drug being used. Although some addicts can withdraw without substitute drugs (Robins 1973), the vast majority of addicts will require some help with detoxification and the withdrawal symptoms associated with this process. In order to relieve these symptoms, the guidelines offer suggestions for a number of substitute drugs for the various types of addiction problems.

Once the decision to prescribe has been taken, the next question is 'how much?' Clearly, the patient's health will be paramount, so the dose has to be one that will not place the patient in jeopardy of overdosing, especially with methadone, a drug commonly prescribed to opiate addicts. The DoH guidelines in tandem with the British National Formulary suggest doses based on the severity of the withdrawal symptoms, with the overall aim of minimising the suffering endured by the withdrawing addict. Once the initial withdrawal period is over, the doctor, following consultation with the patient, must then decide on the next step in the policing of problematic drug use.

The DoH *et al.* (2007: 52) note that ' ... patients may not cease all illicit drug use immediately ... eliminating all illicit drug misuse ... may take months or years'. Thus it becomes necessary to establish a maintenance programme. This is a long-term approach to problematic drug use that can, in some cases, continue for a number of years before the patient is ready to reduce their prescription drug intake. The patient will receive a regular supply of a prescription drug that is of an appropriate dose. The amount of drug will be enough to stave off withdrawal symptoms, provide a measure of stability, yet not be sufficient to induce 'signs of intoxication' (DoH *et al.* 2007).

Compliance is a very important aspect of the socio-medical professions' approach to treating this client group. The DoH *et al.* (2007: 52–54) guidelines contain a section on assessing and responding to progress and failure to progress. For example, the DoH Guidelines offer a number of points of advice concerning the manner in which the doctor can build the trust and confidence of the addicted patient, thus aiding compliance. These include building a good therapeutic relationship that allows the discussion of drug-related problems without the patient fearing expulsion from treatment. However, the DoH also advises doctors to employ other tactics that can be seen to be more controlling.

These could include random urine tests designed to ascertain if the patient is still using illicit drugs, daily pick ups of the substitute drug, and supervised consumption of the substitute drug, the latter only being relaxed when 'subject to assessment of the patient's compliance' (DoH *et al.* 2007: 50). The relaxation of supervised consumption can also be used as a form of incentive to comply: as the DoH *et al.* note (2007: 51) the relaxation of supervised consumption can be used as an incentive if there has been a period of drug-free urine samples for example.

Overarching all of the above is the ability of the medical professions to prescribe substitute drugs. Clearly, this power is an important part of the medical profession's identity and forms a substantial part of their professional power base, at the same time carrying with it an enormous responsibility, the latter point being made forcibly by the DoH *et al.*'s guidelines. However, it also ensures that the socio-medical professions wield large amounts of control over their patients, especially those patients who are dependent upon drugs: in itself, the threat of a loss of prescription becomes an encouragement for the patient to comply. Nevertheless, doctors can, and do, end treatment programmes due to the non-compliance of the patient. Whilst this is understandable, it also provides the medic with a considerable ability to 'police' the lifestyle of the addict patient, due largely to the fact that non-compliance will lead, ultimately, to a withdrawal of legal, substitute drugs. When this happens, the addict will almost always be forced to return to using illicit drugs, and the concomitant risks associated with that lifestyle.

Arguably, the power to prescribe is at the heart of the medical profession's 'policing policy' in relation to problematic drug users. Without retention of the right to withdraw prescriptions, doctors quickly lose their professional identity, as well as the all-important ability of being able to control their patient's behaviour. As Whitaker and McLeod (1998: 366) point out, 'the line between "substitute prescribing" and simply giving drug users legal drugs, thus decriminalising that part of their drug use is indistinct'. Building upon the paradox that the possession of medically approved and supervised drug use automatically decriminalises drug users, Self (1992) has colourfully pointed out that doctors can become '[drug] dealers by appointment to H.M. Government'. This point is taken up more forcibly by Strang *et al.* (1994: 202) who suggest that there is some concern doctors could become 'overpaid grocers', if they are forced to merely act as signatories on prescriptions.

Although prescriptions are now part of an overall care package, for many addicts the prescription is seen as 'the whole treatment' (Read 1995), thus allowing the power to prescribe to be employed as a form of 'carrot and stick' in the policing of problematic drug users. It is a carrot in as much that if the addict is able to convince the doctor that their problem is sufficient, their attitude is correct, and that they are able to comply with the agreed treatment plan, they will be rewarded with a prescription. On the other hand, it becomes a stick, because failure to comply will almost certainly lead to a withdrawal of the prescription, which for many will cause a return to illicit drug use.

From this perspective, it can be seen that the work of doctors in dealing with problematic, heavy-end users becomes a form of policing. There are clear elements of surveillance: the weekly appointments, supervised consumption and random urine tests being the most obvious. There is also the element of sanction: reviews of the treatment plan, a revocation of home consumption and a cessation of treatment and prescription. Using a combination of these approaches allows doctors to control drug addicts. It also forces addicts to conform, if not to society's mores of a drug-free life, then certainly to the medical profession's conception of a 'good' patient.

Conclusion

What this chapter has tried to do is alert the reader to the fact that the British state (alongside almost every other Western democracy) makes a significant effort to police the use of controlled drugs. In Britain's case, the state employs two different sectors – medicine and the law – to carry out this task, thereby running the risk of importing a number of differences and similarities in the manner in which the state polices drug use. In terms of similarities, both sectors use the tactics of surveillance and sanction in an effort to ensure conformity. However, the difference lies in the effect of the sanctions each sector employs. These are dramatically different, with one, the law, treating the drug user as a criminal, and therefore by implication as 'bad', whereas the other, medicine, treats the drug user as a patient, and therefore as 'ill'.

In this way, contact with either arm of the British system is framed within competing discourses of knowledge, and brings dramatically different social consequences: at the same time a drug user can be defined as a criminal and as a patient, and receive the concomitant actions and responses both roles carry with them. At one level there is very little wrong with this. Indeed, it could be argued that policing drug use this way upholds the law, thus supporting the consensual view of right and wrong, as well as fulfilling the social expectation that sick people will be treated and, if possible, cured. However, that perspective ignores three points: first, as we have seen, a substantial minority of the population does not share the consensus that the use and possession of every substance controlled under the MDA should be proscribed; second, not every addicted patient receives the appropriate treatment as a matter of course; and third, which discourse should take precedence in instances where both sectors lay claim to the same person?

There are other, deeper, critiques of the British state's response to illicit drugs, revolving around issues of organisational needs. For party political reasons, legal 'policing' is often presented as being wholly domestic-led, conveniently ignoring the fact that international law is very often the driver, or at the very least, acts to set the parameters of, domestic drug policies, thereby limiting the nature of the domestic response. Equally, medical 'policing' is nearly always presented as being wholly concerned with 'treatment', 'prevention' and 'cure', ignoring the fact that at the same time it is promoting the relatively recent moral perspective that 'luxurious' use of certain substances is wrong. As well as this, medical control of drug addiction further cements the medics' ownership of deciding who is eligible to receive certain drugs. The result is that referral to the general direction of British drug policy often obscures highly relevant points, thus limiting the extent and nature of debate.

These are points that will be returned to in some of the following chapters, which examines these and other issues inherent in contemporary British drug policy. The next chapter moves the book in a different direction, abandoning its somewhat parochial concerns with all things British, and widening the debate to examine illicit drug production in a global context.

Suggested further reading

DoH *et al.* (2007) *Drug misuse and dependence: UK guidelines on clinical management*, London: Department of Health (England).

Reiner, R. (2000) *The Politics of the Police* (3rd edition), Oxford: Oxford University Press.

Questions and areas for reflection

1. The 1971 Misuse of Drugs Act and the drug classifications are 40 years old, and despite some revisions many have called for a complete overhaul of drug legislation in Britain. Do you agree with those calls?
2. Why do we prescribe substitute drugs such as methadone and subutex, instead of prescribing opium?
3. Are problematic drug users 'ill'? Should they be seen as 'deserving patients' in the manner that other people with chronic illnesses are?

4 Illicit drug use

Class, gender and ethnicity

Introduction

This is a new chapter and its purpose is to provide a warning to students working in this area not to assume that the effects of illicit drug use fall evenly on all sections of the population. Whilst it is true that drug use transcends gender, class and race the manner in which that occurs, and, in some cases, the types of drugs consumed, is not consistent across different social groups. In many respects this is unsurprising as there is a large body of literature in the social sciences that demonstrates aspects of inequality of life experience, consumption patterns and provision of services. However, as with all specific areas it is important that the exact manner in which inequality manifests is understood, not least because it may serve to improve services.

This chapter begins by outlining the normalisation thesis (Parker *et al.* 1998) both in its original form and the revisit that Howard Parker and colleagues conducted in 2002 (Parker *et al.* 2002). From there, it offers a more in-depth look at the use of illicit drugs in terms of gender, social class and race and ethnicity in order to explore the effects of social and cultural pressures on different social groups. For example, we know that many female problematic drug users who are committing crime often resort to prostitution, yet prostitution is not currently one of the trigger offences used to determine suitability for drug intervention programmes. Equally, we know that drug use when conducted by males can be explained as 'normal' risk-taking behaviour, but when undertaken by women it is seen as doubly deviant. The chapter concludes with an examination of the manner in which the media reports on illicit drug use in relation to gender, class and race and will argue that the media's 'horror-distortion' techniques often provide a false impression regarding the extent and nature of drug use. However, before starting on that journey, it is important to offer a brief reminder of the current state of illicit drug use in contemporary British society.

Normalisation theory: some basic concepts

Parker and his colleagues started their work from the premise that more young Britons than ever before were taking illicit drugs but that this was being explained in a number of competing and confusing ways. Accordingly, they set out with the aim of better understanding the contexts and pressures that lead to the widespread use of illicit drugs amongst young people. In order to achieve this, the research team undertook a longitudinal study of 700 young people in the North West of England. They made the initial contact with them when they were aged 14 and then they were subsequently contacted by the research team annually for up to the next five years. Specifically the team asked them a series of questions about:

> ... personal and family circumstances, their disposable income, use of leisure and perspectives on personal and social relationships ... their tobacco, alcohol and illicit drug use. As they matured we felt able to pursue more complex issues ... including their attitudes towards drug use and drug users, their assessment of the health education they received, and their experiences at parties and nightclubs. For those who took drugs ... we felt able to ask them to describe their motivations for their use of individual drugs and what they experienced in doing so.
>
> (Parker *et al.* 1998: 32)

As a result of this research Parker and colleagues were able to offer a fascinating account of the role and impact illicit substances had on the lives of young people growing up in late twentieth century Britain. This is not the place to detail those findings (rather readers are urged to go to the original source: Parker *et al.* 1998), but it is important to review the seven key conclusions, as they hold, in my opinion, clear indicators as to why illicit drug use remains widespread amongst young people 20 years on. However, prior to that it is important to define the central concepts of Parker *et al.*'s thesis.

Normalisation and recreational use

The starting point for Parker *et al.*'s work is that they are concerned with some not all drugs: more specifically those drugs they term 'recreational' (they note cannabis as the primary drug), followed by nitrates, amphetamine, LSD and ecstasy, and that these are the drugs that are readily associated with 'recreational' use. Heroin and, at that point in the illicit drug taking-chronology, cocaine were not included, nor were the actions and lives of daily or chaotic poly-drug users due to Parker *et al.*'s assertions that those drugs and the patterns of use that can accompany them were not accepted by recreational users – in short that type of drug use with those drugs is seen as 'deviant' even by those young people who have themselves used illicit drugs. As an aside, it could be suggested that if a similar study were undertaken today cocaine may now be included as a 'recreational' substance that is culturally accommodated.

Rather, normalisation refers to the moving of a formerly deviant, marginalised activity into the centre of youth culture. It does not mean, as Parker and colleagues categorically state, 'it's normal for all young people to take drugs' (Parker *et al.* 1998: 152). In order for a clear definition to emerge and to demonstrate that illicit drugs have moved closer to the centre of youth culture in the United Kingdom, Parker and colleagues identify six key features each of which will be reviewed in turn (Parker *et al.* 1998: 153–59).

Drugs availability

Central in the thesis is the increased availability of drugs as without the opportunity to try drugs, the normalisation of drug taking could not have begun. Parker *et al.* argue their research demonstrates that drugs are more available than ever before, and importantly drugs are available in almost all the social situations young people find themselves in, to the point that by the time they are 18 almost all young people will have been in a position where drugs have been available to them.

Drug trying

Parker *et al.* identify the fact that, methodological flaws notwithstanding, self-report studies have demonstrated that the numbers of young people who admit to trying an illicit drug rose steadily during the 1990s, to the extent that between five to six in ten young people had a tried an illicit drug at least once. Interestingly, and this is germane to this chapter, Parker *et al.* note that gender and class differences in drug trying were also closing during that period. Parker *et al.* make the point that if drug use transcends all the usual differences associated with 'deviant' activity (education, social class, ethnicity, low self-esteem), it can be argued that drug trying ceases to be 'deviant'.

Drug use

In Parker *et al.*'s research around 25 per cent of young people became regular recreational users. They argue that for the majority the drug that dominates regular use is cannabis,' and this is because the users have made a sophisticated cost-benefit analysis regarding their drug taking. However, Parker *et al.* note the influence of the 1990s dance scene and the manner in which this facilitated the transition from adolescent drug using patterns into a more nuanced and culturally informed drug taking career.

Being drugwise

For me, this facet of the normalisation thesis is one of the most important, as it refers to the knowledge that most young people, even those who do not or have ever taken an illicit substance, exhibit. Parker and colleagues posit that being drugwise is a necessity given the ubiquity of illicit drugs in the social lives of young people. In turn, such ubiquity leads to the need for all young people to re-asses, re-confirm and often re-negotiate their drug status. It is especially important to note that even amongst abstainers the 'sensible' use of illicit drugs are accommodated and tolerated, which indicates an increased tolerance and another move toward normalisation.

Future intentions

Parker *et al.*'s work demonstrated that drug use remained a future possibility for many of their sample even for those who had previously tried and used drugs but had since abstained from use.

Cultural accommodation of the illicit

The researchers argue that, unlike the physically and psychologically addictive drugs heroin and crack cocaine, the recreational substances used by their sample do not lead young people into a recognisable deviant subculture. Rather, recreational use becomes part and parcel of busy young people's lives, and as a result the purchase and consumption of illicit drugs is just one more facet of their lives in the same way that holidays, shopping, drinking and clubbing are. Thus, in the eyes of Parker and colleagues, the formerly deviant activity of illicit drug taking has moved from the periphery of youth culture and is moving ever onward to the centre ground.

We can further explore this by looking at culture and consumption. It is difficult to disagree with Courtwright (2001: 96) who argues that it is impossible to disentangle the use of psychotropic substances and culture. Clearly, contemporary culture in Britain is fluid at present (Blackman 2004) and, I wish to argue, based on the sequence work conducted by Parker *et al.*, that we are seeing the development of a culture that sees the recreational use of certain proscribed substances as being in some instances 'normal', or at least to be *expected* in certain situations and amongst certain social groups and therefore of no great consequence. I would suggest that amongst a significant minority of the young and a lesser minority of the general population, the recreational use of illicit drugs has ceased to become the subject of a moral dilemma and is rapidly moving away from even being viewed as 'wrong'.

Instead illicit drug use has become what Felson (2002) has termed a 'crime of everyday life'. By that it is meant that people who would otherwise be described as the law abiding majority and see themselves as respectable citizens have no moral problem in breaking drug laws, and view their actions as an acceptable cultural activity rather than a serious crime. Thus, illicit drug taking for some of the population in contemporary Britain has become akin to other 'types of crime [that] fall into the grey zone of morality' (Karstedt and Farrall 2006: 1011), which include breaking red traffic lights, making fraudulent insurance claims, and undertaking or paying for work done in the black economy. Karstedt and Farrall (2006) expand on this in terms of the moral economy of day-to-day living and make some interesting claims in regard to crimes of everyday life. In particular, they see activity that falls into the grey zone of morality not as being the sole preserve of individual morality but rather as indicative of the overall moral state of society.

They suggest that our current morality is linked to the promotion of consumerism and that neo-liberal economic policies have transformed how we conceive of individuals and our relationship with the state and civil society, with an accompanying effect on the shape of our shared morality. Specifically, these changes encourage: (1) self-advancement by seeing the world as entrepreneurial and thus full of negotiable risks; (2) consumerism being declared as sovereign in a de-regulated and risk-heavy market place that places all relationships into consumer-based ones; and (3) consumerism leading to a reshaping of the relationship between individuals, the state, the law and morality, thus shifting definitions of fair, just, legitimate and moral toward consumer- and market-led perceptions. In essence, contemporary culture revolves around choice, freedom to consume and the ability to make calculated 'lifestyle' choices, which are furnished and encouraged by a largely unregulated market.

For some of the population, taking and sharing (and thus in legal terms dealing in) illicit drugs becomes just another consumption choice that fits with a market-led, consumer focused, collective morality (Van-Ree 2002). Drug use falls into the grey zone of morality where an activity becomes placed on a continuum from illegal to shady. However, the law lacks either legitimacy or enforceability in the eyes of the transgressor and their peer group. As Karstedt and Farrall (2006: 1030) note: 'Citizens discuss justifications and techniques of committing crimes of everyday life with considerable ease, thus creating a moral climate which encourages such types of behaviour.' As a result, for a significant minority of the population taking some types of illicit drugs becomes devoid of questions about right and wrong, and choices about drug using are made as individuals, often regardless of gender, social class or ethnic origin.

Thus, many of the old barriers to drug taking are being broken down and drug trying and drug taking now transcend all aspects and areas of society, yet paradoxically, and I would suggest wrongly, there are still differences in the manner in which we view drug use by women, ethnic minorities and certain social classes. With that in mind, the next section of the chapter moves to explore drug taking in terms of gender, class and race.

Women and drug use

The starting point for this section is best encapsulated by Anderson (2008: 17) who notes that:

> Substance abusing women live simultaneously in the 'legal' and 'illegal' worlds and that women's involvement in the illicit drug world, like their involvement in legitimate social activities, is multi-faceted and offers both positive and negative consequences.

Clearly then what the author is saying is that it is important to avoid any uni-dimensional view of women who use drugs. In essence, such views can be distilled into two approaches: one is that women who use illicit drugs are victims in the sense that they are powerless and in the thrall of a dominant male or second, they are villains who fail to conform to social expectations of what a 'good' woman should be.

This is important in both our understanding of drug use and our responses to it, inasmuch that the manner in which drug use is perceived and reported will impact on the manner in which the user is viewed and treated by wider society. If we look backwards at the literature, this has been recognised for some time: for example, Taylor (1993) noted that the majority of drug research is conducted on young males, which led, in turn, to Barber (1995) questioning the impact and worth of service and treatment because most research and provision was based on a male-centred model. This recognition of a gendered approach to drug services was subsequently recognised by the government; in 2001 the Home Office noted that there was a continuing tendency to concentrate service provision on the needs of white male users (Home Office 2001).

To an extent this is unsurprising. The most recent NTDMS report (DoH, 2009) highlights the fact that the majority of those in treatment are white males with a mean age of 33. Equally, the most recent Home Office *Drug Misuse Declared* work (Home Office 2009) notes that, in terms of last year use, men report drug use around twice as high as women. However, the fact that the majority of drug users appear to be white males does not excuse either the academic or practice communities from having a partial view and approach to drug use.

That said there have been some authors who have had a long-term interest in women drug users. Key amongst these is Elizabeth Ettore. Ettore's work is premised on the belief that we cannot understand female drug use without reference to the social construction of women's role in wider society. In her recent work she has distilled a number of her earlier themes in an attempt to understand the cultural foundations and contemporary impact of female drug use. In it, she challenges the concept of pollution. She notes that many of the moral and paternalistic approaches to drug use are based on blaming the user for polluting their bodies, as well as their immediate social environments. This idea of the 'polluted' drug user is exacerbated for women, primarily because of the roles that they occupy in society: that of the bearer of emotional burdens and that of homemaker and mother. Thus, women drug users are seen as not only polluting and contaminating their own bodies but are often seen as being culpable for polluting and contaminating the private/family space (Ettore 2007: 230–31).

Ettore continues by noting that this idea of contamination and pollution is increased again should the female drug user be pregnant: 'she characterises a body which is "doubly polluted" … she consumes illegal drugs contaminating her body. In turn, these drugs are seen as having contaminated the foetus'

(Ettore 2007: 231). Thus pregnant women become feared for the damage they do to their unborn child. Renzetti encapsulates this belief by claiming that: 'the *female* drug addict ... is a target of derision for her traits: her promiscuity, her lack of will, her neglect of her children and those close to her, her selfishness, her self pity and her self loathing' (Renzetti 2008: xiii, original emphasis).

However, Ettore and others (see for example, Maher 1996: Fraser and Valentine 2005 amongst others) have challenged the stereotypical view of female drug users being pathological and passive, and have begun to produce a body of work that sees women drug users as rational actors concerned with controlling their use in order to ensure they maximize their power, their empowerment and their agency in the same way that male users do. Such a shift in the narrative surrounding female drug users is necessary because, as Anderson (2008: 3) succinctly notes: 'persistent focus on women's victimization and/or the consequences they encounter in criminal contexts denies not only an understanding of the benefits they obtain from illicit drug world interaction but also how they exercise agency and mobilize resources to achieve a sense of control in their lives'.

In summary then, the 'traditional' view of female drug users is/was to view them as essentially victims in the sense that they are powerless and in the thrall of a dominant male, or they are villains who fail to conform to social expectations of what a 'good' woman should be. However, this view is beginning to change, largely due to the work of some of the authors mentioned above, amongst many others. As a result, some of the more recent drug research work, and certainly some new policy initiatives (see below and Chapter 10) have begun to recognise the need for a far more nuanced and informed approach to women's drug use that previous eras have provided. However, as we shall see below in this chapter, those old stereotypes still persist in the reporting of drug use.

Social class and drug use

There are ongoing debates in sociology about the nature of what is and what is not 'social class' with some (for example Bourdieu's 1984 work *Distinction*), arguing that in postmodern societies heterogeneity, cultural fragmentation and boundary transgression have all caused the 'traditional' markers of social class to disappear, making it difficult to determine social class by consumption patterns. Equally, some members of society have been able to become socially mobile and move out of their 'class of origin' (Gilleard *et al.* 2005) and into a different social group based on their role and income. This chapter is not the place to become embroiled in such debates. Rather, I have chosen to use the Home Office's approach to questions surrounding the social status of drug users, and use the 'A Classification Of Residential Neighbourhoods' (ACORN) system of identifying consumers by income. For me, this has a 'common sense' appeal; whilst there may be fragmentation and social class boundary crossing in consumer behaviour, levels of disposable income still have a great impact on consumption patterns. With that in mind, this section reviews the evidence relating to illicit drug use and, for lack of a better term, social class.

A cursory glance at the media tells us that illicit drug use spans all social groups. There have been a number of high profile people with privileged backgrounds, up to and including members of the royal family, who have admitted drug use. Indeed, some of the people who have control of the nation's drug laws have admitted drug use: Jacqui Smith, the former British Home Secretary, admitted to cannabis use whilst being a student (Johnston and Moore 2007), and remained in office. Interestingly, cannabis is one of the drugs that the parents of the Edlington 'torture boys' were publicly castigated for exposing their sons to (Rayner 2010). Readers may wish to reflect on the different media reactions to those cases: whilst the substance is the same, the implicit distinctions between the users and the personal and social impact of their drug use speaks volumes about the manner in which drug use is viewed and reported. As Neale (2006: 1) points out, the social position of a drug user 'is not likely to be invoked as an explanation for university students smoking cannabis; clubbers using ecstasy ... sports people taking performance enhancing drugs; or city executives and media personalities snorting lines of cocaine'.

Nevertheless, evidence suggests that there are differences between income groups where illicit drug use is concerned. Illicit drugs, stripped of any moral or paternalistic perspectives about their use can be seen as simply another commodity that can be bought or sold. Just as with licit commodities there are price variations, with some goods being cheaper than others. Put simply some social groups are financially more able to purchase some goods than others. This rings true for all goods including illicit drugs. Evidence from the Home Office supports this. For example, the Home Office notes that cocaine use was at its highest in areas classified as 'urban prosperity' than any other household type. Conversely, cannabis use was higher in households with an income of less than £10,000 per annum than any other type (Home Office 2009: 44). Arguably, this difference in use pattern can be explained by reference to the relative price of the different drugs, with cocaine being more expensive per use than cannabis.

Thus, it is possible to suggest that amongst recreational drug users there will be a difference in consumption patterns, but that this is likely to mirror other consumption patterns and will be based around disposable income and not necessarily social class. The area where social class becomes most pronounced is amongst the problematic drug using population but this is a separate group with its own distinct set of problems, and this will be dealt with in detail in another chapter.

Ethnicity and drug use

Clearly, if illicit drug use transcends social barriers then drugs will be used by people from ethnic minority groups, yet, the manner in which some sections of society have viewed drug users from ethnic minorities has not always been the same as drug users from the white population; this is largely to do with the position of the 'dangerous other' in drug mythology. The role of the 'dangerous other' has always been prominent in much of the reporting of drug use, and often otherness is related, implicitly or explicitly, to ethnicity: in Chapter 1 I noted that the media made much of the role of Chinese and Jamaicans in two high-profile drug-related deaths in the 1920s. As Khan (2006: 56 original emphasis) notes, society is quick to demonise those who, often wrongly, are associated as being 'the main providers and purveyors of such substances – the "*others*", the visible minorities'.

However, whilst it is of course true that some drug users and some drug dealers will be from ethnic minority groups, many others will be from the white population; the harms suffered by users and communities do not vary considerably from ethnic group to ethnic group. Indeed, if we examine the ethnic background of those in treatment by far the largest group is white British (82 per cent) and no other ethnic group accounts for more than 3 per cent of clients (DoH 2009: 1). Arguably, those relatively low percentages have conspired, alongside some myths around ethnic minority drug use (such as Afro-Caribbeans favour crack, South Asians only use cannabis and neither group injects), to marginalise ethnic minority groups' needs in terms of drug treatment and information.

For example, Sangster *et al.* (2002), in a report commissioned by the Home Office, noted that: 'There is a growing concern that drug services are aimed at White people and have failed to develop in ways that would make them more accessible to Black and ethnic-minority users'. Since then, there have been some developments that have moved areas of provision away from a 'one size fits all, white male users dominated' approach to service delivery: as Khan (2006: 55) points out Macpherson opened the door for opportunities to tackle race and social justice, but much remains to be done. In many ways, the marginalisation of the needs of ethnic minorities should be unsurprising as it reflects many other areas of service provision in Britain. It is worth reminding ourselves at this stage that it is just over ten years since the Macpherson inquiry, and whilst much has been done to address many of the problems that report highlighted, there is still much to be done.

As all the above sections have illustrated, illicit drug use has, arguably, become normalised in British society, and whilst it is undoubtedly true that drug users, irrespective of their gender, social class or ethnic background will share some common features, experiences and needs, it is also equally true that they will have their own unique set of circumstances and needs. Perhaps what is required is an approach to illicit drug use that ceases to attempt to generalise and instead seeks to understand on an individual, case-by-case basis, based on informed nuances rather than ill-informed stereotyping.

However, as the following section will attempt to show, achieving that level of understanding may be problematic due to the manner in which the media – the vehicle through which most of the population 'learns' about illicit drug use – reports drug-taking behaviour.

The media: horror-distortion reporting of drug use

Whilst the actual complexity of the situation surrounding illicit drug use is recognised by professionals and academics working in the field, the same cannot be said of the tabloids, which seemingly adopt a simplistic vision of drug use and drug users. The media perceive drug use through what are essentially morality-based polar opposite viewpoints seeing drug users either as ill, adopting the role of a patient and therefore deserving of treatment and sympathy, or as bad, unrepentant hedonists who are often supplying and encouraging others to take drugs and therefore deserving of our rage and contempt. In short this dichotomous view encourages the general population to conceive of illicit drug use and users as either a corrupted innocent or a hedonistic ogre.

In policy terms illicit drug use can be defined as a criminal problem or a medical problem, or more frequently in twenty-first century Britain as a combination of both (Barton 1999). However, the media almost always choose to see illicit drug use as a moral/criminal problem first, with any reference to treatment coming in the guise as a visit to 'rehab' or 'a clinic'. Moreover, whilst research seems to indicate that most drug use is experimental and infrequent: media attention is biased toward the minority of users whose use has become problematic. Although this is a distortion of reality it seems to have an effect on the public and policy-makers (Blackman 2004).

We are all aware of the tabloid press and their use of lurid headlines and images in their portrayal of illicit drug use. Recently, Kerry Katona seems to be the current scapegoat of the tabloids, but in different times the examples used could have been Pete Doherty, Craig Charles, Michael Barrymore, Brian Harvey and even Sir Paul McCartney. In the case of this Knight of the Realm it is worth recalling that he was arrested, imprisoned and then deported from Japan in 1980 for attempting to import 219 grams (7.7 ounces) of cannabis, his fourth prosecution for illicit drug possession and his second for importation (Wasserman 2006). Regardless of the subject the reporting perpetuates the fairy tale distinction between ogre and innocent. Thus, in terms of facilitating a much-needed discussion on where we take illicit drug policy in the twenty-first century, the manner in which the media 'deal with' illicit drugs becomes of paramount importance as it is the media that shapes and often constructs public opinion.

For example, Levi (2006: 1083), in discussing the influence of the media in crime reporting, suggests that:

> ... the media shapes crime discourses and may well influence public perceptions of harmfulness and of what the 'law and order problem' consists of with consequent effects on:

- Enforcement resources (including policing powers);
- The decision making of juries and other tribunals ...

The media can also directly cause us to re-think policy as well as 'illuminate the politics of representation of some social groups and try to account for this' (Levi 2006: 1039). Reiner (2002: 402–404) argues that when the media report on crime they represent 'hegemony in action', which occurs as a result of (a) the conservative nature of the press that leads to the middle of the road majority options becoming the 'common sense' view; (b) the need for stories to be newsworthy, which explains the over-representation of lurid crimes; and (c) the structural determinants of news-making, which allows criminal justice organisations to become the primary definers of crime news. This echoes the work of Felson (2002: 2), who suggests that the media indulge in 'horror-distortion sequences' and as a result there are 'ten fallacies' about crime the media perpetuate, with the result that 'public misinformation grows, with new stories building on public acceptance of past misconceptions. So it is no accident that crime becomes distorted in the public mind'.

This is arguably the case with the British press and the reporting of illicit drug use, and the result is that the general public are often misinformed about drug use, viewing all drugs as dangerous and drug users as either 'mad or bad'. As Khan (2006: 55–56) notes, this creates a dangerous set of circumstances, not least because it allows the construction and reconstruction of minority user groups, the demonisation of substances and the people that use them and perceptions (and sometimes policies) that are based on nothing more than stereotyped assumptions about gender, class and race.

Conclusion

To summarise, this chapter has suggested that the use of illicit drugs has become normalised amongst certain sections of the population, making drug use widespread and not confined to a particular social group. It has demonstrated that many of the assumptions about motivations for use and patterns of use amongst women, minorities and social groups are, at best, misguided. However, it has also argued that the reporting of drug use by the media is informed by misguided, simplistic and stereotyped perceptions, which create fear and demonisation of drugs and drug users.

As a result, public perceptions of drug use become skewed by atypical examples that do not reflect the lived reality or experience of most illicit drug users. The drug-related stories the public are fed by the media are little more than fairy tale-like morality stories, which divide drug users into hedonistic ogres or naïve innocents and imply seduction, contamination via spell-casting and happy endings, in which redemption and 'saving' come as a result either of the love and support of an innocent or the interventions of quasi-medical clinics. Whilst this may sell papers, such an approach does little to pave the way for a much-needed debate as to the future direction of British drug policy, in an era where public morality and concern seems to be moving against current policy and law. Until we tire of such stories the chances of politicians making significant policy changes to match the reality of the drug milieu in the twenty-first century seems as unlikely as Beauty not saving the Beast.

Selected further reading

Bennett, T. & Holloway, K. (2005) *Understanding Drugs Alcohol and Crime*, Open University Press: Maidenhead.

Ettore, E. (2007) 'Women, drugs and popular culture', in Manning, P. (ed.) *Drugs and popular culture: drugs, media and identity in contemporary society*, Willan: Cullumpton.

Karstedt, S. & Farrall, G. (2006) The Moral Economy of Everyday Crime, *The British Journal of Criminology*, 46 (6), 1011–1036.

Khan, K. (2006) 'Race, Politics and drugs', in Hughes, R., Lart, R. & Higate, P. (2005) *Drugs: policy and politics*, Open University Press: Maidenhead.

Reiner, R. (2002) 'Media Made Criminality: The representations of crime in the mass media', in, Maguire, M., Morgan, R. & Reiner, R. (eds) *The Oxford Handbook of Criminology*, (3rd edition) Oxford University Press: Oxford.

Taylor, A. (1993) *Women Drug users: An ethnography of a female injecting community*, Oxford: Oxford University Press

Questions and areas for reflection

1. Why do young men appear to use illicit substances more than young women?
2. Why might a 'one size fit all' drug treatment system fail some minority groups?
3. Do you consider the normalisation theory to be valid? If so, what are its implications for future drug policy?

5 Illicit drugs

Growth and production

Introduction

The aim of this chapter is to alert the reader to the fact that the British 'drug problem' is only a small part of a global phenomenon and that the extent of the global illicit drug industry is such that it makes combating it difficult. Moreover, this chapter also marks the beginnings of a change of direction in the manner in which 'drugs' will be conceived. Once stripped of any moral viewpoint on the 'rights' and 'wrongs' of trading or buying illicit drugs it becomes clear that they are a valuable and sought after commodity, and as such hold the potential to be politically and socially important commodities. In short, a burgeoning and productive supply industry has built up in reaction to what seems to be an insatiable global demand. As is always the case in these instances, there are large profits to be made by those entrepreneurs able and willing to enter the market.

In order to do this the chapter has to cover a great deal of information. It begins by illustrating the size of the global illicit drug production industry. From there, the chapter identifies the three main plant-based illicit drugs and their primary countries of origin. The next section examines the impact illicit drug production has on the developing nations by focusing on the economic, political and social situation of one nation, Afghanistan. Following this, the chapter moves away from plant-based substances to examine the production of synthetic drugs in Europe. By way of conclusion, the chapter ends with a section on the problems the global nature of illicit drug production pose in relation to the local disruption of supply.

The inclusion of this chapter serves two purposes. First, it alerts the reader to the size and nature of the illicit drug industry, in order to demonstrate the complexity of the situation and the sheer size of the task faced by individual nations in attempting to combat their domestic drug problem. Second, and related to the former point, the chapter serves to partially answer one of the most often asked questions in the drug debate: that of 'why not stop the product at source?' This seemingly straightforward idea is, as will be demonstrated, fraught with major difficulties and holds the potential to unleash drastic unforeseen consequences within the producing nations, as well has holding the potential for international repercussions.

Drug production as a global phenomenon

There is a danger that illegal drugs and the problems they carry in their wake can be seen as a purely domestic concern. This perspective is wrong and adopting such a view of the illegal drug industry simply ensures a very partial view and restricted understanding of the complexities in controlling the demand and supply of illegal drugs. Illegal drugs are nothing if they are not the product of a huge international industry of impressive proportions. Just as in any attempt to gauge the exact nature of domestic consumption, providing definitive figures that relate to the international illicit drug industry is difficult, due to the clandestine nature of the business. This becomes clear in the literature where, for example, the United Nations International Drug Control Programme (UNDCP) (2001) notes that estimates of the annual turnover for the illicit drug industry vary from $100 billion to $1000 billion per annum. Despite the high levels of vagueness, there is a consensus that the illicit drug industry is of formidable stature, with the following quote, although being a decade old, still being representative:

> The international [illicit] drug trade is now worth an estimated $400 billion annually. Only the arms industry has a bigger turnover than this. Like car making, pharmaceuticals or even banking, the drug trade has become a truly global industry: it knows no frontiers and has no particular national identity.
>
> (Williams and Milani 1999: 4)

Building on this, and providing a scale by which to judge the size of the illicit drug industry, the UNDCP (2001) posits that illicit drugs account for 8 per cent of all global trade, thus outranking the worldwide trade in iron and steel and motor vehicles, and running roughly parallel to the global trade in textiles, oil and gas and world tourism. Perhaps the best example of the size of the illicit drug industry is a comparison of the global illicit drug trade with global licit drug trade: the UNDCP estimates that the illicit trade is at least double that of its legal counterpart. This level of growth, coupled to the size of the turnover of the illicit drug industry, becomes all the more amazing when it is remembered that British Customs and Excise only had its first major heroin seizure 40 years ago. Broadening this to provide a European dimension, the United Nations Educational, Scientific and Cultural Organisation (UNESCO) (Williams and Milani 1999: 3) notes that in 1970, 54 kilos of heroin and 1.1 kilos of cocaine were seized by European authorities: less than three decades later (1997), this had reached ten tons and 39 tons respectively. The EMCDDA (2009) notes that between 2007 and 2009 there was an

8.5 per cent increase in heroin seizures in Europe and in the same year 120,607 kgs of cocaine was seized.

There are a number of economic and political reasons for this expansion. First, as with any number of global industries, the changing nature of the world economic and political situation is a significant factor. The worldwide impact of free market economics has meant that there are fewer controls placed on the movement and import and export of goods across and between countries. There has also been the restructuring of the political situation in Europe, with the demise of the communist blocs in Eastern Europe, and their concomitant restrictions on trade and movements, leading to an overall 'freeing up' of the global market place. The cost of air travel and airfreight has fallen dramatically, allowing much greater movement of people and goods across the globe, opening up more routes for the smuggler. Banking and commerce have seen a lifting of restrictions, and the introduction of new technology, allowing the movement of money in an unprecedented scale, both in terms of volume and speed.

Of equal importance is the volatile nature of the political situation in many of the drug-producing countries, which allows all manner of non-governmental factions to control various drug-producing regions, often becoming *de facto* governments in themselves. In short, changes in global communication and technology, aided by uncertainty in the world political order, have created conditions where the movement of goods and money around the globe is far easier than ever before. Amongst those businesses benefiting from this are the illicit drug traffickers.

This global nature of the illicit drug industry poses considerable problems for national governments, and arguably has a greater impact on some national economies than many of the licit multinationals operating in today's economic world. At this stage, it is perhaps important to note a division between the types of products used by the illicit drug industry, as the nature and origin of the 'product' has a significant bearing on the impact the drug industry has upon a region or country. Essentially, there are three types of drug that are of concern to this book: those drugs derived from plant products or plant products that have undergone some form of semi-synthetic process; synthetic drugs that are manufactured from other chemicals; and to a lesser degree, licit drugs that are diverted from their intended medical use. Here, only the first two concern us.

Much of the attention of the remainder of the chapter focuses on the global impact of the production of plant-based drugs. The rationale for this is that these substances very often have a significant relationship with the producing country in terms of economics, politics and social conditions (Morrison 1997). Equally important is the potential that addressing drug production in these nations holds for global politics and global economics. On the other hand, the manufacture of synthetic drugs, which most often takes place within the more industrialised nations of a region, still impacts on nation states, but tends to have a less strategic, more peripheral impact on the producing countries' political and economic infrastructures, especially so in the West. With that in mind the next section provides an overview of the three main types of plant-based drugs and their countries of origin.

Types of drugs and their primary countries of origins

The UNDCP (1996: 127) emphasises the importance of plant-based drugs by stating categorically: 'The largest share of drugs consumed illicitly are plant-based products'. Of these, there are three main types of plant that feed the illicit drug industry: cannabis satvia, the coca bush and the opium poppy. It is these three plants, either in their pure form or semi-synthesised, that are the main raw product for the plant-based illicit drug industry. This section provides an overview of the main areas of production and the 'best-guess' output figures.

Dealing with them in alphabetical order, the first plant product is the cannabis satvia. This plant is probably the most versatile of the three, as it occurs naturally throughout the world and is readily adaptable to indoor cultivation. Indeed, the United Nations Office on Drugs and Crime (UNODC) (2009) notes that some of the most potent strains of the crop are grown indoors. The result is that cannabis production is not confined to relatively small geographical regions, as are the other two, but is produced worldwide under a variety of conditions. Nevertheless, there are some areas that specialise in large-scale cultivation of cannabis, namely the US, the Republic of South Africa, Morocco, the Central Asian Republics of the Commonwealth of Independent States, Afghanistan, Pakistan, Columbia, Mexico and Jamaica, although it should be noted according to the UNODC (2009) Afghanistan has recently become a major producer.

Because cannabis can be grown 'at home', and thus produced almost anywhere across the globe, it is difficult to begin to even estimate the level of global production, a point noted by the UNODC (2009: 12) who bemoans the 'absence of reliable information on global cannabis cultivation'. However, as an indicator of the scale of production they point to the figures for 2008, where there was an estimated cannabis herb production of 13,300 metric tons to 66,100 metric tons. In terms of cannabis resin, the UN estimates that production in 2008 ranged from 2,200 metric tons to 9,900 metric tons.

The next plant product is the coca bush, which, when semi-synthesised, is the plant base for drugs such as cocaine and crack cocaine. In terms of location of production, this plant is almost the diametric opposite of cannabis satvia, inasmuch that its natural growing region is concentrated in the Andean region of South America, which allows three countries – Peru, Columbia and Bolivia – to dominate world production. This is reflected in the UNODC's (2009) figures, which claim that over 98 per cent of all the world's coca is produced by these three nations. Other nations do contribute to the overall global output, notably Ecuador, Brazil, Venezuela, Panama and

Guyana, but their output is insignificant in relation to the 'big three' producing nations (Williams and Milani 1999).

The plant itself is fairly easy to cultivate and can begin to return the farmer a yield within two years of planting. It is hardy and therefore requires little in the way of maintenance, but harvesting the leaves can be labour intensive. Production of coca leaf can be broken down by country, where, in the year ending August 2007, Bolivia produced an estimated 113 metric tons of cocaine, Columbia produced 430 metric tons of cocaine and Peru produced 302 metric tons. These figures are reflected in the amount of land given over to coca bush cultivation in each of the major producing nations: Bolivia had 30,500 hectares in cultivation, Columbia 81,000 hectares and Peru 56,100, making the coca bush a major crop in each country. Looking at farm gate prices, in 2007 Peruvian growers received just over $2.5 USD per kg of coca leaf, compared to $4.1 USD per kg in Bolivia (UNODC 2009: 233–52). In terms of turning that raw material into cocaine or cocaine derivatives, the UNODC estimates that in the year ending August 2007, the potential worldwide output of cocaine HCI was 984 metric tons.

The final plant is the opium poppy, which is the plant base for heroin and opium. Again, this is a fairly easy plant to cultivate but is labour intensive in harvesting and does need some attention during growth. There are two main regions which, when combined, are responsible for the majority of the world's opium poppy. These are the regions known as the 'Golden Crescent', incorporating Afghanistan, the Islamic Republic of Iran and Pakistan, and the 'Golden Triangle', which comprises of the People's Democratic Republic of Lao, Myanmar and Thailand.

However, production has recently shifted to Columbia and the Central Asian states of the former Soviet Union. Evidence seems to suggest that these relative newcomers have the potential to become major suppliers of the opium poppy. It is important to note, however, the UNODC (2009: 3) has identified: 'In 2007, Afghanistan alone accounted for 92% of global opium production'.

Examining in more detail the output of the two main producers, in 2007, Afghanistan produced 8,200 metric tons of opium (which is a staggering 24 per cent higher than the 2006 *global* opium production) and Myanmar 460 metric tons. Again, the scale of this level of production is visible in the amount of land given over to cultivation, with Afghanistan having 193,000 hectares and Myanmar 27,700 hectares; the Afghans being more productive and providing a better kilo per hectare output. The farm gate prices for opium in these two countries are $111 USD per kilogram in Afghanistan and $265 USD per kilogram in Myanmar (UNODC 2009: 233–52).

By way of an introduction to the next section, it is important to draw attention to the nature of the producing nations, the manner in which these crops are produced and by whom. Almost all of the nations that produce plant-based drugs are what is known as 'developing nations', that is, nations that have not yet reached the stage of industrialisation, are reliant upon a mainly agrarian-based form of production and have a low Gross National Product (GNP) (Fuller 1990: 432). The UNODC (2009) agrees, noting with some inevitability that the vast majority of plant-based illicit drugs producing nations are always amongst the world's poorest, both in terms of gross domestic product (GDP) and GNP. The farmers that grow the crops are almost always poor subsistence farmers who cultivate the plants safe in the knowledge that, unlike the situation with some other crops they produce, they can sell their yields and obtain enough money to sustain their families.

Morrison (1997) provides an interesting discussion on the driving forces of illicit drug production, which draws on the economic, political and social situation in the producing nations. She argues that drug sources are either 'concentrated' or 'diffuse', with the former generating the bulk of global drug supplies from a small number of sources, as in the case of opium and Afghanistan, and the latter characterised by a wide range of sources aimed at supplying local markets, as in the case of cannabis. In the case of some of the developing nations involved in concentrated drug production Morrison (1997: 127) has noted three contributing factors, all of which enhance the potential for illicit drug production. These are:

- weak law enforcement caused by either corruption or insurgency;
- economic insecurity, especially in rural areas;
- isolated rural areas.

All three are visible in the chosen example, Afghanistan.

Drug production as an economic and political problem: the case of Afghanistan

Stripped of moral judgments, the growth of the plants that feed the world's illicit drug business becomes a simple economic exercise – a job of work, undertaken to provide an income, sustain life and make profits. Evidence these two quotes:

> We are not cultivating opium to have a luxury life. We have no food, no cloth, and no shelter. The basic needs of the human being. Therefore we are searching for the means to at least cover these needs.
>
> (Afghan farmer talking to UNODC worker, Helmand province 2007)

> ... opium production can ensure survival ... It should be noted that survival in this case refers not only to food, clothes, housing and repayments of existing debts, but also basic necessities such as healthcare.
>
> (both taken from MacDonald 2007: 65)

Clearly, this cycle of cultivation, harvest and sale is a part of the process of plant crop production for the farmer, and, even if the farmer is aware and concerned about the end destination and use of their crop, his primary concern must be the price per kilo the buyer is prepared to give him, for, as the quotes above illustrate, it is on this, and often this alone, that the quality of his and his family's life depends. In simple economic terms, if the farmer can get more per kilo for opium than saffron (a substitute crop in some areas of Afghanistan), the farmer will almost always produce opium.

This section of the chapter seeks to explore the impact the cultivation of plant-based drugs has on the economic and political landscape of an individual country. Afghanistan has been chosen because it represents a nation where production of opium is rooted historically, opium production has huge significance economically, and, interestingly and appositely for this work, the amount of surveillance taking place in Afghanistan, coupled with the fact that the country is to all intents and purposes being co-governed by the international community at present, means that the international community has unprecedented knowledge about the scope and location of production and therefore has opportunities to 'do something' about drug production in a way never before possible.

Afghanistan's economy and demography: a brief review

It is important to note from the outset of this section that data on Afghanistan is thin on the ground. Macdonald (2007: 18) notes that it is one of the least researched countries on the planet: a look at the World Bank's website confirms this (http://web.worldbank.org) where there is a proliferation of blank spaces in tables that are generally comprehensive and detailed overviews – indeed the World Bank is unable even to give population statistics. There are a number of reasons for this, which will be returned to below.

However, we do know for certain that Afghanistan is one of a number of countries in the South Asian region of the globe and covers an area of roughly 647,500 square kilometres (as a comparison Britain covers an area of around 241,000 square kilometres). In 2008, Afghanistan had an estimated population of 32,738,376 (compared to Britain which has a population of just over 61 million). The average life expectancy is 44 years (compared to Britain where life expectancy is 78.5 years) with an infant mortality rate of 165 per thousand live births: the Afghan-Web (2009) notes that 25 per cent of Afghan children fail to live beyond their fifth birthday.

It is on the United Nations' list of least developed countries, which makes it one of the poorest 49 nation states. Using the United Nations Office of the High Representative for the Least Developed Countries, Landlocked Developing Countries and the Small Island Developing States (UN-OHRLLS) data we can estimate that the average income in USD is $800 per annum (compared to Britain which has an average income of $36,600 per annum). The majority of the population suffers from shortages of what in the West are considered staple requirements: housing, clean water, electricity, medical care and jobs. Bearing in mind that figures are unreliable and contestable, the Revolutionary Association of the Women of Afghanistan (RAWA) (2009) estimates that some 20 million Afghans (around 20 to 30 per cent of the population) are living in poverty.

Afghanistan's economy reflects the fact that the country has seen decades of conflict. Whilst the economic situation has improved since the fall of the Taliban in 2002, this is largely because of the influx of international aid, which based on the pledges at the Berlin Donors Conference for Afghan reconstruction in March 2004 reached \$8.9 billion for the period 2004–09. Arguably, for the foreseeable future, reliance on aid will continue due in large part to widespread criminality, social insecurity and the Afghan government's inability to ensure the rule of law exists in all areas of the country. Thus, whilst the international community is committed to support Afghanistan there remains a number of challenges to regeneration and poverty relief. Chief amongst those are the expanding poppy cultivation and a growing opium trade which generates in the region of \$4 billion in illicit economic activity. Other long-term problems, which arguably flow from such a large illicit business as the opium trade, include: budget sustainability, job creation, corruption, government capacity and rebuilding war torn infrastructure. Arguably the roots of these problems lie in the history of the country to which this chapter now turns.

As noted, Afghanistan is a large country with tracts of land that are under-populated and isolated with high levels of poverty, and there are also very high levels of insecurity making it a classic example of Morrison's (1997) typology of illicit drug production prerequisites.

Opium is produced in 22 of Afghanistan's 34 provinces, with the more remote southern provinces accounting for 67 per cent of total production, but of those the Hilmand province accounts for 53 per cent of total cultivation. In terms of area, in 2007, 193,000 hectares were under poppy cultivation. The economic importance of opium production in the provinces can be seen by examining the percentage of families involved in its production: in Hilmand 93 per cent of families have some involvement in poppy cultivation with 3.3 million or 14.3 per cent of the total population being involved in opium production (UNODC 2009). The reason for the centrality of opium production to the Afghan people is in the geo-political history of the area and it is to this that the section now turns.

Afghanistan: a brief recent history

Afghanistan has always been an area where conflict is never far from the surface. However, since 1979, which saw the Soviet invasion of Afghanistan, the country has been in an almost perpetual state of conflict. Briefly, the then ruling party of Afghanistan, the Marxist People's Democratic Party of Afghanistan (PDPA), requested Soviet assistance in the fight against the

Islamist mujahedeen resistance. What followed was a bloody, under-reported war. Macdonald (2007: 43–44) suggests that over one million Afghans were killed, with as many as another five million fleeing into neighbouring Pakistan and Iran.

Following the Soviet withdrawal in 1988 the country was plunged into internal turmoil and riven by a power struggle between the Taliban and the United Front (later to become the Northern Alliance). This proved to be a particularly brutal time with Amnesty International (1999) describing the situation as one where:

> Local military commanders and factional groups fight for control in a country where laws are meaningless and systematic human rights abuses are a daily occurrence ... and the victims are almost always ordinary civilians.

In addition to abuses to the person, both groups engaged in systematic destruction of villages and established crops in a scorched earth policy, which means that infrastructure and crops were destroyed in order that little of use was left for opposition troops to use. The net result of the Soviet invasion and the civil war was the total destabilisation of both the social and economic infrastructures of Afghanistan, leading to widespread and deeply entrenched poverty.

The civil war ended in 1996 when the Taliban gained overall control of the majority of the country. The Taliban emerged from a mixture of the mujahedeen fighters and Pashtun tribesmen who had spent time in the Pakistan-based religious schools or madrassas. This group practised a form of Wahhabism which is an orthodox form of Sunni Islam. Once in power, the Taliban introduced an extreme and authoritarian form of Islam that resulted in the banning of many established and imported cultural activities, ranging from the traditional cultural activity of kite flying to the more recent development of watching television. Women were effectively banned from public life and when they did appear in public were forced to cover themselves from head to toe. Enforcement of these new regulations was the responsibility of the Ministry for the Promotion of Virtue and Suppression of Vice. However, just as in the case of the Soviet war, the world at large reacted to this with a mixture of indifference and ignorance.

It was not until the terrorist attacks on the World Trade Centre in September 2001 that the majority of the world became aware of Afghanistan and the plight of its people. However, initial global attention proved to be a double-edged sword for the Afghans, as it led to another bout of conflict which, at the time of writing, is still ongoing.

Sage (1991: 327) notes the effects of sustained economic and social collapse arguing, rather prophetically, that conditions such as these produce fertile ground for 'subterranean economies', such as the production of plant-based drugs. The need to overcome poverty, the abandonment by any form of government, and the absence of security and formal law and order enhances the 'attractiveness of the only sector still expanding' (Macdonald 1989: 78), which in the case of Afghanistan is opium production. The problem is that whilst opium production can act as a buffer against poverty for the Afghans, it increases the problem of heroin abuse in the West, hence the demands 'to do something' about the historically high levels of production and it is to this the chapter now turns.

Eradication and alternative production

Essentially there are two options in any drug policy – the reduction of production or the reduction of consumption: the latter will be looked at in another chapter and the remainder of this section looks at the impact of eradication and the attractiveness of alternative production. Before that however, it is important to examine why and how the Afghan opium industry operates.

Martin and Symansky (2009) suggest five reasons why opium production has become the chief export for Afghanistan:

- good cultivation conditions
- high morphine content
- insecurity and institutional weakness
- poor infrastructure
- rural poverty.

The production of opium makes good economic sense for the farmers who, in the main, have relatively small amounts of land, commonly around two hectares (UNODC 2009), especially as the traders and traffickers often provide the growers with seeds and fertilizers, and also take delivery of the crop at the farm gate, thus relieving the farmer of storage and transportation costs. Added to this is the high return on the crop: Martin and Symansky (2009) compare the income per hectare of opium against wheat and rice and note that the gross revenue for opium per hectare is $5,385 USD compared to $282 USD for wheat and $947 USD for rice. As a result the same authors suggest that opium production accounts for 27 per cent of all economic activity in Afghanistan. Whilst it is important to note that this has declined sharply in recent years, the fact that an illicit activity accounts for more than a quarter of economic activity illustrates the centrality of opium production to the Afghan economy.

It must also be remembered that with economic activity of this scale not all the effects are negative. Martin and Symansky (2009: 31–33) provide a breakdown of the pluses and minuses of opium production on the Afghan economy, which is reproduced in tabular form below:

Table 5.1 Positives and negatives to the Afghan economy of opium production.

Advantages to Afghan economy of opium production	*Disadvantages to Afghan economy of opium production*
Allows and encourages consumption of licit goods by farmers thus stimulating demand in areas of the licit economy.	High levels of illicit income can have a negative effect on investment and can create widespread corruption and weak sub-national administration.
Larger players in the illicit market may save and/or invest their profits which may fuel investment and growth in the wider economy – for example much of the rebuilding in Kabul may be financed partly by opium money.	Savings being held overseas and/or being held in Afghanistan but in USD weakens the central bank's reserves. Equally, the true impact on the Afghan economy of the opium trade is not recorded and therefore makes economic data at best skewed and at worst meaningless.
Demand for labour in the opium market can cause an overall rise in wages as licit industries compete for labour. As a result, living standards rise nationally.	The presence of such a large illicit industry deters licit foreign investment in Afghan companies.
	The illicit nature of the opium trade means that tax revenues are lost. Equally, the illicit nature of the industry means that government expends resources in combating it, making any gains to the economy through opium marginal at best.

Source: Adapted from Martin and Symersky (2009).

Geo-politically, the problem for the West is how to reduce this dependency without further destabilising and alienating a population that is already suffering widespread deprivation and social and economic insecurity. The policy dilemma is that forced eradication will create absolute poverty; the farmer will lose all income and alternative production will increase relative poverty as the farmer will suffer a reduction in income. In addition, the entrenched nature of opium production and the economic instability that the country has experienced in the past three decades means that many farmers have opium-related debts, which increase the unattractiveness of alternative crops. Finally, although the negatives from the opium industry probably outweigh the positives, the immediate removal of an industry which accounts for in excess of 25 per cent of all economic activity could have unprecedented repercussions, not just for Afghanistan but for the rest of the world. That is not to say that action is not being taken: it is and it is a mixture of the stick and carrot approach with education, interdiction, substitution and eradication all being used in an effort to reduce production.

The aim of this section has been to alert the reader as to the complexity of the situation and the difficulties of implanting the 'common sense' option of total eradication. Put simply, total eradication would not work; it would produce more problems than it solved, further alienate a dissolute and confused population, further destabilise a fragile state, and lead to long term dependency on international aid. As the UNODC (2009) notes, it is not poverty *per se* which is the driver of the Afghan opium industry (although quite clearly it is an important factor): rather it is the lack of security both in terms of law and order and social stability. There is a correlation between opium production and lack of security and, arguably, total eradication would exacerbate rather than alleviate the security situation. It appears that a by-product of a weak and insecure Afghan state is opium production, and arguably the West's efforts need to be concentrated on remedying that rather than punishing an already downtrodden peasant class, who are making a logical and understandable economic decision to cultivate a profitable crop.

The production of synthetic drugs in Europe

Without doubt, illicit drug production in Europe is big business, but its economic and political impact on the individual nation states is less visible and of a subtler nature than that of the developing nations. The difference between the economic and political impact of illicit drug production in the developing and the industrialised nations is graphically illustrated by Medina (1991), who commented that: 'For the U.S. it's like cutting off a finger because you have gangrene. For Bolivia, it's like having a tumour in your head, which you cannot cure simply by an amputation'.

Nevertheless, the production of synthetic drugs does have some consequences for those nations where this occurs. The types of drugs under the spotlight in this section include amphetamine-type stimulants (ATS), ecstasy and LSD. In order to simplify the text the acronym ATS will be used to describe all synthetic drugs unless otherwise stated.

There are parallels between the plant-based and ATS industries, especially in economic terms. For example, the production of plant-based drugs occurs because of climatic reasons, and much of the synthesising process takes place close to the growing regions, with export of the refined product to consumer nations, thus mirroring other agrarian industries in developing nations. Likewise, the production of ATS mirrors many of the factors visible in licit industries in developed nations.

For example, Morrison (1997: 125) notes that many of the ATS producing factories are to be found in developed countries where there is an established licit chemical and pharmaceutical industry. Morrison provides a clear economic logic behind this decision: 'By setting up alongside the licit industry, producers of synthetic drugs lowered their production costs through easy access to knowledge, equipment and chemicals ... and had a ready made market for drugs'. Interestingly, and perhaps mirroring economic developments in licit industries, the UNODC (2009: 12–13) notes there is an emerging trend for production to be 'shift[ed] ... from developed to less developed countries as ... interest from transnational crime grows ...' creating 'operations of previously unimaginable size and sophistication ... '.

Fuller (1990: Chapter 13) provides an overview of reasons why industries locate in particular regions; his thesis can easily be applied to ATS industry globally. There are two opposing forces at play in the location of production: closeness to raw materials and closeness to the market. In businesses where there is a gap between raw material and market, industry tends to locate production close to raw materials and ship the refined goods, which weigh less, thus reducing transport costs. As has been demonstrated, the majority of ATS factories utilise their closeness to licit chemical industries and thus are close to raw materials. Given the importance of the production of the licit precursors to South and South East Asian economies it will come as no surprise the UNODC notes: whilst trafficking of ATS tend to be intra-regional, the precursor chemicals come predominantly from the Asian region.

The next determinant of location is the requirement to have access to skilled labour. Again, closeness to licit chemical and pharmaceutical industries ensures that there are reliable and regular sources of chemists, or people with chemical knowledge, to supervise the production process. There are also what Fuller (1990) terms non-economic factors. In the ATS industry, this may translate as a lenient approach to the enforcement of laws; the availability of secluded or isolated areas close to centres of populations within which to locate the factory; or the proximity to an intra-regional distribution centre, such as a busy sea port or airport. This pattern is visible in the global manufacture of ATS, leading to the 'local' nature of this particular section of the illicit drug trade. It appears that in each region of the world there are one or two countries that act as main producers for that area. Unlike plant-based illicit drugs, there are no producing nations that dominate globally due to the fact that 'like cannabis ATS can be produced anywhere at relatively low cost' (UNODC 2009: 12).

Where plant-based illicit drugs and their synthetic counterparts differ is the means by which estimates of production are calculated. Much of the estimation for plant-based products comes as a result of satellite and aerial photographs showing the extent of cultivation, allowing 'best-guess' estimates of final harvest totals. This is obviously not possible in the case of illicit drugs produced in factories. Instead, we are forced to rely on seizure data. It is worth remembering at this point that Chapter 3 noted a 10 per cent seizure rate is the maximum any Customs and Excise force can reasonably claim. Based on that, it is possible to argue that these figures represent, at the most, only 10 per cent of overall production.

However, one of the strong points of seizure figures, when allied to economic theory relating to the location of production, is that it enables us to 'best-guess' key areas of production. Thus, if, for example, French customs officers seize a large shipment of ATS coming from the Netherlands into France, there is a strong probability that the ATS will have been manufactured within the Netherlands, due to the economic factors identified above. Examining the seizure figures from countries across Europe highlights this. With those caveats in mind, the next section of the chapter reviews the known data relating to illicit synthetic drugs in Europe. All the following statistical data is derived from the UNODC (2009: 233–55) unless otherwise stated.

The ATS market is hugely profitable with an estimated 400 per cent mark up on prices in a global market estimated to be worth $65 billion annually. Concentrating on Europe, which the UNODC claim has one of the most established ATS markets in the world, figures show in 2006, 610 ATS laboratories were dismantled and 9521.1 kgs of ATS were seized across Europe as a whole. However, whilst these figures are of interest, arguably more interesting is the shifting patterns of production across Europe. Indeed, just as it is possible to link geo-political factors to the production of plant-based substances, geo-political changes have also impacted on ATS production.

In the previous edition of this book, I claimed that 'the domination of European ATS production and distribution by the Netherlands appears to be under some threat from some of the Eastern European countries, notably Poland and the Czech Republic'. This threat has clearly become a reality as the next section demonstrates. However, once again it is important to reiterate the point that although we can use the data to identify trends and patterns, the clandestine nature of the illicit drug industry means that we need to maintain caution in claiming any 'truths'.

That said we are able to begin to compile a picture of where ATS production seems most prevalent. In terms of ATS laboratories reported, seven countries dominated: the Russian Federation, Poland, the Netherlands, Germany, Bulgaria, Belgium and Turkey. However, when we look at this in more detail it is still the Netherlands that is the country seen by the rest of Europe as dominating the ATS 'scene' – although perhaps not in terms of manufacture. This can be seen in the number of times a country is mentioned as being the source of ATS. Two countries dominate these figures with the Netherlands being mentioned in 28 per cent and Poland being mentioned 17 per cent of the time for amphetamine, and the Netherlands being cited in 43 per cent of cases when ecstasy is being discussed.

How do we begin to make sense of this data? First it is probable that increased efforts by law enforcement agencies in the Netherlands have seen a reduction in production. For example, and in line with Fuller's (1990) typology outlined above, we have seen an increase in production of ATS in the Netherlands' neighbour Belgium, which would suggest that the producers have simply moved over the border – a task which has been made easy by the removal of border controls in many areas of mainland Europe. Equally, there has been a reduction in the seizure of the precursor chemicals in the Netherlands, which again suggests a reduction in production.

Seemingly, production is moving away from 'old' Western Europe and into the emerging 'new' Eastern European states of Poland, the Russian Federation and the Czech Republic. Again, we can look to a combination of economic and social factors for reasons behind this shift and these would include relative economic and social instability caused by the shift in political structure; lower levels of law enforcement in the emerging states mirrored by higher levels of law enforcement activity in the 'traditional' Western

European producers; greater ease of access to either licit or illicit sources of precursor materials.

However, the question still remains as to why the Netherlands dominates the market at least in terms of involvement in the ATS industry. Arguably the answer lies in the fact that it is a major shipping nation and also that it is close to the largest market for ATS in Europe: the United Kingdom, which again leads us back to Fuller's (1990) work and the importance of production and distribution being close to the market.

There is one other significant change in the nature of ATS production in Europe worthy of mention, that is in the shifting nature of the scale of production and, especially for ecstasy, the location of production. Looking at the former point first, in the previous edition it was noted that many of the ATS laboratories in Europe were 'kitchen' type setups where relatively small scale production took place. Whilst this is still the case in some areas, for example the Czech Republic and Moldova, the trend in both old and new Europe seems to be for larger factories producing relatively substantial amounts of ATS.

In terms of location of production it is still the case that the majority of ATS consumed in Europe is, in all probability, manufactured within the region. However, it is increasingly the case that ecstasy-type substances are being produced in North America, Oceania and a number of emerging countries of South East Asia. Arguably this is because access to precursor chemicals is easier in those areas than Europe, leading to a shift in production in order to continue to maximise not only production but also profit.

Clearly, the production and distribution of ATS creates a significant amount of money and wealth for some of those involved in the business. It also creates employment, not only for the chemists but for all those involved in distribution networks. Equally, it is possible to suggest that developments in the location and nature of production have been as a direct result of geo-political shifts in Europe, especially in the emerging 'new' European states. However, it is clear that whilst important, the production of ATS does not directly impact on the GDP of the producing nations in Europe in the same way that the production of plant-based substances does on countries in the Andes or Asia.

Conclusion

The aim of this chapter was to impress upon the reader the sheer scale of the global illicit drug industry and give an indication of the kind of power and influence an industry of such magnitude has on some nation states, especially those in the developing world. By highlighting this aspect of the industry, it is hoped that some recognition of the difficulties in halting production at source has as a policy. Although phrases such as 'no coca no cocaine' or 'The logic is simple. The cheapest and safest way to eradicate narcotics is to destroy them at source' (Bush 1989, in Hoffman 1989) have simplistic, 'common sense' rings to them, the economic, political and social consequences are fraught with difficulties, as the Afghan experience shows, and require a more nuanced and cerebral approach than that advocated by the former US president.

The problem for the producing nations lies in the fact that plant-based drug production plays a major part in their economy. Indeed, for many peasant farmers illicit drug production is their primary source of income, without which their quality of life would suffer a significant deterioration. In pure economic terms, unless the government or international community can offer a suitable replacement crop that provides a similar income, offer a long-term compensation package, or provide alternative means of employment, and guarantee law and order and social stability, the peasant farmers will continue to produce plant-based drugs from economic necessity.

Forced eradication, whilst combating the drug-production problem for that harvest, does little more than alienate the farmers and growers from their government, creating conditions of resentment and resistance. This is dangerous enough in countries where there is a stable regime; in countries where there is a strained relationship between the centre and periphery, or where there are credible alternatives to the government, it becomes akin to a form of political Russian roulette. The Bolivian experience has shown that once a government has adopted an eradication policy that has seen questions being asked about human rights violations, as well as strengthening the resolve of, and support for, alternative forms of government, it becomes difficult to regain the support of the people.

The problems for the international community lie in the fact that in the event of internal strife the international community can be called in to act as a form of 'policeman', or forced to launch humanitarian aid missions. Moreover, a policy of eradication of the sources of plant-based drugs also supposes that the international political community can defeat, or at least change, the behaviour of one of the largest and fastest growing global industries. Nation states seem powerless to control the activities of licit multinationals as the recent global banking crisis so vividly demonstrated, why should we assume they can control the behaviour of illicit multinationals?

Therein lies the problem. The global illicit drug industry, when any moral questions or viewpoints are removed, is a major economic force, wields huge economic power and is able to exert a concomitant degree of political and social pressure at all levels, be they local, national or international. It may be that in order to control and 'regulate' the illicit drug industry we need to adopt an economic perspective that allows us to view drugs as a market commodity and use the laws of the market as controlling factors. This idea is further explored in Chapter seven.

Suggested further reading

European Monitoring Centre for Drugs and Drug Addiction (2009) *2009 Annual Report on the state of the drug problem in Europe*, available at http://www.emcdda.europa.eu/publications/annual-report/2009 accessed 15 November 2009.

MacDonald, D. (2007) *Drugs in Afghanistan: opium, outlaws and scorpion tales*, London: Pluto Press.

Martin. E., & Symansky, S. (2009) Macroeconomic impact of the drug economy and counter narcotics efforts, in Buddenberg, D & Byrd, W.A. (eds) *Afghanistan Drug Industry: structure, functioning, dynamics and implications for counter narcotic policy*, available at www.unodc.org/paf/ afg/publications/afghanistan_drug_industry_pdf accessed 17 November 2009.

United Nations Office on Drugs and Crime (2008) *Is poverty driving the Afghan opium boom?* New York: UNODC.

United Nations Office on Drugs and Crime (2009) *World Drug Report*, New York: UN.

Questions and areas for reflection

1. Critically assess crop eradication as a policy option. Do the benefits outweigh the costs?
2. Economic theory would suggest that if demand falls, supply will also fall. That being the case, should Western nations who are the largest consumers of illicit drugs do more to reduce demand?
3. Given the scale of the illicit drug industry in terms of its profit and political influence, is it realistic to continue to try to 'deal' with it as a criminal enterprise?

6 The geo-politics of illicit drug production and distribution

Introduction

In many respects this chapter is a continuation of the previous chapter, not least because the developments that have occurred in Afghanistan since 2001 can be seen to reflect much wider global problems than the war on terror. Globalisation has become a double-edged sword for the international community: on the one hand it has allowed an opening up of the world and created a number of opportunities in terms of trade, travel and cross-cultural exchanges. On the other hand it has also aided the creation of global problems in the shape of an increase in transnational organised crime, international terrorism and a global market in all forms of smuggled goods. In order to address these problems, the international community needs to work together, but much of the work is led and conducted by Western nations. This often leads to the presence of Western troops in sovereign territories and can lead to destabilisation of governments. Thus, 'dealing with' transnational criminal activity is fraught with problems.

This chapter seeks to provide a basic introduction to geo-politics. This is important because, as Chapter 5 demonstrated, many of the drugs that cause the West problems originate in countries that are distant both geographically and in terms of their socio-political and economic make up. This chapter begins by an examination of the basic concepts of geo-politics with a view to locating the global illicit drug trade as a geo-political force that exercises the minds and policies of Western governments. This is then demonstrated by looking at the role of politics and 'narco-terrorism' with particular reference to America's 'war on drugs'.

Geo-politics: a brief conceptual overview

Geo-politics has its academic and conceptual base in human geography, which causes a few problems as it is an area with no one single definition. Rather than strive for an all encompassing definition it is probably better to give an overview of the sorts of areas human geography covers. The discipline's interest goes beyond simply locating a place on a map: for example, rather than identify where Saltash is located in Cornwall, human geographers examine the underlying characteristics of the town: for example, the transport system, the location of the shopping areas, the prevailing weather patterns and so on. They are also interested in the relationships between different places. So, for our purposes what, if any, drug taking goes on in Saltash; where is it located and where do the drugs come from? Thus, from a human geography perspective, fully understanding a place requires in-depth knowledge of its economy, the manner in which it is socially organised and its political structures.

However, human geography moves beyond the 'place' and is also interested in 'space'. Bal and Bryson (1991: 174) contend that 'human culture is made up of signs, each of which stands for something other than itself, and the people inhabiting that culture busy themselves making sense of those signs'. Human geography suggests that this includes the buildings, land and spaces that make up our urban and rural environment: landscapes therefore contain and convey meanings and serve purposes beyond the obvious and the construction and interpretation of these meanings are formed in a subjective, but socially and culturally nuanced fashion. This perspective is perhaps best summarised by Crawshaw's (2001: 68) observation that 'space is never neutral' and Rose's (1993: 1, original emphasis) contention that there is a qualitative difference between 'space' and 'place':

> Space is something to be accessed and can be defined as open to scientifically rational measurements of location, whereas *'place'* is something created and open to human interpretation and significant ... to be human is to live in a world that is filled with significant places: to be human is to have and to know your place ...

Thus, human geography is interested in place and space; the inter-relatedness of spaces and places, how they are constructed, physically, socially and politically and the fluidity of that construction. However, each of those aspects of human life has a scale. Flint (2006: 11–12) uses the example of economics. For him, economics can be personal – your own wealth or lack of it – it can be local – the strength or weakness of the local economy – it can be national – as in the case of the UK's economic fortunes – regional – in relation to the EU economy – or global. Each one of those examples has a place on a scale starting at the micro personal level and moving to finish as a global phenomenon.

Clearly, your individual economic fortune is different from global economics. However, the key point is that despite the different places each one has in terms of scale they are all related: individual economic well-being is ultimately dependant on the global economy, as many of those who have lost jobs in the current global recession will testify. In this way, there is inter-relatedness between the actions of each component part, be that an individual actor, a group of workers, a trade union, a political party or a nation state. However, and this begins the move to discuss geo-politics, the larger the scale the less we as individuals are aware of our part in the action.

Again, as in the case of human geography, there is a lack of an agreed definition as to what geo-politics is. However, Flint (2006) suggests that we employ a four-point schema in order to be able to provide a critical analysis of world politics, and in our case, the relationship between world politics and the illicit drug trade. The first is that there is a relationship between statesmanship and geo-politics. It is clear from even a cursory glance at history that nation states have competed for territory and the natural resources within them. Second, geo-politics is a way of viewing the world in as much that the world is a knowable and transparent place. This perspective has led to a critique from some feminist writers with the main thrust of the critique being that the key theorists are often white, male, of Western origin and often come from privileged positions making their viewpoint 'partial'. Third, geo-politics depends on 'situated knowledge'. That is, there is much more to the world than simply nation states competing for territory: some conflicts erupt around race, gender, sexuality, others stem from the actions of businesses or insurgent groups. To confine a definition of geo-politics to nation states would therefore provide only a partial view of the world. Finally, there is what O'Tuathail (1996) has called critical geo-politics. This relates to the practice of identifying the impact of power relations in geo-political statements and the manner in which those statements impact on our understanding and restrict policy options. For example, 'the spread of democracy' can be seen to mean the implementation of Western style democracy at the cost of any other form of collective decision making.

To summarise then, geo-politics is a complex area that asks us to examine both the uniqueness and inter-relatedness of space and place, and the manner in which scale is important in understanding that inter-relatedness. We are able to do this by using one or all of the four lenses above. We need to examine events to see the impact of statesmanship and the need to control or influence resources; what perspective of the world the various protagonists are coming from; the nature of the conflict – is it state versus state or is the conflict around other problem areas such as gender or ethnicity; and what is the impact of the power relations inherent in geo-political statements? Do these statements block policy options for example?

The above is a brief and somewhat simplistic overview of a fascinating subject area but the object of including an albeit truncated overview is to allow you to begin to understand the complexity and immense difficulties Western nations have in attempting to deal with the global drug trade. When done well it is a delicate balancing act that manages to exert pressure on the drug-producing nations without overly destabilising the precarious relationships between the places and spaces that create individual, local and national identities; when done poorly Western intervention can and has led to insurgency, revolution and, frankly, the breaking of international legislation by Western governments. As always, the best way to make this clear is to use an example and accordingly the chapter now turns its attention to the US's involvement in Columbia.

Columbia: a recent political history

Columbia is an excellent example to use in order to make sense of some of the concepts outlined above. For example, in demonstrating the links between space and place there can be little doubt that even to people with only a cursory interest in illicit drugs Columbia is a name that is synonymous with cocaine. As a result, Columbia *the space* can be located on a map in the Andean region of South America and Columbia *the place* resonates with the global cocaine trade. Equally, if we examine the impact of individuals and scale Columbia once again proves a useful tool: the individual coca bush grower will have his own economic and social reason for growing and harvesting the crop; collectively the actions of many coca farmers create conditions where Western governments feel it necessary to intervene. As a result, the coca farmer makes a few thousand dollars per annum whilst the US has sent more than \$6 billion to Columbia since 2000 (Kushner 2009).

Columbia is also a good example to use in an attempt to understand the impact that foreign involvement can have on the political, economic and social development of nations largely because Columbia was the first state to receive official counter-insurgency and military aid from the United States of America, as well as being one of the first states to receive aid from the World Bank (Chasteen 2001). As a result, we are able to better understand the long-term effect of outside interference.

As a nation, the Republic of Columbia has existed since 1886. It is also important to note that, unlike many nations in South America, it has a tradition of democracy, albeit tinged with some violent clashes between the two main political parties, the Liberal and Conservatives (which will be examined in more detail below). Modern Columbia has an estimated population of 44.6 million people and is the fourth largest economy in South America. It also has the most unequal distribution of wealth in South America. The population of Columbia is concentrated into two main areas: the Andean Highlands and the Caribbean coast. Of the rest, the eastern lowland region that comprises of 54 per cent of the total area of the country has only 3 per cent of the population. Importantly for us, the last four decades have seen a population shift from rural areas into the urban areas (CIA 2009).

However, from our perspective it is the manner in which the country has been governed, especially in the context of other global political developments, which is of paramount importance in enabling our understanding of modern Columbia, meaning the historical starting point will be 1959. This year marks the date that Fidel Castro took power in Cuba, effectively placing an ally of the Soviet Union in America's 'backyard'. As a result of that, halting the spread of communist governments in South America became a central part of the US's foreign policy. Columbia, because of political developments discussed below, was seen by the US as potentially being the next state in South America to fall into the hands of communist control as a direct result of the rural peasants' reaction to what is known as '*la violencia*'.

In order to understand this period it is necessary to understand the nature of politics in Columbia during this period. Historically, two parties domi-nated Columbian politics: the right wing Conservatives and the left of centre Liberals. Both of these parties were controlled by urban elites and represented the interests of urban landholders and industrialists. Alongside this ran the *Partido Comunista Columbiano* (PCC), which was the Columbian Communist Party formed in 1930. From the outset, the majority of support for the PCC came from the rural peasants; the PCC had a history of rural militancy espe-cially around the vexed question of land rights and ownership. Thus, by the 1940s Columbia had three parties vying for control, two of which represented the land-owning urban elites and one which represented the marginalised rural peasantry.

La violencia was a ten year period of conflict between the Liberal and Con-servative parties. It ran from 1948 to 1958 and saw a period of intense poli-tical violence. During this period around 300,000 Columbians were killed, the majority of whom were from rural areas and included peasants, labourers, sharecroppers and the landless (Richani 2002). Whilst elements of *la violencia* were as a result of left wing and right wing factions of the main political parties attacking each other, there is also evidence to suggest that, irrespective of whether the liberals or conservatives were in control, the state used *la vio-lencia* to launch systematic attacks on the PCC and its supporters (Richani 2002).

La violencia came to an end in 1958 as the result of a truce between the urban elite leaders of the Liberal and Conservative parties. This truce was known as the National Front agreement. In short, the truce called for the sharing of political office by the two main parties, with all administrative and legislative duties being divided equally irrespective of any electoral results. In effect, power and control of the country was placed in the hands of a ruling elite creating a quasi-dictatorship in a seemingly democratic system. In essence, the National Front agreement curtailed the growth of the PCC as a radical element in Columbian politics: no matter how popular it became it could never gain power because it was not part of the National Front agree-ment. Power remained in the hands of (and arguably worked for) a few members of a rich urban elite.

Running parallel to this, and reflecting the manner in which the National Front agreement was used by the ruling elite to cement their own positions of power and wealth, came a reform in the manner in which land ownership and control occurred. Briefly, this involved the maximisation of capital through the expansion of capitalist operated farms at the expense of the small tradi-tional peasant holdings. This was facilitated via a series of legislative changes passed by the National Front agreement coalition. As a result of the forced creation of large commercial farms there was a displacement of small peasant farmers and an increase in landlessness amongst the rural poor. As Brittain (2010: 73) notes:

> The land reform acted as a legitimate method for large landholders, in cooperation with the state, to formally consolidate lands, while, first, ensuring a legal mode of ownership that enabled the owners to call on the state to 'protect' interests through coercive means of displacement, violence, torture and intimidation; and second, creating a landless, or below subsistence reserve army of labour forced to sell its labour power for their (family's) continued existence. This was arranged by large landholders who sought to evict tenants and re-hire them as labourers.

The same author states that as a result of the National Front agreement and the land reforms three critical socio-economic events occurred:

1. the creation of a reserve army of labour in urban and rural areas, thus depressing wages;
2. the monopolization of rural land by an urban elite;
3. the exclusion of mobilised peasant groups from the process of political change.

(Brittain 2010: 7–8)

Thus, by the end of the 1950s Columbia's political, social and economic milieu could be characterised as one of simmering, state-sponsored violence against political opposition, the cementation of economic power in the hands of an urban elite and the systematic denial of land ownership and political representation to the peasant class and rural poor.

Enter Fueraz Armadas Revolucionarias Columbianas-Ejercito del Pueblo

In an effort to resist these forms of repression, but especially the violent attacks from state organisations, peasants, under the guidance of PCC officials, set up self-defence groups. Many scholars (for example Livingstone 2003) see the setting up of these groups as the beginnings of *de facto* independent republics, autonomous from central government and run by and for the peasant class. LeGrand (2003: 176) notes that these enclaves were a 'real peasant movement, a response to official violence and military repression'. It is from these groups that a new, more radical group informed by Marxist–Leninist principles emerged: *Fueraz Armadas Revolucionarias Columbianas-Ejercito del Pueblo* better known as FARC-EP. From the outset, FARC-EP has promoted a radical change in Columbia through revolution, and has become the longest-lasting guerrilla group in South America. It is viewed in polar opposites: for example Escribano (2003: 299) views FARC-EP as 'the most important military and political force in South America opposing imperialism', whilst the US government has classified FARC-EP as the most dangerous terrorist organisation in the Southern Hemisphere.

FARC-EP was formally created on 27 May 1964. The catalyst for the movement was a series of US-supported military attacks on Marquetalia, a small hamlet in the Tolima province. Marquetalia was a PCC controlled hamlet that had successfully resisted central state interference and had set up an alternative communist controlled autonomous region. Clearly, such a site of resistance was dangerous for the ruling elite and accordingly the full might of the Columbian military, acting under the guidance and advice of senior US military advisors, was used to regain state control from the communist part officials. Interestingly, many see the US involvement in this attack, especially in terms of devising tactics and approaches to counteract guerrilla warfare, as a 'practice run' for the Vietnam war; for instance the Columbian Air force used US supplied napalm to bomb large tracts of the Marquetalia valley (Hylton 2006).

Whilst the campaign was a short-term success, inasmuch that the state regained control of Marquetalia, arguably it created a longer term problem for both Columbia and the US. Following the battle for Marquetalia the revolutionary movement gained support from the rural population, and consequently the numbers of guerrilla fighters at FARC-EP's disposal grew as well as its political influence, to the extent that by the beginning of the 1990s in excess of 50 per cent of municipalities had some form of FARC-EP influence. Indeed, in many isolated rural areas FARC-EP were a *de facto* government taking responsibility for the education and welfare of the population, raising taxes and offering security and protection.

In the intervening period between the 1960s and today FARC-EP has arguably gone from strength to strength, although it is fair to say that the last few years have seen a weakening of its position. At its zenith it was an alternative power and had full control over a number of regions of Columbia. It was successful in resisting Columbian government attacks both from the official military and the right-wing paramilitaries who were working for the Columbian state (Brittain 2010). How you view the strength of FARC-EP will depend on your own ideological viewpoint: to some in the West they are seen as a bastion against the US's neo-imperialism, whilst to others they are seen as little more than drug-dealing criminals hiding behind a façade of revolutionary rhetoric. What is incontrovertible is that in their efforts to combat and remove this alternative power base both the Columbian and US governments have spent billions of dollars and lost thousands of lives, and it is to this and the geo-political justification and consequences of such actions that the chapter now turns its attention.

Combating FARC-EP: narco-politics and America's 'war on drugs'

Kushner (2009) writing in *Newsweek* graphically illustrates the cost of combating FARC-EP in the past decade:

> Since 2000, the United States has sent more than $6 billion to Bogota [the capital of Columbia] to help Uribe and his predecessor stabilise the

Andean region, staunch the flow of drugs into America's cities and cut drug production. In what is known as Plan Columbia, Washington sent pilots and choppers to Columbia, trained commandos and furnished weapons to fight traffickers and terrorists.

Moreover, it is not only the US that has involved itself with combating FARC-EP. Reporting for the *Guardian* newspaper in 2003, Pallister, Brodzinsky and Bowcott note that, despite concerns about serious abuses carried out by the military and growing concerns by human rights groups, at the very least the British government has:

- provided SAS training of narco police;
- supplied military advice to the Columbia army's counter-guerrilla units;
- supplied increasing amounts of military hardware and intelligence equipment;
- assisted in setting up an intelligence centre and a joint intelligence committee.

How then do we make sense of this Western involvement in South American politics? How can this amount of intervention be justified? In order to fully understand this we must examine how the presence of aid and advisors is justified by Western governments and what are its wider aims beyond simply supporting a South American government in its fight against communism, and the answer can be found in geo-politics.

The initial decision to back Columbian governments in their war against FARC-EP must be seen in the context of the Cold War. That era was a period in recent world history when, in essence, the globe was divided into two power blocs: one – the West – was ostensibly pro-democracy and sought to promote and sustain the capitalist economic system. The major player here was the US backed by Western Europe with support from Westernised nations in the pacific; the second was the Soviet Union which controlled vast areas of Eastern Europe. These two giant superpowers had direct influence over much of the world and in areas where they did not have direct territorial control – Latin America, Africa and some areas of South East Asia – both power blocs engaged in a form of Imperialism, using aid as a tool to gain a hands-off form of control.

Geographically, the US was protected from a direct military invasion force from the West and East by the Atlantic and Pacific oceans, although a missile strike remained the most likely first strike aggressive action. However, the proximity of South America meant that that area was seen as a potential launching base for ground attacks. Thus it was no surprise that the US became very concerned about Castro's communist party gaining power in Cuba, which is only a short distance from mainland US. That concern grew as Castro forged an alliance with the Soviet Union and allowed a Soviet missile base to be located on the island. For the first time the US had a communist state in its 'backyard'. As a result of this, a large part of American foreign policy in the period 1960–90 was aimed at stopping the spread of communism globally, but with special attention being paid to Latin America, hence the initial interest in Columbia (for a full account of the Cuban Missile Crisis and subsequent developments in American foreign policy see Weldes 1999 amongst many others).

Running roughly parallel to this, as a response to the counter-culture hippy movement that originated in California in the 1960s, America became embroiled in an internal 'war' that was aimed at protecting the 'American dream', especially the negative effects that illicit drug use had on the core fabric of American society. Again, it is necessary to be aware of American cultural and social mores of the time. America was, at that time, a conservative, deeply religious country, and the anti-establishment stance of the counter-culture movement was seen as a real threat to the status quo.

In order to combat this 'threat from within', in 1969 the then president, Richard Nixon, coined the phrase 'war on drugs', and put into place a series of measures aimed to combat the threat illicit drugs posed to American youth and society. The degree of threat that Nixon saw in drugs is illustrated in this excerpt from a speech he made in 1971:

> The threat of narcotics among our people is one which properly frightens many Americans. It comes quietly into homes and destroys children, it moves in to neighbourhoods and breaks the fibre of community which makes neighbours ... we have the moral resources to do the job ...
>
> (Nixon 1971: 22)

Consecutive presidents followed suit in terms of waging the drug war but Ronald Reagan escalated the war on drugs to the level that it currently holds. In 1982 Reagan made a speech in which he stated that illicit drugs were a threat to America's national security (Reagan 1982). Arguably it is at this point the conflation of the US's domestic illicit drug policy and American foreign policy, especially toward the Andean region of South America, occurred, thus justifying and continuing large-scale US involvement in internal Columbian affairs. In a stroke Reagan had turned the blame away from domestic consumers of illicit drugs and placed America's drug problem firmly in the hands of the foreign producers and, moreover, had defined drug production as a threat to national security. This was given further weight by Reagan's republican colleague George Bush (Senior) who, when running for president in 1988, stated categorically that:

> The logic is simple ... The cheapest and safest way to eradicate narcotics is to destroy them at their sources ... We need to wipe out crops wherever they are grown.
>
> (Bush 1989)

As a result of the linking of domestic drug problems with national security, the respective Presidents provided the US with a reason, and subsequent legislation, to intervene in the domestic affairs of drug-producing nations, thereby allowing American 'forces to carry out direct actions, militaristic or otherwise, in regions other than their national jurisdiction' (Brittain 2010: 141). Of course, it also helped that in the main cocaine-producing nation, Columbia, there was a long established and very successful left wing guerrilla group to blame – FARC-EP. At a stroke the US was able to conduct its war on communism and its war on drugs as a joint endeavour away from American soil and thus protect American society from the 'twin evils' of communism and cocaine.

Conflating communism and cocaine: geo-politics in action

To re-cap, as noted in Chapter 5, the coca leaf is of great social and cultural significance to the indigenous peoples of the Andean region. Contemporarily it is the source of a guaranteed and relatively high and stable income for those peasant farmers that grow coca for cocaine production. Equally, in Columbia, those same peasant settlements have long been the target for state violence, forced eviction from their land, a form of political disenfranchisement following the banning of the PCC, and in some areas virtual abandonment by the Columbian government in terms of social and structural infrastructure. In many rural areas the FARC-EP has become the *de facto* government and has taken responsibility for education, health care, road building and land re-distribution (Cooper 2002). That is not to say that FARC-EP is without blame: it is not. It is an avowedly revolutionary party that has, and still continues to, use violence and warfare to meet its aim of creating a Marxist–Leninist state in Columbia.

On the other side of the coin are the elected Columbian government and the legitimate rulers of the state. Given the democratic nature of Columbian politics it is to be assumed that their policies have been ratified by any electoral mandate, thus making any armed opposition an illegal resistance. Equally, given that the US has identified illicit drugs as a problem of national security and that Columbia is one of the key producers of at least one illicit substance, it makes sense and justifies American involvement in Columbian affairs, especially if, as is the case, the Columbian government has asked for US assistance in 'dealing with' FARC-EP who have been identified as a key player in the international drug trade.

However, this justification depends exclusively on FARC-EP being major players in cocaine production and supply and it is vital that the US–Columbian alliance can 'prove' this to be the case. The established wisdom seems to suggest that is the case (see for example LeGrand 2003), and certainly American propaganda is keen to emphasise that perspective. The basic argument is that FARC-EP leaders at all stages of the organisation have abandoned their Marxist–Leninist revolutionary principles and become just another one of many drug cartels. According to Brittain (2010: 90) analysts such as LeGrand (2003) have come to the conclusion that FARC-EP has indeed abandoned its ideological base and has developed a strategic coca alliance in order to create personal wealth throughout the organisation.

Reinforcing this message to national and global audiences assumes great importance for the US and Columbian governments not least because as Suarez (in Kraul 2006) noted 'if you reduce FARC to just a drug cartel, you make the possibility of negotiating a political settlement more difficult'. Thus, linking cocaine to communism has potentially negated any chance of a political end to the Columbian civil war, and has delegitimised FARC-EP's claim to be a *bona fide* revolutionary party. Geo-politically that covers at least three of the points made above – geo-politics as a way of viewing the world; geo-politics as 'situated knowledge'; and the identification of the impact of power relations in geo-political statements and the manner in which those statements impact on our understanding and restrict policy options.

However, the true extent of FARC-EP's involvement in the cocaine industry is subject to some debate and may be more complex than the simple explanation that the guerrillas are just another drug cartel. For example, it would be naive in the extreme to claim that FARC-EP is not aware of coca production in the regions it controls and all authors recognise this: FARC-EP is clearly aware of the coca industry in the regions it controls (Holmes *et al.* 2006; Peceny and Durnan 2006). However, the debate, and thus much of the legitimacy for US involvement, revolves around how, why and which aspects of the coca industry FARC-EP is involved in. The answers to those questions from the US–Columbian alliance viewpoint are clear:

- *how* – by using armed force and fear to control large tracts of coca producing land;
- *why* – because there is enormous wealth and power to be had from large scale involvement and also to fund insurrection and terrorism in Columbia;
- *which* – all aspects of the cocaine trade including the transportation, distribution, and marketing of cocaine in Western nations.

Thus the US–Columbian alliance has been able to conflate the cocaine industry with communist revolution, effectively delegitimise FARC-EP as a political party and define FARC-EP as both a terrorist organisation and a drug cartel. However, if we examine those same questions from a different geo-political lens the answers could be different, thus putting into doubt the US–Columbian alliance's policy.

Looking at each in turn, if we look at *how* FARC-EP are involved in the cocaine trade it has been argued that FARC-EP are involved only in offering security and economic protection for the peasant farmers growing coca in the regions they control. In the previous chapter it was noted that for the majority of peasant growers illicit drugs make sound economic sense, inasmuch that the yields and price per hectare outstrips that of legitimate crops. FARC-EP's argument is that it is their duty to ensure the peasants they represent live lives which are economically stable. As a result, FARC-EP have concentrated their efforts in ensuring that there is a taxation system in place that places levies and taxes on the production of coca and coca paste. As Chernick (1996: 35) notes, FARC-EP are not 'another cartel. Their role in the coca trade is exhorting a percentage of the commercial transaction of coca and coca paste ... '. Richani (2002) claims that the money raised through this tax system is then distributed throughout local communities to provided social amenities, infrastructure and support that are not provided by central government.

If we turn our attention to the *why* question it is possible to argue that FARC-EP are not involved in the cocaine industry to gain personal power and wealth but rather as a political response to the Columbian government's policies around land ownership. They recognise that, as a consequence of the land reforms which took place in the 1960s and 1970s, and subsequent shift from tenant farmer to wage earner that occurred as a result of these reforms, many peasants suffered from low wages and poverty. As a consequence peasants were forced into producing illicit crops simply to survive. Thus, whilst ideologically FARC-EP is opposed to coca production, it takes a pragmatic view of coca production as an economic short-term necessity for the people they represent. However, taking the longer-term view, it has been suggested that FARC-EP are active in encouraging and promoting the production of alternative crops in an effort to significantly reduce the production of coca, having previously worked with the UN on alternative social development projects (Labrousse 2005).

Finally, examining the *which* question, it is possible to claim that FARC-EP have little *direct* involvement in the coca trade. Clearly they are aware that it exists and indeed do generate revenue from it via taxes on production. Equally, they protect the peasants that produce coca via ensuring that 'fair' prices are paid and, occasionally, protecting land used for coca production from state forces seeking to forcibly eradicate crops. However, unlike the cocaine cartels that they are compared to, FARC-EP claim they are not involved directly either in the production or the distribution of cocaine. Moreover, unlike the cartels they do not take money directly from coca production, do not gain personal wealth from coca production and are working toward creating conditions where the areas they control depend on alternative crop production (Brittain 2010).

Based on the preceding three paragraphs we could produce a second set of bullet points based on a different geo-political understanding of the situation that is different to the US–Columbian alliance's and, in turn, would lead to a different policy option:

- *how* – by creating and implementing a tax and income redistribution programme that ensures social and economic stability for the peasants they represent;

- *why* – as a legitimate political response to unfair land reforms and to protect the economic and social well-being of the people they represent;
- *which* – none directly but where they are involved it is mainly the production aspects of the cocaine trade in terms of protecting the peasant farmers they represent.

Thus, a different geo-political reading of FARC-EP's involvement with coca could see the movement as only indirect and has occurred as a legitimate political struggle working in response to unfair (and arguably unconstitutional) land reforms and in opposition to a corrupt Columbian government that is little more than a puppet of an imperialistic American state.

Conclusion

The purpose of this chapter has been to alert the reader to the fact that there is an inter-relatedness to many aspects of the production, distribution, marketing and taking of illicit drugs. Moreover, exactly how that is viewed and who the 'villains' are is often not the product of 'facts' but the product of a particular set of circumstances and, arguably more importantly, how those circumstances are used, defined, interpreted and 'sold' by competing parties.

This is evident in the way in which geo-politics has shaped Columbia's response to its involvement in the cocaine trade. Over the past six decades the Columbian cocaine industry and the often impoverished peasants who produce the raw materials have been affected by and ultimately incorporated into:

- the US's fight against global communism;
- the reaction of the US to Castro's seizing power in Cuba;
- the result of a violent conflict for the control of Columbian resources;
- a radical reform of land ownership rights in Columbia;
- a Marxist–Leninist response to those reforms;
- the resulting civil war in Columbia and the creation of alternative power bases and autonomous territories within Columbia;
- the inability of the Columbian government to fully control the country;
- a growth in the use of illicit recreational drugs in Western society;
- the decision by neo-Conservative politicians in the US to brand illicit drug use as a threat to US national security, thus allowing the US into Columbian politics;
- latterly the decision by the US to brand FARC-EP as a terrorist organisation.

All of the above have joined together to create a particular, ideologically based perspective on cocaine, communism and revolution in Columbia and all have led to the creation of a particular set of policies aimed at combating both the cocaine trade, an alternative political future for the Columbian people and the maintenance of American hegemony within South America. As demonstrated above, viewing cocaine and communism through a slightly different geo-political lens would, arguably, create a different perspective and a different set of policies. Hopefully, what has emerged from this and the previous chapter is that whilst illicit drug use poses serious repercussions for individuals, communities and nation states, the solution to the 'drug problem' cannot be at those levels alone. Rather, what is needed in any debate about drug policy is a recognition of the geo-political importance of winning the 'drug war' to the West, but particularly to American foreign policy aims.

Selected additional reading

Benavie, A. (2009) *Drugs: America's holy war*, London: Routledge.

Brittain, J.J. (2010) *Revolutionary Social Change in Columbia: the origin and direction of FARC-EP*, New York: Pluto Press.

Flint, C. (2006) *Introduction to Geopolitics*, London: Routledge.

Richani, N. (2002) *Systems of violence: the political economy of war and peace in Columbia*, New York: State University of New York Press.

The *New York Times* archive, especially with reference to the drug-related speeches by Richard Nixon, Ronald Reagan and George Bush Senior.

Questions and areas for reflection

1. What do you understand by the term 'geo-politics'? In your opinion is it relevant to the study of illicit drug use?
2. Is illicit drug use 'a threat to national security' as President Reagan suggested? If not, what other reasons might the US have for becoming involved in South American politics?
3. Ideology and political preferences clearly impact on how situations and events are seen and interpreted. With that in mind, in your opinion what should be the limits of Western governments' intervention in drug-producing nations' internal politics?

7 Illicit drugs

Markets and market forces

Introduction

Chapters 5 and 6 established the fact that there are economic and political dimensions to the illicit drug industry, alongside the better known medical, moral and social aspects. It also noted that for some illicit drug-producing nations the economic and political consequences of a too-rapid reduction of output could lead to economic and political de-stabilisation. However, the use of economics and economic theory to make sense of illicit drugs provides an alternative view: one that sees illicit drugs like any other tradable commodity. As a consequence, this allows the use of economic theory as an alternative policy dynamic. This chapter builds upon that idea. Again, illicit drugs are stripped of any moral content and seen only as a commodity to be traded, and thus subject to the laws of economics, in the same way as butter, eggs or cars.

As noted, the cultivation and production of drugs has become an important and sometimes integral part of many countries' economic development, and given the centrality to those economies that illicit drug production holds there is a persuasive reason as seeing illicit drugs as simply commodities. If this approach is adopted, and there seems to be few good reasons why it should be, there is a need to examine the nature of market-based relationships that surround drug users. The logical extension of this being that the market mechanism, including the laws of supply and demand, holds the potential to control the illicit drug market.

Thus there is a need to undertake a market-based review of the illicit drug milieu in order to ascertain the ways illicit drug markets resemble legitimate markets, and the ways in which they vary. In order to achieve this there are a number of requirements to be fulfilled. First and foremost there is the need to understand the value of illicit drugs in relation to other commodities. Then there is the need for an excursion into economics and economic theory in order to understand the market mechanism and the nature of markets. Following this, the chapter will examine the work of a number of authors who have applied economic analysis to the workings of the drug markets.

Before entering into the world of markets and economics, it is perhaps important to pause to consider why there is need to study this particular aspect of the world of illicit drugs. Broadly speaking, there are two policy approaches in response to the growth of illicit drug use. The first is harm reduction, which is dealt with elsewhere. The second can be called the demand reduction approach. Essentially, this approach is aimed at reducing the use of drugs by forcing up the 'cost' of drug use to an unacceptably high level.

Here, 'cost' can be either the monetary value of the drug or relate to non-monetary cost such as the certainty of a prison sentence for those caught dealing in illicit drugs, or to emphasise the harm drugs can do to the user's health. If this is seen as a determinant of policy, it can be argued that successful prohibition will drive the price of drugs to levels way above that which we could expect if the same drugs were legal. Moreover, if we add vigorous enforcement of the illicit drug market into the equation, which would include seizure of imports, as well as high profile policing of dealers and users, we should see the cost rise above an acceptable level. This high price, in both monetary and non-monetary terms should lead to a fall in demand, supply and ultimately use.

If we view illicit drugs as a commodity it allows us to compare their value to other tradable commodities. For example, looking at retail sales, Caulkins and Reuter (1998: 595) claim that illicit drugs have an 'extraordinary high per unit weight'. Using figures derived from the Office of National Drug Control Policy (ONDCP) (1997: 10–11), based in Washington DC, they claim that marijuana is literally worth its weight in gold, with cocaine and heroin being 'one and two orders of magnitude more expensive per unit weight than gold'. In turn, the expensive nature of illicit drugs means that they represent a significant part of the user's income, unless the user is wealthy. Thus cost, already high, may affect demand if prices rise above a certain level. This leads us inexorably toward the economic theories of supply and demand and the price elasticity of demand.

Supply and demand

It is important to state from the outset that this work is not being written by an economist. That said, it is necessary that these two relatively straightforward economic theories are explained in order that the reader can make sense of their potential application to the illicit drug market. With that in mind, added to the fact that the majority of readers of this text will not have an economics background, the following section will provide a very basic overview of the laws of supply and demand and price elasticity of demand. I make no apologies for the level at which this is pitched: it will be adequate for the purposes of the text.

Illicit drugs are commodities; that is, they are goods that can be exchanged for other goods, or, more likely in our capitalist economy, money. As such they will have both a value and a price. From the outset, it is important to stress that value and price are not one and the same thing. Fuller (1990) notes that values are subjective things, with some people valuing goods far higher than other people may. Harvey (1998: 27, original emphasis) explains thus:

> ... people always *want* something. A want is significant in economics only when a person is prepared to give up something in order to satisfy it. As the strength of the different wants varies, so will the amounts which people are willing to give up. In other words, different goods have a different *value* to them. Value is measured in terms of opportunity cost.

For our purposes we can visualise value and opportunity cost in this way. A recreational drug user may wish to purchase some amphetamine in order to attend an all night session at a club. The value of that amphetamine is calculated at what that person is prepared to give up (the opportunity cost) in order to purchase the drug. In this instance, it may be two hours worth of pay, plus the prospect of a criminal record if they are found in possession of an illicit substance.

In order to obtain that good (in this example, amphetamine) the drug user will need to exchange something with the seller. In developed Western nations such as the UK, we tend to use what is in economic terms a 'medium of exchange' – but this is more usually referred to as money – to facilitate this exchange. Thus, the value of the good is expressed in terms of money. In this way, we are able to measure the market value of the good by referring to its price. Thus, for Harvey (1998: 27) a definition of price becomes 'the value of a commodity or service measured in terms of the standard monetary unit'. The buyer then decides whether the cost, that is the amount of money they are going to have to give up in order to satisfy their want, plus the possibility of a criminal record, plus possible negative effects in terms of health, is worth the value they place on the good.

These exchanges take place in what economists call 'the market'. The market is an important concept in economics for, by studying the changes in price that take place in a market, markets are able to provide signals about what people want and what they are prepared to forgo in order to satisfy their want. Again, it is important to conceive of the 'market' in theoretical terms. In such terms the market is not a formal structure, such as a shop or auction ring, but *'all those buyers and sellers of a good who influence its price'* (Harvey 1998: 28, original emphasis). Harvey also notes that within markets the price of a good tends to become the same across the whole range of buyers and sellers, thus establishing a 'market price'. Markets are created as a response to demand and that demand is satisfied by the supply of a good or service.

The two concepts of demand and supply are important parts of economic theory, and are, according to economists, subject to laws that determine their actions upon each other. Looking first at demand, it is important to note that economics are concerned with effective demand. This refers to the amount people are able to afford and willing to buy at each price. For example, a drug user may want to buy some heroin but is unable to afford it. Therefore the want is not an effective demand as they are unable or unwilling to buy at the current price.

Turning attention to supply, this is taken to mean 'the quantity a producer is prepared to put onto the market at a particular price during a particular time period' (Fuller 1990: 38). Supply is determined by cost, and, as we will see, the illicit drug market has some unusual costs attached to it, some monetary, others not. Cost tends to rise as supply is increased for several reasons, including the employment of more workers, more spent on packaging and so on. Once costs have risen to a level beyond which the producer feels is acceptable, the producer will leave the market and cease trading in that particular commodity. Thus, the economic law of supply says that more of a good will be supplied at a higher price than at a lower price (Fuller 1990: 38).

By combining these two laws, it is possible to calculate the equilibrium price, which is the point that represents the 'market price'. By the same token, it is also possible to see other aspects of the market relationship. For example, if demand remains the same but supply falls, then prices will rise, with the converse being true. Again, this has implications for the illicit drug market. For example, if a crop eradication programme reduced the supply of heroin into the UK, but demand remained the same, the price of heroin rises. However, if the state could create conditions where the price of an illicit drug rises, economic theory tells us that demand will fall as more and more would-be consumers decide that the price is higher than the value or opportunity cost. Equally if the supplier's production costs rise above a certain level, then the supplier will leave the market.

This rise in 'cost' for the consumer and the producer could be anything from a rise in the actual price to an increase in policing, the certainty of a prison sentence if caught, mandatory drug testing of prisoners, loss of employment and so on. Therefore, economic theory would seem to support a policy of ensuring the 'cost' of drug use, both in terms of price and production costs, remains as high as possible. There is, however, one more economic theory that needs to be considered, and that is the theory of price elasticity of demand. This refers to the susceptibility of demand to price. For some goods and for some consumers there is a strong degree of price elasticity. This is taken to mean that consumers are highly responsive to price changes and will alter their consumption pattern as soon as the price rises.

The opposite extreme is where demand is inelastic. This means that consumers will continue to demand a good irrespective of price rise. Fuller (1990: 59) provides four factors that influence price elasticity: (1) the number and closeness of substitutes; (2) the proportion of income the good accounts for; (3) whether the good is a necessity or a luxury; (4) the influence of habit. It should be clear that factors (1) and (4) have a resonance when discussing illicit drug consumption, and this is a point that will be returned to.

To summarise this section, it is possible to claim that there is a relationship between demand and supply. In most situations, economic theory dictates that as prices rise so demand will fall. Economic theory also tells us that costs rise as production rises. However, if any or all of the above four factors of price elasticity of demand are present it may be the case that demand remains constant amongst some consumers despite price rises. These approaches have obvious implications for illicit drug policy, and applying economic analysis to policy provides a fascinating, alternative glimpse of the illicit drug scene, and is one which will be returned to at the end of the chapter.

Market factors and their effect on prices

One of the things that economics may help us understand is the reason for the relatively high per unit price of illicit drugs. It will be recalled that most illicit drugs are at least worth their weight in gold, which begs the question why crudely refined plant products or cheaply produced chemicals are so expensive? Economic theory would point to the costs of production and it is to this the chapter's attention now turns, especially to the work of Caulkins and Reuter (1998). These two American academics have produced one of the most fascinating insights into the economics of the illicit drug market. Their work relates specifically to the situation in the US, but it can be assumed that, broadly speaking, the same market conditions exist across the globe. Their work will now be reviewed in some detail. It is important to note that, although they base their work on 1990 prices, meaning that *actual* prices will have changed, the percentages quoted at each stage should remain broadly constant.

In essence, Caulkins and Reuter attempt to explain why illicit drug prices are relatively high, and use cocaine as their example. They begin their argument by outlining the nature of production costs that could be expected for most small businesses. Some costs that a licit business would face are much lower, or totally absent, for the illicit drug business. For example, for cocaine, the raw material costs are very low: in Peru the farm gate price for sun dried coca leaves is $2.5 USD per kilo (UNODC 2008b: 111). The illicit drug entrepreneur does not pay taxes, neither do they pay conventional import or export duties. Conventional shipping prices are low. If we look at a conventional method of transportation – the post – Peruvian Serpost can send a parcel weighing a kilo between Peru and Britain for £31.13. Packaging of illicit drugs tends to be minimal, accounting for as little as 0.25–0.5 per cent of the retail price (Caulkins *et al.* 1999). The illicit nature of the product means that promotional costs, such as advertising, are negligible. Drug dealers tend not to need shelf space, storage or specialist premises, and tend not to hold large amounts of product in stock. In short the cost of raw materials, import, packaging, marketing and supplying are negligible. Therefore, it can be seen that some of the costs faced by licit businesses are not applicable to the illicit drug business. Their costs are somewhat different: Caulkins and Reuter (1998) have identified four key costs that pertain to illicit drugs. Please note that inflation means that these prices will be higher.

Import costs

Although conventional shipping prices are low, there is a high import cost. For example, Caulkins and Reuter remark on the fact that the wholesale price of cocaine is about $1,500 per kilogram in Colombia. This rises to $15,000 per kilo, wholesale, inside the US, denoting a cost associated with bringing the product across the border. Clearly, this is not linked to taxes but must reflect another type of 'cost', most likely to be associated with risk compensation (see below). Retail sales in the US move the price up to $110,000 per kilo. Based on this, Caulkins and Reuter (1998: 597) estimate that 12 per cent of the total retail value of cocaine is attributable to import costs.

Labour cost

Labour costs tend to be high in the illicit drug industry. There are a number of examples of this, such as the fact that packaging tends to be done by hand instead of by machines. Caulkins and Reuter point to the fact that simple machines, such as those used in the packaging of sugar, could reduce the cost dramatically. However, the clandestine nature of the business makes it risky, therefore 'costly', in terms of detection by police or competitors, to have fixed machinery. Equally, selling drugs tends to be done by crews, each of whom has a specific task. In their studies, Caulkins *et al.* (1999: 233) identified crews of up to six who are paid by the hour to sell drugs from a 'spot'. Although many of these low-level employees are relatively poorly paid, their wages still incur a cost to the entrepreneur. Based on their figures for the US cocaine market, Caulkins and Reuter (1998: 597) estimate that 13 per cent of the retail cost of cocaine comes from labour costs.

Cost of product and asset seizure

Part of the ongoing 'war on drugs' is the seizure of both goods and assets of illicit drug businesses. Drug seizures and confiscation can be part of the work of the Customs and Excise Agency or specialist police units of a country. Financial investigation can be undertaken by taxation squads that deal with the money laundering activities, often leading to the sequestration of assets of known and convicted traders in illicit drugs. Caulkins and Reuter (1998: 598) suggest that the cost of seizures of both kinds accounts for about 8–11 per cent of the retail price of cocaine.

Risk compensation

The illicit drug business is fraught with risks and compensation for actual or potential risks also can be considered to be a cost. As Chapter 2 noted drug dealers get much higher sentences than those offenders charged and convicted on possession offences. Likewise, there is competition amongst illicit drug

Table 7.1. Estimates of the magnitude of cost components for cocaine sold at retail, 1990

Wholesale price in Columbia	1%
Importing of drug	12%
Retail labour	13%
Higher-level labour	3%
Drug and asset seizures	8–11%
Money laundering fees	2–4%
Packaging, processing and inventory cost	2%
Compensation for risk of prison	23.6%
Compensation for physical risk	33%

Source: Caulkins and Reuter 1998: 600.

businesses. The very nature of the business means that inter-firm disputes are sometimes settled by resorting to violence, leading to the injury or death of a participant in the illicit drug business. Caulkins and Reuter have made some calculations regarding the US situation. They suggest that the average drug dealer could expect $43,500 per annum for each year spent in prison, which, based on the number of drug dealers incarcerated in American prisons, represents about 23.6 per cent of the US retail price for cocaine in that illicit drug market. Equally, drug dealers need to be compensated for death or injury. Caulkins and Reuter (1998) argue that this needs to be higher than prison compensation and accounts for 33 per cent of the retail price of cocaine. They summarise their findings on the price determinants of cocaine in tabular form.

There are, of course, slight differences between the illicit drug market in the US and the illicit drug market in Britain. For example, up until a few years ago it would have been possible to argue that threat of physical injury was appreciably lower in Britain than in the US, thus reducing the extent of compensation required against threat of physical injury. This is arguably still the case, although there appears to be a rising level of drug-related violence within Britain with both the Joseph Rowntree Foundation (2005) and the Home Office (2007) noting that the carrying of weapons by those involved in the drug market is becoming the norm. Nevertheless, even given the differences, the fact appears to remain that the highest influence on the price of illicit drugs is compensation for risk. As Caulkins and Reuter (1998: 605) argue, 'the extraordinarily high prices ... are clearly a function of their illegality', and the need for those in the illicit drug business to be able to compensate for the costs such illegality carry in their wake. Again, this has implications for policy that will be explored in the final section of this chapter.

Having reviewed the factors on price within a predominantly US-based context, it is time to return to more domestic concerns and provide an overview of the British illicit drug business. For this, the chapter turns its attention to the work of Lewis (1994) and the Matrix Knowledge Group (Home Office 2007), who provide an examination of the nature of the British illicit drug market.

British drug markets: composition and key players

In some of the earliest work examining the British drug markets, Lewis (1994) structured his outline of illicit heroin markets in Britain around a model for New York drug markets devised in 1969 by Preble and Casey. They offered a six-level hierarchy of the market, which, as Lewis (1994: 45) comments, 'remains relevant to European markets as a point of departure rather than a blueprint'. Some of the most recent findings on the British market comes from the Joseph Rowntree Foundation (2005), the Matrix Knowledge Group (MKG) (Home Office 2007) and McSweeney *et al.* (2008), the latter providing a comprehensive review of the literature relating to the British drug market. In many respects the more recent work builds on Lewis's original material. Before reviewing the research on British drug market composition there are three key points that need to be made.

First, both Lewis (1994: 46) and the MKG (Home Office 2007) suggest that the British drug market is flexible in terms of entry. This is partly because of the absence of organised criminal gangs such as the Mafia. Second, the British drug market is complex and multi-layered, with constant exit and entry of individuals. This means that there are often three or four layers between the importers and the end users. Third, the British market tends to be characterised by sole traders or small businesses. To place this in context, Fuller (1990) suggests that small businesses employ between eight and 15 people. The following section reviews the findings of both Lewis (1994) and the MKG (Home Office 2007).

Both sets of work identify that, just as in many licit markets, there are layers of 'businesses' between the end user of the product and the grower. Both sets of work identify four distinct sets of businesses (although, interestingly, McSweeney *et al.* challenge this, noting that they prefer to think of the structure as tripartite claiming little evidence to support the 'national' level dealer). Lewis (1994) calls them importers and bulk distributors; bulk wholesalers; small-scale wholesalers and apartment dealers; retail sales and user-sellers, and the MKG (Home Office 2007) names them: international; national; local; retail, thus whilst the terminology differs, the nature of the market does not, and it is to this that the chapter now turns.

Importers and bulk distributors or international

MKG (Home Office 2007: 27) defines this stage of the market as 'dealers who bought drugs outside the UK, arranged transportation and sold them, within the UK'. In business terms, this stage of the operation is relatively new for, as Lewis (1994: 46) notes, the 'commercialisation' of the heroin market is relatively recent, only beginning in earnest during the late 1970s and early 1980s. Prior to this, heroin users were denied reliable access to constant supplies of heroin, and constructed co-operative smuggling ventures aimed at meeting the needs of the co-operative, and not for large commercial gain. However, with the expansion of production in South East Asia, and the increasing vigilance of Customs and Excise officials at major ports and airports, this type of import business became increasingly risky. As we have seen above, illicit drug businesses seek compensation for risk, which, when added to the rise in heroin use, set in train the commercialisation of heroin importing.

Lewis (1994: 46) argues that this can be seen by the 'consolidation of a complex, high turnover market' that emerged at the start of the 1980s. He suggests that this signifies a shift in the nature and motive of those involved in importing heroin. Rather than simply importing heroin as a means to ensure personal consumption and make a modest profit to allow future use, heroin importers became major investors, building sophisticated and complex smuggling empires. These businesses tend to be located in big cities, such as London, Manchester and Liverpool. Lewis notes that research and definitive information at this level of the market is perhaps the hardest to come by, because the importers are far removed from the street, often tend to be professional criminals, can be linked to organised crime and are hostile and dangerous groups.

Building on this, the MKG research found that at this level there is a degree of sophistication to the business and that in some cases legitimate trade is used to aid the illicit business. Equally, the same work found that there was a move toward expanding carers and networks; that prison was seen as an occupational hazard; that professional services were often used at this end of the market and that some dealers had long and complex careers as international importers (Home Office 2007: 27–28).

Bulk wholesalers or national

MKG (Home Office 2007: 28) define this group as 'dealers who distributed drugs at national level, e.g. buying drugs in one city and selling in another'. In market terms, this group serves an important role as once the heroin has been imported into Britain (in what will be its purest form in the journey from point of entry to point of use) and has undergone the distribution process, it moves into the hands of the bulk wholesalers. According to Lewis (1994) bulk wholesalers are part of a network that incorporates importers, distributors, bulk wholesalers and house dealers. Within the market, they occupy the ground between 'the large-scale importer/distributor and the low-level wholesaler and dealers' (Lewis 1994: 47). The relationship between these parts of the market is extremely fluid and often distributors will sell directly to low-level dealers.

Lewis informs that bulk wholesalers purchase their products from a number of sources and in a number of forms. For example, the product may be bought in a semi-refined state and converted into heroin. On the other hand, relatively undiluted heroin can be bought either from a distributor or from a place of brokerage where the wholesaler will use their existing contacts. Lewis (1994: 48) suggests that the 'average' bulk wholesaler would buy half-kilo to 100 gram units that are then diluted into 100 to 30 gram units and sold to dealers.

Bulk wholesalers vary in type and can be drawn from a number of sections of society. Lewis posits that they can be:

1. drug entrepreneurs, who in the past may have operated at retail level;
2. legitimate traders, who have developed sidelines as distributors or wholesalers;
3. predatory professional criminals, who have found a lucrative source of income in drugs.

(Lewis 1994: 48)

However, they appear to share a number of common characteristics. Lewis suggest that they are older than either users or retail dealers, being in their 30s and 40s compared to 20s for the latter group. Bulk wholesalers also tend to have criminal records. Although distanced from street-level dealing they are vulnerable, especially when making collections or deliveries. Their presence often goes undetected, however, as the majority of police raids tend to take place at a lower level. In these situations, it is not uncommon to find empty 100 gram bags containing traces of heroin (Lewis 1994: 48), indicating the presence of a higher-level market player.

In bringing this up to date the MKG work also found that the following were characteristics of this group:

- they often had long careers;
- they were very adaptable – moving on to new drugs and new methods;
- they dealt in a variety of drugs;
- the majority had progressed their careers through unstructured means, meeting people in one place and moving on to new drugs through chance and luck;
- they did not work in large networks of people;
- salaried employees were most common at this level; and
- they worked many different roles at this level with lots of variety – transporters/runners and buyers appeared to be particularly important.

(Home Office 2007: 28)

Small-scale wholesalers and apartment dealers or local

MKG (Home Office 2007: 28) defines this group as 'dealers who buy and sell drugs in bulk in one geographical area (e.g. a small region or town)'. Lewis (1994: 48–49) identifies this group as house or apartment dealers. He notes that at this level it is likely that the market player will be a user as well. The MKG research also notes that at this level the distinction between dealer and user becomes blurred, claiming that 'some dealers were users' (Home

Office 2007: 28). Often, these market players are independent sole traders, not being linked to any of the professional criminals or bulk wholesalers. However, there is some cooperation here also: MKG research found that networks were small but that runners were often employed. Lewis found that whilst many of the drug transactions were conducted in what May and Hough (2004) term closed markets – that is the buyer was known to the dealer – many of these dealers worked from houses or used legitimate businesses as cover.

Having a fixed base means that if the police or rival competitors in the market identify the permanent site, the base becomes an easy target. In terms of operation, this section of the market works from two types of base. The first, the legitimate business, is perhaps the most attractive as it allows: (a) good cover inasmuch as prospective heroin consumers can mingle with non-heroin buying customers and (b) profits from the illicit drug trade can be diverted through licit accounts.

The second option, operating from a house or flat, is the riskier of the two. Constant streams of customers to a private dwelling can alert the attention of neighbours and the police, as well as signalling the location of the business to rival sellers. It is not uncommon for this level of market player to employ assistants who can be used to monitor phone calls, vet existing and potential customers and perhaps supervise consumption on the premises. Interestingly enough, and dating the article, Lewis (1994: 49) comments on the centrality of the telephone to the small scale wholesalers and house dealer's business: clearly, the recent explosion of mobile phones and pagers have both enhanced business and, to an extent, reduced risk of detection.

Two other points that Lewis makes are worthy of inclusion here. He notes that if dealer and wholesaler also use heroin, they need to be careful to monitor their own intake. Using too much of their stock for personal consumption can leave them out of profit, in debt and neglectful of security. Hence, for many in this position, business is conducted with the additional pressure of controlling immediate use and gratification in order to secure longer term futures. Second, Lewis (1994: 49) argues that, at this level, some of the transactions resemble the market pre-commercialisation, with barter and exchange taking place in lieu of cash exchanges, or the grouping together of users to buy larger amounts of the drug from bulk wholesalers. This is endorsed by the work of the Joseph Rowntree Foundation (2005: 3) where they note that in some markets dealers are more than happy to accept stolen goods as payment for drugs.

The MKG (Home Office 2007) note that this group deals in smaller quantities than the previous two, mainly working in kilo measures and ounces and that, in terms of structure, there were many more sole traders than at previous levels. Also, there were opportunities for career progression at this level with dealers sometimes moving from selling to users to selling to retailers. However, both sets of research suggest that drug dealing is an integral part of the lives of the people operating at this level.

Retail sales and user-sellers or retail

The MKG research defines this group as 'dealers selling drugs at the street level to users' (Home Office 2007: 28). This is the lowest end of the market, and this is where mainly heroin or cannabis in conjunction with other drugs gets sold. Almost without exception most market players at this level are consumers as well as retailers, and are drawn into the business because of the possibility of regular supplies of drugs, selling to others to ensure their own supplies. However, the commercial world in which these 'day labourers' of the drug trade work is equally as complex as the higher echelons of the market. Although there is little evidence of organised networks it is not uncommon for these retailers to have tens up to hundreds of customers; these customers are drawn from informal networks of users. According to the MKG research dealing is commonplace within the social circles of most retail drug dealers. Equally, most of this group will have had more than one spell in prison and are living what can be seen to be chaotic lives.

Lewis (1994) identifies five categories of user-dealer; appointment dealers; street dealers; network suppliers; user-sellers; and social suppliers. He argues that these categories are useful in an understanding of the market, because it helps us differentiate between wholesale apartment dealers who enter the retail market, aids the realisation that retail sales happen in places other than the street, and demonstrates that there are a number of different consumer networks within the market that are serviced in a variety of ways. This chimes with the work of May and Hough (2004), who identified three types of market: open, semi-open (pubs and clubs) and closed.

Lewis (1994: 50) also suggests that some of these user-sellers occupy a number of different roles in the heroin market, moving between a number of service roles that can encompass selling, transporting, diluting, look out duties and testing products. The common theme running through the business at this level is the high degree of risk faced by the market players: arrests at this level are more common then elsewhere in the market. For this reason, the market has developed a number of 'coping strategies' designed to reduce the likelihood of arrest by the police or aggressive competition by other sellers. These include the appointment system, the use of pagers and mobile phones to arrange meetings and the use of tightly knit networks between sellers and regular customers.

The value of works such as that of Lewis (1994), MKG (Home Office 2007) and to an extent McSweeney *et al.* (2008) is that they serve to reinforce the message that the illicit drug industry is every bit as complex and interrelated as any licit business. Bearing this in mind, it can come as little surprise that economic analysis has been seen by some as holding the potential to act on the illicit drug market. As Caulkins *et al.* (1999: 323) point out: 'drug dealing organisations are ... businesses. Furthermore, they are businesses whose operations the government seeks to regulate'. Theoretically, the employment of economic 'laws' as a controlling mechanism, able to inform policies and shape practice, in much the same way as governments use the same laws to control licit industries, should offer some of the optimal methods of control. The next section of this chapter explores some of the literature surrounding this approach.

Economics as a possible controlling mechanism?

Based on the information supplied above, it is possible to tentatively suggest that policy-makers could look toward economic theory as at least an alternative policy approach. This stance has been taken up by a variety of academics, and, in some instances, has figured in policy documents for police forces across the world. The concluding section of this chapter reviews the key arguments, and provides some thoughts as to the usefulness of economics in steering practice.

To review the situation, the economic 'laws' of supply and demand indicate that as prices rise so demand will fall, and that as costs of production rise, more and more producers will leave the market. In terms of applicability to the illicit drug market, it can be seen that actions by the authorities that raise the price of drugs to the consumer, or increase the cost of production to the supplier, should, in theory, reduce the number of consumers and suppliers. There is one exception to this 'law', and that is where price elasticity of demand is inelastic, meaning that consumers will continue to demand and buy a product irrespective of any rise in price. The implications here for drug policy is that for those users whose drug use is problematic and financed by crime, price rises will only lead to increased crime, due to the fact the user's demand remains constant and increased income is required to service that demand.

These theories have only been tested out on a number of occasions, a point noted by Warner (1993: 353) who claims that 'the state of the art is primitive'. For example, Weatherburn and Lind (1997), writing from an Australian perspective, note that economic theory dictates that in a market where the majority of the product is imported, as in the case of heroin, seizures of large quantities should cause prices to rise, leading to a fall in quantities purchased and consumed. However, they argue that, in the Australian context, there has been no hard evidence to indicate this was the case. This led Weatherburn and Lind (1997: 557–58) to review the literature on price elasticity of demand in relation to heroin addicts. They found that there was a mixed opinion, with some suggesting that despite being addictive, there is a high degree of price elasticity amongst heroin addicts (Kaplan 1983).

Very few studies had been conducted to test this. Weatherburn and Lind (1997: 558) point to the work of Silverman and Spurill (1977), who found that demand for heroin shows little long-run price elasticity, but is price elastic in the short run. Grapendal (1992), who found that addicts tended to base their consumption on their daily income rather then vice-versa, supports this view. In order to further test the applicability of economic theory to 'real life' scenarios, Weatherburn and Lind conducted a longitudinal study of the heroin market in Cabramatta, a suburb of Sydney, NSW. Their findings spread some light on the usefulness of economic theory on supply side enforcement.

In essence, Weatherburn and Lind (1997: 566–68) found no relationship between the amount of heroin seized and either street price or purity levels. They suggest the primary reason for this is that the level of seizures by Customs and Excise are not large enough to impact on the overall market. For example, during a two-year period, Weatherburn and Lind (1997: 566) estimate that seizures only accounted for between 3.7 and 17.2 per cent of all heroin consumed. However, paradoxically, 67 per cent of heroin users, when asked why they were seeking treatment, cited the cost of the drug; 30 per cent cited trouble with the police, which can also be seen as a cost. Moreover, 97 per cent of users cited being tired of the lifestyle as a reason for seeking treatment. Weatherburn and Lind suggest that this indicates an overall disaffection with both types of 'cost'.

They conclude by discussing the nature of the type of policies and the levels at which these need to operate. They suggest that in the case of Australia, seeking to raise the price of heroin via creating a shortage of the drug has failed. However, the fact that there is an agency detailed to *attempt* to do this sends signals to the importers and is factored in as a cost of production, thus having a direct impact on price, due to the need of the importers to compensate for this potential risk. Thus, even giving the impression of attaching more importance to the import and distribution end of the market can influence the street price to some degree, even if interdiction is unable to significantly reduce the amount of a drug entering a country. Weatherburn and Lind (1997: 567) conclude by stating the need for policy-makers to:

> ... address themselves to the question of whether the benefits of a policy designed to moderate the demand for heroin by maintaining street prices can be made to outweigh associated costs.

In economic terms, given that there may only be a slight elasticity of demand for illicit drugs amongst heavy-end users, this point raises implications for the allocation of resources for supply-side enforcement policies, a point taken up by Wagstaff (1989). He notes that because of the nature of the illicit drug industry, it is difficult to map the parameters of the business, making economic analysis fraught with difficulties. Thus, as we have seen in Chapter 2, we have little in the way of accurate indicators of levels or patterns of consumption across the whole population, are reliant on anecdotal information from law enforcement agents and fieldworkers over price, and use samples taken from seizures to measure purity. Wagstaff (1989: 1174) argues that these indicators are often atypical and provide only limited information.

Similarly, he notes that the main rationale for government intervention into illicit drug markets is that there are third party costs imposed by drug use.

This is taken to mean that third parties suffer as a result of drug use in ways such as increased acquisitive crime. These costs, known in economics as external costs, need to be addressed to ensure that the community at large does not suffer the ill effects of drug use. In terms of devising policy, Wagstaff points to two problem areas. First, he notes the need to balance spending on the variety of available drug reduction programmes. There is little point, he argues, in skewing resources to favour a particular approach that, in economic terms, has a lesser impact on external cost. Using economic theory as a driver of policy would demand that each type of drug reduction programme would reach a level where an extra pound spent on each programme would have exactly the same impact on external cost.

Second, he suggests that it makes 'little sense to spend more on reducing drug consumption than there is to be gained from the reduction in external cost' (Wagstaff 1989: 1175). In more detail, Wagstaff (1989: 1175) argues that this raises questions concerning the total level of aggregate spending on reducing illicit drug use. Put simply, economics prompts us to ask the question: 'do the gains society gets from reducing illicit drug consumption match the cost of financing them?' Again, Wagstaff (1989: 1177) returns to the point made by Weatherburn and Lind (1997), that, in terms of supply-side policies, the answer to that question lies in whether demand for illicit drugs is elastic or inelastic. Given that there seems to be, at least in the short run, some price elasticity, the next policy question economics can answer is which segment of the market is the optimum area to target in terms of reducing supply?

This ties neatly into the work of Kleiman and Young (1995). They argue that the illicit drug debate is shaped by economic language, but over-emphasises the dichotomy between supply-side policy and demand-side policy. Instead of concentrating on these arguably simplistic polarities, Kleiman and Young suggest a more holistic approach that focuses on the factors of production visible in the illicit drug market. In this way, it may be possible to identify the factors of production that, in economic terms, are described as 'those factors that can be most readily made scarce relative to others' (Kleiman and Young 1995: 730). In lay terms this refers to the identification of the weakest link in the market operation. The difference between this perspective and the others is that it allows targeting of both demand and supply, and is therefore not reliant on the nebulous and somewhat unproven concept of price elasticity.

Conclusion

To some extent, economic theory is able to allow us a differently focused look at the world of illicit drugs. It does this by stripping away any connotations of morality and demands that we see illicit drugs as a commodity, subject to laws and pressures more readily associated with commonplace goods such as eggs and butter. However, for this to work to its fullest extent, we need to assume that the illicit drug market place is identical to that of licit goods.

Moreover, economic theory and therefore economic analysis is centred on the availability of information – there is a need to be fully aware of all the actions of all the participants.

Just as in the case of trying to measure the extent of illicit drug use, the clandestine nature of the illicit drug market inhibits our ability to obtain accurate information. Thus, put simply, we do not have all the necessary information to use economic theory to its fullest. Nevertheless, that does not render economic theory superfluous to understanding. Its strength lies in the fact that it makes us aware of the impact of costs and benefits, and as we will see in the final chapter, can provide us with pertinent questions concerning the 'value' of pursuing particular polices. That is for the future. The immediate concerns revolve around the manner in which costs and payments affect both the user and the communities they inhabit. This, then, becomes the focus of the next chapter.

Suggested further reading

Home Office (2007) *The Illicit drug trade in the United Kingdom* (2nd edition), Home Office online report 20/07 accessed 21 October 2009.

Joseph Rowntree Foundation (2005) *Understanding drug selling in local communities*, November, New York: Joseph Rowntree Foundation.

May, T. & Hough, M. (2004) Drug Markets and Distribution Systems, *Addiction, Research and Theory* 12 (6), 549–563.

McSweeney, T., Turnbull, P.J. & Hough, M. (2008) *Tackling Drug Markets and Distribution Networks in the UK: a review of the recent literature*, London: UK Drugs Policy Commission.

Questions and areas for reflection

1. What do you understand by the economic terms 'supply', 'demand' and 'elasticity of demand'? How do these affect your everyday life?
2. Caulkins *et al.* (1999: 323) point out that 'drug dealing organisations are ... businesses. Furthermore, they are businesses whose operations the government seeks to regulate'. Is it feasible to suggest that we can regulate 'hidden' businesses when the state sometimes struggles to regulate legitimate businesses?
3. At what level in the illicit drug market should the state focus its attention?

8 Illicit drugs

Paying for the goods and assessing the costs

Introduction

Having spent the previous three chapters examining global and economic issues inherent in the illicit drug industry, this chapter returns to more domestic concerns. In the previous edition of the book I noted that we needed to pay particular concern to two related 'problem' areas often associated with illicit drug use: (a) those of the drug/crime link, and (b) the damage drug use does to individuals and society, and this is still the case some seven years later.

From the outset it is important to be aware of the centrality the drug/crime link holds for UK policy developments. For example, in 2008 the Home Office produced the following figures:

- problematic drug use could cost around £15.4 billion per annum of which 99 per cent is generated by problematic drug users;
- between 33 and 50 per cent of acquisitive crime is believed to be drug related.
  (Home Office 2008)

This was endorsed by the then Home Secretary Jacqui Smith when she stated that: 'It costs taxpayers millions to deal with the health problems caused by drugs and to tackle the crimes such as burglary, car theft, mugging and robbery which are committed by some users to fund their habit' (Smith 2008). This is an important point because, part of the rationale for the state intervening in illicit drug use lies in the damage caused to the wider community – the external costs. Crime which is linked to drug use is clearly seen as the largest and most important of these 'external costs'.

The chapter begins by exploring the link between illicit drug use and crime. From this point, the chapter moves to offer a typology of illicit drug using offenders, identifying and discussing three distinct, but not mutually exclusive, groups. The purpose of this section is to make a distinction between the costs incurred by recreational users, offenders who use illicit drugs and 'heavy-end' or problematic drug users who are drug dependent and appear to be committing crimes to finance their drug use. It also serves to discuss the nature of the links between illicit drug use and acquisitive crime.

In the final sections, the chapter examines, in detail, the notion of 'cost', and expands the previously made point regarding costs as being monetary and non-monetary, as well as individual and societal.

Just before commencing on that pathway, it is important to point out that, for the purposes of this chapter, 'crime' and 'offending' will be taken to mean what Chaiken and Chaiken (1991) call 'income generating' offences, but which will be referred to here as 'acquisitive crime'. This includes offences such as burglary, shoplifting, fraud, and unlike Chaiken and Chaiken's work, prostitution and other sex crimes. It does not include crimes of violence. This is not to say that drug users do not commit crimes of violence – some clearly do and the consequences of their actions are of concern. However, our focus here is to explore the link between acquisitive property crime and illicit drug use, for it is the link between acquisitive crime and drug use that seems to worry the British state more than the links between crimes of violence and illicit drug use.

The links between illicit drug use and crime

Since the publication of the first edition of this work there has been a growth in the number of books and papers looking specifically at the relationship between drugs and crime (see for example Bean 2004), and students wishing to explore this important area ought to look to those for their in-depth approach. Rather than attempt to duplicate that detail, this chapter is aimed at providing a starting point for understanding.

At one level, there is an obvious link between illicit drugs and crime – any action that contravenes the parameters of the law regarding drugs becomes 'criminal'. Thus, for example, drug dealing, importation and possession are all crimes, making the link between drugs and crime obvious. However, there are other links, far more complex and requiring a much deeper analysis: links that have taxed academics for at least the last 30 years. As evidence, witness the manner in which the ACMD (1995: 11–12) discusses the ways 'drugs' and 'crime' can be viewed:

> Every year thousands of drug misusers come into contact with the criminal justice system. There are three ways in which this occurs:
>
> - because they commit offences under the misuse of drugs legislation, for example the possession or supply of controlled drugs;
> - because their misuse of drugs causes or contributes to other criminal behaviour, for example committing acquisitive crime to help fund their drug misuse, or crime committed under the influence of drugs; or
> - because they commit offences unrelated to their drug misuse.

Although it may now be the mainstay of contemporary policy, recognising and establishing the link between drug use and crime has been a long process: Sutherland and Cressey (1970: 164) stated that 'felons are over represented in the addict population, crime rates are increased considerably by drug addiction'. However, as Chaiken and Chaiken (1991: 281) point out, at that stage the precise link between drugs and crime were not fully thought through or explored.

There have been a number of contemporary attempts to 'think through' the relationship between drugs and crime, and almost without exception the results have been strewn with ambiguity and littered with caveats. To put it bluntly, we are searching for a 'chicken and egg' type understanding of the relationship between crime and drug use. For instance, Newburn and Elliot (1999: 6) are unequivocal in stating that 'it is undeniably the case that crime and drugs are linked'. However, they are more guarded in claiming causality, noting that 'the precise relationship [between crime and drug use] is far from clear'. Bean (2004: 26) neatly summarises the questions around the crime–drug link when he asks:

> Is the link a matter of cause and effect, or is it something more complex? And in which direction does it go? Do drugs lead to crime, or crime to drugs? Or perhaps there is no connection at all and the one remains separate from the other?

So what do we know for certain? We know that there are a number of different types of user, and often these different types of user restrict themselves to set consumption patterns, which in turn appear to have some relationship with offending behaviour. For example, some illicit drug users may infrequently use a combination of alcohol and cannabis, but almost never add cocaine into their consumption pattern; this group shows little evidence of offending. Others may frequently use heroin, cannabis and cocaine, and are persistent offenders. Thus, sweeping statements that link all drug users to acquisitive crime become unfounded and hide a complex situation. This view is not only the view of academics: witness DPAS (2001b: 12, original emphasis), '*Drugs is not one issue, but several. It is not a single problem for which there is only one solution, but a range of issues that need separate but linked solutions*'.

The realities regarding crime and illicit drug use are therefore perhaps better understood if we take as a starting point Chaiken and Chaiken's (1991) assertion that there are different types of users with varying patterns of behaviour, some which includes offending, others that do not. This necessitates the creation of a simple typology of illicit drug users and offending behaviour. This task can be embarked upon by separating out those sections of the population that use illicit drugs into three, broad, but discrete, categories:

1. 'recreational/low frequency user';
2. 'frequent offender/frequent drug user;
3. 'prolific offender/problematic drug user.

Membership of each category can then be ascertained by viewing illicit drug users through four lenses:

1. the nature of drug use;
2. whether drug use is financed by crime;
3. the nature of the relationship between drug use and crime;
4. the 'risk' posed to community in terms of acquisitive crime.

Once this separation of users is completed, the crime–drug link debate becomes clearer and enables a sharper focus to be made. There are two important points to note here. As with all typologies these categories are 'ideal types', and therefore there will be people who do not fit into the compartmentalisation inherent in typologies. Second, movement between categories is possible but not inevitable: a person who begins in Category 1 may, quite quickly, end up in Category 3, but evidence suggests that in the majority of cases this is unlikely.

It is also important to be specific about some of the more quantifiable data such as frequency and persistence. Looking first at frequency, contrary to popular opinion, even the most habitual of criminals seldom offend on a daily basis. Using data derived from research in the US, Chaiken and Chaiken (1991: 287) claim that most offenders commit non-violent offences at low rates. For example, Chaiken and Chaiken (1991: 293) posit that crime days per year may be as low as 11 for some non-drug using offenders.

However, there are small minorities of offenders who commit offences at a very high level of frequency. Coid *et al.* (2001) note that from their sample of drug using offenders who admitted to offences of theft, the mean crime days per six-month period was 44. Bennett and Sibbitt (2000) state that some offenders who use drugs admit to at least 20 offences per month. My own research into prolific drug using offending identified an individual who was committing crimes in excess of two per day (Barton 2005).

Based on these findings it is possible to suggest that people who have more than four crime days per month are frequent offenders. Equally, when examining patterns of illicit drug consumption in the UK (see Chapter 2), it is clear that the vast majority of those who admit to using illicit substances do so on an infrequent basis. For example, only 14.5 per cent of the highest using age group admitted to use in the last month (Home Office 2008a). Based on those assumptions, it is possible to begin to construct a typology of illicit drug users and their relationship to crime and risk.

Category 1: the low frequency/recreational user

Research findings offer no evidence to support the theory that use of an illicit drug leads inexorably to involvement in acquisitive crime. In fact, according to Chaiken and Chaiken (1991: 290), the link between acquisitive crime and illicit drug use is not even the predominant pattern for the vast majority of illicit drug users. On reflection, this finding is unsurprising. As series after series of BCS figures indicate, large percentages of the population admit to taking illicit drugs at least once in their lives, and there is no evidence whatsoever to support the assertion that all of those people have at one time or another committed acquisitive crime in order to purchase illicit drugs, a point endorsed by reference to the recorded crime figures. Moreover, this group's drug use is not expensive: 'Most casual drug use is inexpensive – at least in the same order of magnitude as drinking alcohol and there is no evidence that anything but a small proportion of such misuse (*sic*) is financed by crime' (Hough 1996: 10). Indeed, as Hughes and Anthony (2006: 76) point out, historically this group has never been the target of policy concern, nor has the criminal justice system been interested in them.

In terms of looking at this group through the four analytical lenses outlined above, it can be claimed that the nature of this group's drug use is recreational and mainly infrequent. It is unlikely that their drug use will be financed by crime, making the nature of the relationship between drug use and acquisitive crime low to non-existent. The 'risk' posed to community in terms of acquisitive crime and drug consumption is low. Thus, it appears that the majority of people who use illicit drugs do so in an experimental and relatively unproblematic fashion, failing to become involved in acquisitive crime in any significant form.

Category 2: frequent offender/frequent drug user

Whilst it is possible to claim that the majority of those people who have *ever* used an illicit drug have done so in an unproblematic manner, there are numbers of users for whom drug use and/or offending behaviour has a significant impact upon their life. However, that knowledge poses an interesting, chicken and egg type question for the researcher and policy-maker in deciding which came first: frequent drug use or frequent offending behaviour. This has generated a wealth of literature and it is to some of this the chapter now turns.

UK-based research shows that many of those offenders who offend on a frequent basis are also frequent drug users (Wallace and Eastham 1994; Coid *et al.* 2001; Barton 2005), giving rise to speculation as to the relationship between frequent offending and the frequency of illicit drug use. This is supported by recent Home Office research, which conducted urine analysis on arrestees and found that there are high percentages of offenders who use illicit drugs (Bennett and Holloway 2005). Thus, it becomes difficult to refute claims that for *some* offenders their offending behaviour runs at least parallel with illicit drug use. Chaiken and Chaiken (1991), in reviewing the US research, recognise this, but caution that although for some offenders use of illicit drugs may be the primary cause of onset, participation and frequency in offending, for the vast majority of offenders illicit drug use is not the cause of offending behaviour.

Hammersley *et al.* (1989) and Hammersley *et al.* (1990), conducting research in Scotland, echo these US-based findings. They undertook two sets of research, one on prisoners and non-prisoners with offending histories and the other on teenage users of licit and illicit drugs. In both studies Hammersley and colleagues found that illicit drug use did not cause the onset of offending behaviour, neither did frequent illicit drug use determine the frequency of criminal activity. They suggest that day-to-day criminal activity was a better explanation of drug use than daily drug use was of crime. They note that readily available income allows increased consumption of a number of goods, including illicit drugs. In turn the availability of disposable income, set in an environment where drug use is normalised, can lead to increased and, for some, ultimately problematic use. Thus, for Hammersly *et al.* (1989, 1990) being involved in a criminal environment is more likely to lead to drug use than *vice-versa*.

This is worthy of expansion, because, often, implicit in the messages of the media and politicians, and certainly the main thrust of policy, is the assertion that illicit drug use *causes* crime. In some cases this may be true: however for many individuals offending behaviour pre-dates drug dependency. Searching for causality in the social sciences is very often a complex process, devoid of 'right' answers. However, the complexity inherent in this situation can be simplified by viewing it diagrammatically. Figure 8.1, which has been adapted from Hough (1996: 11), contains three interlocking figures. Take note that the figures are not to scale and it is not intended that they map the precise overlap between each of the categories. Rather, they are intended to demonstrate the relationship between drug use and offending and highlight the different pathways into problematic drug use.

The largest circle represents all illicit drug users, and relates to Category 1 in the typology offered here. The triangle relates to all those involved in acquisitive crime, with the oblong representing those drug users whose use has become problematic. It can be seen that some offenders overlap with drug users, and these relate to Category 2 in our typology.

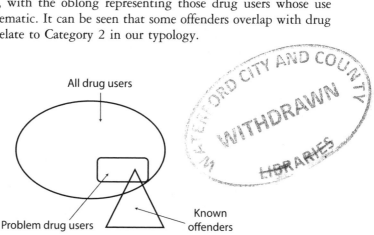

Figure 8.1 The relationship between drug use and offending

According to researchers such as Hammersley *et al.* (1988, 1990) and Chaiken and Chaiken (1991), routes into Categories 2 and 3 are more likely to come from the offending pathway than from the drug using pathway. Thus, as Hammersley notes, being involved in a social group where offending and drug taking is the norm provides a greater chance that individuals will move from offending into drug use and then sometimes, but not always, onwards into problematic drug use. Although it is possible for those that use illicit drugs and come from non-offending social groups, such as those in Category 1, to move into Categories 2 and 3, the likelihood is lower.

This argument is clarified and endorsed by Coid *et al.* (2001). In their research into the crime/drug link they found that some acquisitive offences such as shoplifting, theft and burglary preceded drug dependence. For example, Coid *et al.* (2001: 47) found that, amongst their cohort, the mean age for first burglary was 17 years, whereas the mean age for first opiate use amongst those that had committed burglary was 20.2 years. However, offending pre-dating opiate dependence only relates to certain types of offences: in the same work, Coid *et al.* note that 75 per cent of those who admitted offences of prostitution committed their first offence *after* they were drug dependent. Again, these findings are reflected in some current research that I am undertaking, where Category 3 drug users admit to offences such as shoplifting at ages as young as ten, which predates any use of any substance.

In many ways, Hough (1996: 5–11) further clarifies this theme. He suggests that offences where there is a drug and crime link can be viewed in one of two ways: as either *drug-related* or *drug-driven*. In detail, Hough employs the ACMD distinction between casual users and problem drug users. Problem drug users are identified as:

> … anyone who experiences social, psychological, physical or legal pro-
> blems related to intoxification and/or regular excessive consumption and/
> or dependence of his/her own use of drugs or other chemical sub-
> stances … [it also] includes anyone whose drug misuse involves, or could
> lead to the sharing of injecting equipment.
>
> (Hough 1996: 5)

Hough qualifies this statement and warns not to take the above as an implication that 'recreational' or 'casual' drug use is unproblematic – he argues that it is not problem free and can lead to both legal and medical complications. Nevertheless, for Hough, the area of linkage between drugs and crime revolves around those users whose drug consumption has become problematic.

On this basis, Hough (1996: 10–11) offers his analytical dichotomy of offences with links to drug use. He argues for the need to examine both the motivations for committing the offence and the nature of what the proceeds from offending are spent on. He suggests that some recreational drug users who commit acquisitive crimes may use some of the proceeds of crime on drugs. However, they are equally likely to use the proceeds on a plethora of consumer goods and/or staple essentials such as food and rent. In this instance, drug purchase can be seen as an incidental item of expenditure and therefore lacking any form of causality, demonstrating only a tenuous link between drugs and crime, and locating them firmly in Category 1 users, outlined above.

Moving along the continuum, Hough (1996: 11) recognises that 'some non-dependent drug users consume a volume of drugs which would be beyond their means if it were not for the income they derive from crime'. Once again this does not constitute a causal link between drug use and crime; it does, however, begin to increase the strength of the relationship between the two variables. By way of illustration, Hough suggests that a non-dependent drug user may be motivated to burgle in order to finance a 'good time', but be indifferent as to whether that 'good time' is fuelled by alcohol or illicit drugs. Thus, the nature of the offence is *drug related*.

Bearing this in mind, it is possible to begin to create a Category 2 drug user. For this group drug use will have become regular and relatively frequent, and probably will have moved into regular cocaine and/or amphetamine use. The nature of the relationship between drug use and crime is one where offending and drug use is frequent with drug-related crime taking place. Drug consumption will be financed at least partially by crime. Overall, this group poses a medium to high risk to their community in terms of offending behaviour.

Category 3: prolific offender/problematic drug user

At the polar extreme of the continuum is the offender whose motivation to offend is directly related to drug purchase and consumption. The ACMD (1995: 12) defines this group as: 'those individuals, some of whose offending is associated with misuse of drugs either causally or because of the influence of drugs on their behaviour'. Hough argues that this group of offenders commits crimes 'specifically to buy a preferred illegal drug'. As Hough notes (1996: 11, original emphasis), offences 'committed by [this group] can be regarded as *drug-driven*'. Coid *et al.* (2001: 44–45) reinforce this perspective. They note that from their sample, in the month prior to interview only 19 per cent had managed to keep their expenditure on illicit drugs within the limits of their legal income; the remaining 81 per cent had resorted to acquisitive crime in order to finance drug consumption.

Arguably, it is possible to suggest that it is this category, for which drug use has reached problematic levels, that the link between crime and illicit drug use is at its strongest, with offending behaviour and drug consumption being frequent in the extreme. Bean (2004: 8), looking at the offending behaviour of this group, suggests that 'An out-of-control male drug user is likely to commit 80–100 crimes per year'. Coid *et al.* (2001: 67), reporting on the drug consumption patterns, note that the mean monthly total of days a heroin dependent offender uses opiates is 24.2, using on average 0.54 of a

Table 8.1. A typology of the crime/drug relationships.

Category	drug use	finance	nature of risk	crime/drug link
1	recreational/experimental	legal means	none	low
2	frequent/recreational	legal/illegal mix	drug related	medium
3	frequent/problematic	virtually all illegal	drug driven	high

gram per day. When heroin is unavailable the same group will use a number of other substances.

In spite of this evidence, claiming any sort of causality for each and every type of offence remains problematic: as Bean (2004: 9) continues: 'Offenders might say they burgled because they were drug takers but they were burglars in any case'. Perhaps a better way is to study the *types* of crime this group commits and examine changes in offending *patterns* pre- and post-dependency. For example, it seems from Coid *et al.*'s (2001) work that some types of offences predated problematic drug use. Equally, however, some types of offences *post-date* problematic use. It may be the case that problematic drug use causes certain offenders, whose offending pre-dated problematic use, to become engaged in offences that, hitherto, they shied away from. *Possibly, then and only then, could causality between drug use and crime be claimed.*

However, such a detailed analysis is beyond the scope of this work. For our purposes we need to concentrate on fitting this group into our analytical framework. Based on this evidence, it appears the nature of drug use for this group is problematic and extremely frequent. Drug use is, effectively, totally financed by crime. The nature of the relationship between drug use and crime is that crime is drug driven. This group poses a high risk to their community in terms of acquisitive crime. In trying to clarify and end this complex argument, it may be beneficial to the reader to present the above information in a table form.

As a final thought on this matter, and as a way of introducing the next section, it is worth quoting Edmunds *et al.* (1999: 7):

> For the 97 per cent of people who engage in casual or recreational drug use there is little evidence of clear links between drug use and acquisitive crime. For the three per cent of problem users, the evidence of a link is overwhelming.

In essence, the 'problem' population in terms of their drug use and offending behaviour could be as few as 130,000 people, probably not rising to much above 200,000. Whilst this number may seem small, the effects of their action have huge ramifications for them as individuals and the communities in which they live. There is a certain irony (or some may see it as poetic justice) that many of this group of offenders who cause extensive harm and cost to society, suffer equally in terms of harm and cost in terms of their individual health and social conditions. Both the 'harm' and 'cost' of illicit drug use, in terms of crime, health and social conditions will now be reviewed.

The 'cost' of drug use and crime

This section of the chapter considers the nature of 'harm' and 'cost', in individual and collective terms. It begins by continuing the theme in the previous section in concentrating on the harm drug driven crime does to society, and, briefly, to the individual drug user. Following that, it explores the harm drug use does to individuals in terms of their health and their social conditions.

Cost, although it can be seen in purely financial terms, is perhaps better understood, and therefore will be conceived of here, as being related to the concept of 'harm'. When policy-makers talk of 'harm' they actually mean the cost of illicit drug use in terms of health and crime to both the individual and the community. For example, public concern over drugs has been expressed by the government in three ways:

- the link between drugs and crime;
- the health risk posed by the spread of HIV and hepatitis;
- the damage to the social fabric caused by high concentrations of the above two points in some urban areas.

(Home Office 1997)

Just over ten years later, as a result of the effects of their first ten-year strategy, the government's 2008 priorities had changed to:

- protecting communities through robust enforcement to tackle drug supply, drug-related crime and anti-social behaviour;
- preventing harm to children, young people and families affected by drug use;
- delivering new approaches to drug treatment and reintegration;
- public information campaigns, communications and community engagement.

(Home Office 2008)

Essentially, all these concerns are linked to the concept of harm (it is worth noting that 'harm reduction' is one of the key phrases used by those working within the drug field). In terms of the health risk, this is related to the harm that drug use does to the individual user, with wider concerns over public health. The concern over crime can be seen to be linked with the harm which drug-driven crime does to the community, with broader worries as to the effect of criminalisation on the user/offender. Taken together, the overall effect of problematic drug use is deemed to be harmful to the fabric of society.

'Cost' and 'harm' in terms of acquisitive crime

Ignoring questions of causality, there can be little doubt that illicit drug use and acquisitive crime share an affinity, especially for the small minority that comprise Category 3 users. This point has been made in a number of publications drawn from a diversity of sources. Although they have been well rehearsed, it is worthwhile to cover them again, in order that the magnitude of offending behaviour may be reviewed. Edmunds *et al.* (1998) provide an official picture, estimating that, as a group, the combined annual expenditure on drugs for Category 3 users could reach £1 billion. Given the discrepancy between licit and illicit income for this group, somewhere in the region of half that could be raised by acquisitve crime per annum. In light of the fact that stolen property is sold on for around one-third of the retail value, this group could be engaged in offending that costs victims up to £1.5 billion per annum.

This perspective has been endorsed by a number of sources. For example, Wallace and Eastham (1994), conducting a piece of action research amongst Category 3 clients of a street drug agency in Plymouth, found that 62 per cent of their sample (27 people) admitted to offending at least once a day. If that figure is rounded down and extended over a 12-month period, those 27 people held the potential to commit somewhere in the region of 9,855 offences over the course of a year. If each crime resulted in goods to the value of £100 being taken, the yearly cost of those 27 people in terms of goods stolen equals £985,500.

Coid *et al.*'s (2001: 75) work, commissioned by the Home Office, found a similar picture. From their sample of Category 3 users, they compared the weekly expenditure on illicit drugs with the weekly licit income. Their findings illustrate the nature of the problem. Coid *et al.* found that the mean weekly expenditure on illicit drugs was £312.40 compared with a mean weekly licit income of £70.45. This left a mean income deficit of £245.80. The mean six-monthly income derived from crime by this group stood at £10,984. However, high as this may appear, this sum is based on mean figures: some of Coid *et al.*'s (2001: 44) disaggregated findings are staggering. For example, some subjects claimed to be spending £280 per day on heroin. Others claimed that their maximum daily spend on opiates stood at £1,000. At the extreme, there was a claimed income deficit of £1,936 per week.

The Home Office has further updated these figures and, based on research conducted in 2005, claim that the average weekly spend *on drugs alone* is:

- £620 per week for heroin users (£32,240 pa);
- £660 per week for cocaine users (£34,320 pa);
- £1,100 for crack users (£57,200 pa).

These are large amounts of money and all of them are above the average national gross wage (that is the wage paid before any deductions such as tax and national insurance) and clearly represent persistent and prolific levels of offending that will damage communities where this takes place. As an example, the following is an excerpt from a police report that informed a piece of research I carried out in 2004–05 (Barton 2005), which demonstrates the impact just one Category 3 offender can have on a community:

Offender 1

History

On initial assessment Offender 1 was understood to have a heroin habit amounting to £300 per day. He was residing in a town in Penwith and was known to be a prolific criminal, committing acquisitive crime, particularly burglaries, theft and other vehicle-related offences in that area.

Prolific Offender Unit

At the time of assessment, 11 July 2003, Offender 1 was linked to 131 crimes.

Since participating with the POU, he has been linked to a further 22 crimes, the last recorded on the 30 April 2004, including six dwelling burglaries and seven counts of theft.

Offender 1 has spent 137 days remanded in prison in the last 12 months.

COST OF RECORDED OFFENCES JULY 2003 TO APRIL 2004

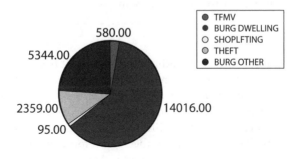

Time spent in prison		Total days
19/08/2003	07/09/2003	19
15/09/2003	16/09/2003	1
30/09/2003	18/11/2003	49
08/03/2004	25/03/2004	17
11/05/2004	30/06/2004	51
	Total	137
	@ cost	£13,289

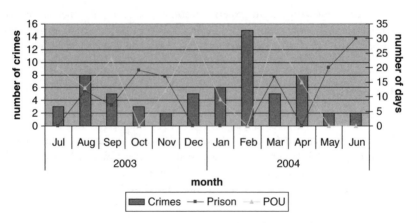

Figure 8.2 Town in rural district burglaries (number of crimes left hand scale; days in prison or under POU supervision right hand scale)

There was a period from 9 January 2004 to 1 March 2004 when the offender was not co-operating with the POU and was not in prison.

This graph provides a visual indication of a dramatic increase in the number of dwelling burglaries in the Penwith town compared with the time when Offender 1 was in prison and/or under POU intervention.

From July 2003 until present, Offender 1's combined total cost of recorded acquisitive crime to the economy is £22,394.

Offenders with this level of offending behaviour will have a negative impact on the quality of life of their (numerous) victims. Mawby and Walklate (1994) note that this will have a number of different effects. First, it will raise the fear of crime amongst victims, amongst those who live in close proximity to and within the wider community (direct and indirect victimisation). Second, the victims themselves may suffer either some form of physical or mental trauma, as well as actual loss of property. For some, especially the low-income, uninsured victim, this may have serious consequences on their ability to replace what are often essential household items. Third, victims can suffer from a loss of time, due to giving statements, becoming involved in legal proceedings and so on. Finally, if the police either fail to clear up the crime, or the offender gets what the victim sees as an 'easy' sentence, the victim can suffer a form of frustration and loss of confidence in the criminal justice process.

Crime can also have a debilitating effect on community relations in terms of creating divided communities and fostering a 'them and us' mentality, where sections of the population become seen as 'dangerous others'. At its worst, this can lead to the creation of a fortress mentality and the use of a 'plethora of high-tech alarm equipment' (Barton 2000: 13). This is often an indiscriminate form of community segregation and involves 'lumping toge-ther' tracts of the community, based on perceptions rather than realities. Thus, it may be the case that all young people are excluded and feared, irrespective of whether they are drug users or not.

There are two other forms of 'cost' associated with drugs and crime. The first is the cost to the government in 'dealing with' drug use. The Home Office states that spending on dealing with illicit drugs will reach £963 million in 2010–11. Whilst not all of this figure is spent on crime-related projects, a substantial amount of that money is, and therefore represents a hefty cost to the taxpayer. The second form of 'cost' is the cost of having a criminal record to the drug user. Whilst in itself having a criminal record is not, in most cases, a direct block on gaining employment, the realities are that many ex-offenders find themselves victims of 'discrimination by application form' and are often unable to find much more than menial employment.

'Cost' and 'harm' in terms of health and social circumstances

This section examines the 'cost' and 'harm' that problematic drug users inflict, mostly on themselves. Ironically, many of those Category 3 drug users who create problems for their community in terms of acquisitive crime suffer most in terms of drug-related ill-health. This is perhaps best sum-marised by Robson (1994: 142), where, writing from a medical perspective, he declares, 'we can only assume that for the vast majority of drug users, their drug use is occasional and spasmodic, or that drugs prove pretty well harmless to most people'. Based on that statement it would appear that, just as in the case with the criminal justice agencies, the majority of illicit drug users do not create a problem for themselves or the health service. Just to make an important point however, that is not to say that drug use is risk free. Robson (1994: 142) notes that all drug taking involves some element of risk. How-ever, it is equally important to remember that evidence seems to suggest the belief that once people start using drugs there will be an inevitable spiral downwards to drug dependency seems to be based more on mythology than fact.

Nevertheless, rare as it is, some people clearly do experience serious prob-lems with their drug use and end up becoming drug dependent (in lay terms many problematic drug users are 'addicted', although the preferred phrase amongst drug workers is 'drug dependent' (Gossop and Grant 1990). For this group of users, it is the consequences of their drug dependency, in health and social terms, which holds the potential to create problematic conditions. This section concentrates upon the nature of those problems faced by drug-depen-dent users.

According to Robson (1994: 153), definitions of drug dependency are dif-ficult to provide, and are always open to challenge. However, he suggests that, in broad terms, being dependent upon something means being caught up in the following cycle:

... a mounting desire to do something; if this is resisted or prevented, a growing anxiety or preoccupation with the act in question; carrying out the act stills the tension, satisfies the desire and briefly eliminates the need; the cycle starts all over again.

Once a person becomes locked into this cycle, their life begins to change. There is a growing preoccupation that intrudes into the person's life, skewing their priorities toward, in our case, an illicit drug. There is a sense of compulsion, which includes an element of the person feeling obliged to do something that they may not really want to do. With this compulsion come the routines that ensure a ready supply, consumption of the drug becomes less dependent on external cues and the person becomes less and less concerned about the consequences of their actions. In some instances, larger quantities of an illicit drug may be needed as tolerance develops.

Dependence may be physical and/or psychological. Physical dependence can manifest itself as withdrawal symptoms if the drug is withheld, especially where opioids are concerned. Psychological dependence can manifest itself as a craving for the drug, which is often triggered by the environment. These can take the shape of 'cues' and can include, amongst many others, a piece of music, being in the company of certain people or the sight of injecting equipment. The exact nature of the harm drug-dependent users experience depends upon a number of factors and varies from user to user, although it is generally accepted that drug-related 'harm' falls into two categories: health condition and social condition.

Health-related harm

Some problematic drug users suffer from health problems prior to their drug-related illnesses. For example, Coid *et al.*'s (2001: 54) work demonstrates that 39 per cent of their sample had experienced some form of depression, whilst small percentages had suffered from serious mental health conditions. Likewise, the same work (2001: 55) noted high percentages of personality disorders amongst the sample. Other work (Wallace and Eastham 1994), recognises the presence of general health problems such as poor dental health and constipation amongst a similar group of drug users.

Gossop and Grant (1990: 5–6) outline the basic medical concerns of drug dependency. They claim that, for the medical profession, these are 'excess mortality and excess morbidity'. The former refers to the death rate amongst drug users when compared to a non-drug using population of the same age range, whilst the latter means the rates of illness amongst drug users when compared to a similar, non-drug using population. Gossop and Grant (1990: 6) note that excess mortality in drug users stems mostly from overdose or (and especially in the case of intravenous drug users [IDUs]), 'the direct access of disease organisms and adulterants into the bloodstream'.

In terms of mortality, and bearing in mind methodological problems and different counting processes, the most recent statistics show that the number of male drug poisoning related deaths in 2008, including those involving both legal and illegal drugs, was 2,075. This was an increase of 8 per cent compared with 2007, and the highest number since 2001. The number of female deaths rose to 853 in 2008, an increase of 17 per cent compared with 2007, after falling for the previous three years. However, when we examine illicit drug-related deaths we can see that there were 897 deaths involving heroin or morphine in 2008. This marks an 8 per cent rise compared to 2007 figures and is the highest recorded number of deaths since 2001. The number of deaths involving methadone also increased from 325 in 2007 to 378 in 2008, a rise of 16 per cent. This is the highest number of deaths involving methadone since 1998, when 398 deaths were recorded. Deaths involving cocaine rose to 235 in 2008, continuing a long-term upward trend since 1993 (Office of National Statistics 2009).

Turning attention to excess morbidity, Gossop and Grant claim that this is related to a complex of factors, including:

> ... the pharmacological and toxicological properties of drug(s) used, the combinations of drugs used, the accessibility of health services ... the nutritional habits and status of drug users, the route of administration, of drugs, the quality of the social network and the social integration of the drug user ...
>
> (Gossop and Grant 1990: 6)

The DoH (1999: 22) provides a clear picture as to how excess morbidity manifests itself in drug users. They claim that amongst drug users the following illnesses are more common than in similar populations:

> ... viral hepatitis [liver disease], bacterial endocarditis [inflammation of the heart], HIV [an attack on the body's immune system], tuberculosis [a communicable disease of the lung], septicaecmia [blood poisoning], pneumonia [disease of the lung], deep vein thrombosis [blood clot in the vein], pulmonary emboli [blood clot in the lung], abscesses and dental disease.

They clarify this somewhat by noting the various component parts of drug use and the specific nature of health-related problems:

A: Drug related:
    side effects (e.g. constipation, hallucinations);
    overdose (e.g. respiratory depression);
    withdrawal (e.g. irritability, fits).
B: Route specific:
    smoking (asthma);

injecting (abscesses, cellulitis).
C: Sharing needles:
syringes and injection;
equipment:
(hepatitis B and C, HIV and other blood-borne viruses).
D: General:
Anaemia, poor nutrition, dental caries and erosion of dentine.

However, whilst these problems are serious for the users, it is worthwhile to examine their known prevalence amongst the drug using population. Be warned, however, that these figures relate to *known* cases: this work has commented more than once on the problems of painting accurate pictures of the illicit drug world.

Looking first at HIV infections, the Health Protection Agency (HPA) (2009: 7), note that HIV infection rates amongst IDUs have been relatively uncommon in the UK and as a result transmission of HIV via injecting has remained stable, with an annual average of 155 reports during the period 1999–2008. However, the infection rate of those who have recently started injecting (that is within the last three years) has risen.

There are two other blood-borne viruses that are worthy of consideration, hepatitis B and hepatitis C. The former is usually acquired in adulthood via sexual activity or injecting drug use and in 2003 injecting drug use was the main identified risk of hepatitis B infection. At present the HPA estimate that one in six injectors has the virus (HPA 2009: 12). There is an effective vaccine for this virus.

Hepatitis C, is, at present the 'most important infectious disease affecting those who inject drugs' (HPA 2009: 8). The same agency report that up to 80 per cent of those who acquire hepatitis C go on to develop chronic infection and run the risk of developing cirrhosis and liver cancer. Reporting for hepatitis C began in 1992; up to 2008, 69,864 reported diagnoses had been reported, of which around 90 per cent are thought to be attributable to injecting users. The HPA (2009: 9) notes that the prevalence of hepatitis C remains high amongst IDUs but this may be due to the fact that more users are being tested rather than increased rates of incidence.

Socially related harm

Not only do problematic drug users run the risk of harming their health, research also demonstrates that many of this group suffer all manner of social problems, ranging from relationship difficulties, to employment problems and housing related stresses. However, it is important to point out that, for many problem drug users, these problems pre-dated their drug use. Coid *et al.* (2001: 51–52) found that a significant proportion of their sample suffered numerous kinds of abuse and neglect as children. For example, they found that 41 per cent came from violent households, 31 per cent grew up in poverty and 14 per cent suffered some form of sexual abuse before the age of 15.

Looking at their current situation, Wallace and Eastham (1994) found that 81 per cent of their sample declared drug use had damaged their relationships. This figure is endorsed by Coid *et al.*'s (2001) later study. Here, examining long-term relationships, the researchers found that 49 per cent of respondents claimed their drug use had a direct consequence on either their divorce or ending of a relationship. Moreover, drug use seems to be a contributory factor in damaging contacts with wider family members, with 35 per cent of Coid *et al.*'s study blaming drug use for causing them to break contact with their family.

Coid *et al.* (2001) and Wallace and Eastham (1994) found that problematic drug users often have problems in obtaining and/or keeping a job; 75 per cent of Wallace and Eastham's sample were unemployed, compared to 77 per cent in Coid *et al.*'s work. Thirty-four per cent of Coid *et al.*'s group cited drug use as a reason for being sacked from a job. Arguably, a corollary of this is that many problematic drug users experience housing problems. For example, Wallace and Eastham found that only 14 per cent of their sample were owner-occupiers. Coid *et al.* found that 39 per cent of their sample were living in some form of temporary accommodation, which included squats and hostels.

On top of these concerns, problematic drug users also have other worries, related to, if not caused by, their drug dependency. Most have debts to family and, in cases where they have formerly held down a job, to banks or loan companies. Equally, they are likely at some time to have sold possessions to pay for drugs, impacting on their quality of life (Coid *et al.* 2001). There are concerns over childcare, with the very real risk of children being taken into care if one or both adults in a relationship are classified as drug dependent (Parker *et al.* 1998). Moreover, the very act of looking for drugs seems, for some, to be a time-consuming worry:

> It takes a lorr a time scoring and that, y'know. You've got no time for anything else. It takes up all your life really. With me working, by the time you get home at 5 o'clock, it might take you 'til 9 o'clock at night to score sometimes. You're sorta running about all the time so you don't get time for anythin' else really.
>
> (Parker *et al.* 1998: 88)

Conclusion

This chapter has examined the 'cost' of illicit drug use and, in so doing, has covered much ground. A great deal of the information reviewed above informs contemporary thinking about the 'drug problem' in the United Kingdom, both in terms of policy making and lay assumptions. Hopefully, the reader will have found it informative as well as offering a slightly clearer perspective on a number of truisms surrounding illicit drug use. Before going on to conclude, it may be a worthwhile exercise to summarise some of the key points that have emerged from the above discussion:

- it would appear that the majority of people who take illicit drugs almost never experience health and/or legal problems;
- there is little evidence to support a 'natural' progression from recreational drug use to problematic drug use – evidence suggests that problematic drug use is infrequent and atypical of most users' experience;
- there is also little in the way of empirical data to support the assertion that drug use leads to crime, except in the minority of cases;
- there is, however, a clear link between problematic drug use and frequent offending;
- there is an equally strong link between problematic drug use and all manner of health and social problems.

What is emerging from research is the fact there is a continuum of illicit drug use with an accompanying continuum of problems. The former continuum moves from the infrequent experimental user along to the drug dependent user, diminishing in number the closer one moves to dependent user. The latter follows a similar pattern, except that, here, problems grow the closer one moves toward the drug dependent user. What has also emerged is the fact that this is a relatively small group of people who cause a disproportionate level of harm to wider society, in terms of acquisitve crime, hence the thrust of much current drug policy. Similarly, often the same people cause themselves and their immediate significant others a large degree of harm in terms of health and social problems.

Despite the fact that, however atypical it may be, some illicit drug users experience severe problems in terms of criminal justice, health, illness and social care, drug use continues to be a growing part of a significant minority of the UK population's life. This is in spite of repeated warnings, drug prevention campaigns, the statutory requirement to include drug education on the national curriculum for schools, the harmful effects of illicit drugs being part of a number of popular soap operas and repeated exhortations from sections of the media imploring the young to resist the temptations of illicit drugs. This begs the question 'what can be done?' The next chapter reviews the policies in place that aim to address this question.

Suggested further reading

Bean, P. (2004) *Drugs and Crime* (2nd edition), Cullumpton: Willan Publishing.

Health Prevention Agency (2009) *Shooting up: infections among injecting drug users in the United Kingdom 2008*, London: HPA.

Home Office (2008) *Drugs: protecting families and communities: the 2008 drug strategy*, London: Home Office.

United Kingdom Drug Policy Commission (2008) *Supporting the supporters: families of drug misusers*, http available www.ukdpc.org.uk/reports.shtml accessed 21 June 2009.

Questions and areas for reflection

1. The justification for maintenance prescribing originates from the 1926 Rolleston Committee. Given that over 80 years has passed since then, do we need to revisit the debate?
2. To what extent do you agree with the statement 'in terms of illicit drug users the state is more concerned with preventing acquisitive crime than treating drug use'?
3. Do we need a more nuanced approach to describing drug use and drug users?

9 Policing the problem

Current trends in UK drug policy

Introduction

One of the intentions of this work has been to alert the reader to the complex nature of the illicit drug scene. At one and the same time illicit drug use in the UK is seen as morally wrong, and thus subject to legal sanctions, as well as being pharmaceutically dangerous, making it in need of control by the medical profession. Yet, despite this formidable level of official sanction and concern, a significant minority of the British population claims some form of illicit drug use. Equally, the UK, whilst having its own 'drug problem', is subject to the pressure and influence of a huge global illicit drug industry that grows, manufactures and distributes a product for which there is a seemingly inexorable demand. In some producing countries, the illicit drug industry has a major impact on economic well being, making it difficult to impose meaningful sanctions. In an effort to control this global 'problem' the UK, alongside a host of other nations, has become a signatory to international anti-drug treaties, which in turn influences and runs parallel to domestic policies.

It is the development of these domestic policies that informs this penultimate chapter. As we shall see, the last two decades have seen a rise in activity in the drug policy area, which has become increasingly frenetic in the very recent past. When I wrote the first version of this book, I noted that 'it is without doubt that, at the time of writing (January 2002), the UK seems to be entering a watershed period in drug policy', and I quoted the DPAS publication: *'Let's Get Real'* (DPAS 2001) as evidence of that. However, hindsight being a wonderful thing, I am now not so sure that much has changed. Essentially, what this chapter aims to do is to chart the development of British policy from the 'just say no' approach of the early 1980s through to the criminal justice dominated approach of the early twenty-first century.

The chapter begins with a brief excursion into some of the literature that describes the policy-making processes, the impact of policy communities, and the problems of joint working. It then looks at the claims for a 'British system' and identifies two distinct policy communities. This is a necessary diversion, as it alerts the reader to the difficulties and tensions in policy formation, as well as providing a theoretical framework through which to view policy. From there, the chapter identifies policy options and trawls through the various policy documents, noting how the government's approach changes over time. In so doing, it searches for factors that influence change. It concludes with some thoughts on the possible future direction of policy.

Policy making, policy communities and joint working

This brief section is included for the benefit of those readers who may not have a background in policy studies. Often, when made aware of a 'social problem' such as illicit drug use, the response of the public and some sections of the media are to call for 'something to be done'. Sometimes, public and media opinion champions the 'common sense' approach to making new policy, calling for the 'obvious' solution and using lurid details to make their points: *ergo* 'Legal drug teen ripped his scrotum off' (the *Sun*, 26 November 2009), so if the *Sun* is to be believed, every person that takes that particular substance (in this case mephadrone) runs a real risk of self-mutilation, and the policy answer is to ban the substance and lock up the suppliers. The reality is that policy making and implementation is seldom that simple. Policy making and ensuring that new policy is delivered in an efficient and effective manner is a complex process and requires a strange and unpredictable amalgam of inputs.

There are two important points to recognise. First, policy is not made in a vacuum. By that, it is meant that policy often reflects contemporary social events and socially accepted norms. Change in social norms often leads to change in policy. Second, and linked to the former point, policy-makers, both nationally and locally, almost never operate with a *'tabula rasa'* or clean sheet. This means new proposals for policy are constrained by a mixture of present and previous policies for 'dealing with' any particular problem. In our example, contemporary policy-makers need to contend with a number of pre-existing givens: the Home Office control over policy, international treaties, local policing arrangements, and so on. This means that any construction of policy needs to recognise that, whatever the desired aims may be, new policy must, in the short term at least, fit into any existing frameworks. This also brings into play the next constraint on policy-makers: existing organisational structures and working practices. In the field of illicit drugs this would include the historic division between health and law as well as the myriad of non-governmental organisations supplying services to drug users.

Policy making also suffers from something called the 'implementation gap' (Colebatch 1998). This is due to the fact that those who make national policy almost never implement their decisions: that is left to any number of organisations spread across the country. This can create differences between the aims of policy as devised by policy-makers at a national level, and the manner in which that policy is delivered by organisations at a local level. For example, until the middle of the decade, there was no official indication from central government that policy relating to cannabis should be changed. However, as Kaal (1998) notes, the use of cautions by English police forces for cannabis, both in terms of possession and supply, rose by more than 50 per cent during the period 1987–95. This would suggest that long before David Blunkett's recommendations police forces had 'downgraded' cannabis use.

The makers of policy need also to contend with the standard operating procedures of the different organisations that implement policy. These standard operating procedures relate to the manner in which organisations go about their day-to-day work and can be both formal (written rules and procedures) and informal ('that's the way we've always done things here'). Informal standard operating procedures have an enormous impact on the manner in which individuals see themselves and their work. One only needs to read the work of Reiner (2000: 85–107) on the manner in which 'cop culture' affects new police recruits to understand its power. In turn, such entrenched and self-perpetuating world views impact on the manner in which organisations and workers view the general public, other organisations and their employees, and social problems and problematic groups. This impacts on another important aspect of policy making and implementation – joint working.

This is not so much of a problem where organisations share ideologies and can form policy communities. For example, health, social services and most voluntary sector street drug agencies all share an ideology that can be broadly defined as 'welfarist', meaning that they seek to provide a caring, harm reduction-based approach to illicit drug use. This allows them to view illicit drug use and illicit drug users in broadly the same way, as well as being able to concentrate on the problems drug use poses for the *individual* drug user, leading inexorably to a treatment-based ideology. However, the police, the courts, and latterly the probation service, are, by virtue of their organisational remit, almost forced to take a law and order stance to illicit drug use. This often means that these organisations view drug use first and foremost in terms of the risk and damage it does to *society*, meaning that the logical approach would be punishment.

As a result, joint working – the coming together of a number of agencies to address a social problem – can take place more easily between like-minded organisations and individuals who share a similar ideology. Historically, in terms of illicit drug policy, the gap between the law and order policy community and the welfarist policy community has not been a problem, as each section seemingly worked in isolation from the other. However, the last 20 years has seen an explosion in the requirement for agencies from all policy communities to end sectoral isolationism and devise strategies designed to promote and cement joint working. This has reached a point where it is almost impossible to launch a new policy that does not require some form of joint working. In some instances, joint working has occurred voluntarily and in others it has been reliant upon government policy.

A 'British system'?

Before moving on to explore and examine the changing face of British drug policy, it is important, given the above discussion, to make one thing very clear; the exact nature of the illicit drug policy community, particularly its dominant discourse and constituent parts. Chapter 1 noted that some commentators have identified a 'British system' in terms of drug policy, where it is claimed that there is a degree of medicalisation, which allows a less punitive and more treatment-based approach to illicit drug use. Chapter 1 was purposefully ambiguous as to the veracity of such claims. This is due to the fact that, alongside writers such as Strang and Gossop (1994), it is believed here that no such system exists, especially in the form claimed by some North American writers who contrast the 'criminalisation' stance of the US to the (supposed) 'medicalisation' approach of the UK (e.g. Trebach 1982).

At most, what we once had in Britain was a dual approach to the 'drug problem', with the criminal justice system and the medical profession having significant, but isolated, inputs, thus making claims to separate domains of expertise over the 'drug problem'. As a result, historically, Britain cultivated a situation where creating drug policy bred an ongoing power struggle between, on the one hand, the Home Office, seeking to maintain the dominance of criminal law and punishment over the other hand, the Department of Health (or one of its other guises over the years), who seek to pursue medical dominance over illicit drugs. Witness the words of the former British deputy drug 'tsar' Mike Trace, who claims that British drug policy has been weakened by the 'constant battles between criminal justice agencies and the Department of Health over policy aims' (Trace, in Travis 2001: 3).

This dual approach allowed entry for two different professional discourses into the drug policy field: treatment and punishment. It also allowed professionals from entirely different ideological, professional and practical backgrounds liberty to contest for the ownership of the 'problem'. Taking a Focauldian perspective, this ensures that the 'problem' will become defined by each side in a manner calculated to emphasise their own discourse and preferred 'solution', and at the same time each discourse will be attempting to weaken the claim of the competing discourse and its solution. On top of this, politics, and the needs of politicians, has to be added to any policy equation: 'the drug problem' is an emotive issue, and one being seen to be 'soft' on it can lose as many votes as they gain. Moreover, it is highly newsworthy and the political classes are acutely aware of the dangers of upsetting the moralistic tabloid press, which views illicit drug use through uni-dimensional lenses. All of these factors have some influence upon the shape of British drug policy.

As we will see below, the 'British system' of drug policy, far from being led by the medics, has, both historically and contemporaneously, been the domain of the criminal justice agencies: our first instinct has been to punish, then, depending on the drug, treat. As an example, Dorn and South (1994: 294) refer to the policy surrounding the use of amphetamine:

> ... social concern over the use of this drug [amphetamine] in particular by working class youth ... led to its criminalization in the 1960s and, subsequently, more attention from the police than from the health sector. Indeed, the manner in which Britain responds to amphetamine may be seen as symptomatic of its general drug policy; here is a drug that can certainly be associated with a range of social and health problems ... Yet the typical British response is to process the user as an offender. British System?

Thus, it is possible to claim that the dominant policy community in British drug policy is law and order, hence the domination of the criminal justice discourse. This is borne out by the fact that the key government department has always been the Home Office; a locus of control that shows no immanent sign of change.

However, it would be mistaken to believe that this makes drug policy the sole domain of the criminal justice agencies. Thanks largely to the continued efforts of the medics to 'own', or at the very least have some direct input into, policies designed to address the drug problem, the British illicit drug policy community is large and diverse. In policy terms the dual approach to dealing with illicit drug use, set in train by Rolleston in 1926, has continued to the present day and, due to the extension of the welfare state and the concomitant growth of welfarist agencies (Kemshall 2002) has expanded in the last two decades. In policy terms this means that there is an in-built requirement for some form of joint working within any policy moves. Moreover, change in wider social policy, which has led to 'joined-up working' becoming central to government policy (Barton and Quinn 2001) has simply increased the joint working imperative.

What this entails is the creation of two possible policy directions. First, policy can be aimed at reducing and controlling the degree to which illicit drugs are supplied and/or used. There are a number of possible ways in which such a policy could be implemented – vigorous enforcing of the law, strong border controls and high levels of Customs and Excise activity as well as a proactive education campaign. Second, policy could take the direction that significantly reducing supply and use is beyond the remit of the government (especially in light of the normalisation thesis) and that policy should move in the direction of reducing demand and impacting upon the harm illicit drug use does to individuals and communities. In many respects it is possible to view the first option as a 'hard' law and order-based approach, and to view the second as more welfare- and medicine-oriented.

The above points provide this chapter with an analytical framework through which to view contemporary British drug policy. It enables the chapter to review contemporary policy developments through three related but separate lenses. First, policy will be examined for signs of the domination of the criminal justice discourse and the manner in which this has been achieved. Second, illicit drug policy will be viewed in terms of the extent to which joint working has been championed, and the manner in which the 'joined-up' approach has been embraced by policy-makers and practitioners alike. Third we can search for evidence of policy moving either toward reducing drug supply or reducing demand.

The 1980s: policy formulation in a time of a rising tide of illicit drug use

Chapter 1 outlined policy developments up to the end of the 1960s, noting along the way the duality of the approach to dealing with illicit drugs. However, despite there being at least two policy sectors working within the illicit drug policy area, there was little evidence of joint working. As one commentator notes: 'Until recently, both approaches worked largely in isolation from each other' (Barton 1999: 145). Indeed, questions could be asked of this period as to whether Britain had a 'drugs policy' *per se*. Strang and Gossop (1994: 343–44) suggest: 'It has not been the way of things in the U.K. to construct formal drugs policy. Policy changes are often seen to have occurred only with the benefit of hindsight'. However, the same authors suggest that, paradoxically, this may be the strength of the British approach as it enables a 'particular capacity for evolution'.

To briefly summarise, the situation as Britain entered the 1980s was one of reliance on specialist clinics to offer substitute drugs in order to manage dependence or withdrawal and reduce demand for 'street drugs'. In many of these clinics there was an air of pessimism pervading drug workers, caused by a realisation that 'nothing works', and at best the interventions of the drug workers may have been little more than the social control of addiction (Strang and Gossop 1994). Outside of that, the police were still prosecuting those found in possession. Indeed, the criminal justice domination of drug policy was an outstanding feature. As Dorn and South (1994: 296) comment, 'heroin/methadone prescribing ... constitute islands of exception within the framework of historically hegemonic criminal law responses'.

It is possible to claim that, as Britain entered the 1980s, the 'masterly inactivity' (Downes 1977: 89) that had characterised British drug policy up to that date was exposed as wanting in the wake of a rising tide of drug use. In turn, the growing political interest in, and politicisation of, the 'drug problem' paved the way for a number of policy developments. Equally, in line with broader social policy, the 1980s began a period of change in the drug field where sectoral isolationism came under increasing pressure, and there was a widening and broadening of policy approaches. To a degree, this upsurge of government interest in illicit drug use was fuelled by a series of moral panics over 'the new heroin users' (Matthews 1995: 3).

In the vanguard of this era of change was the Advisory Council on the Misuse of Drugs (ACMD). It will be recalled that the ACMD was established as part of the 1971 MDA, with a remit to be a standing committee reporting back to the government on drug-related issues. In 1982, the ACMD published *Treatment and Rehabilitation*. This gave recognition to the fact that oral methadone was fast becoming the preferred treatment option, and those specialist clinics were increasingly being seen as only a partial solution to a burgeoning drug problem. The ACMD (1982) recommended that there should be a change in policy and a widening of the policy community. Amongst other things they suggested that there should be greater emphasis on local provision of prescription drugs and care for the addict, the locus of which should be the GP. The era of the specialist seemed to be doomed.

What the 1982 ACMD document also marked was the beginnings of official recognition that 'drug misuse requires collaboration between a wide range of public services and the specialist voluntary and independent sectors who work with drug misusers' (Howard *et al.* 1994: ix). However, despite further documents published in 1984, 1988 and 1989 (ACMD 1984, 1988, 1989), as well as the DHSS setting up collaborative guidelines in 1985 and 1986 (DHSS 1982, 1984), all of which called for greater collaboration between agencies, actual joint working on the ground was 'never ... adequately fulfilled' (Howard *et al.* 1994: ix).

Arguably, this is because there was a growing disparity between the government's hardline 'just say no/heroin screws you up' approach to the problem, when contrasted with some of the independent drug agencies' more realistic, harm reduction-based approach. Moreover, given the cross-sectoral nature of interventions, it is not surprising that joint working was never fully embraced. If we are to use our analytical lenses to view this period, it is obvious that the law and order discourse dominates. Moreover, there is a clear indication that the aim of government policy was to attempt to control and reduce supply, with demand reduction and harm reduction becoming more visible, but wrapped up in wider concerns over the transmission of HIV.

The criminal justice-led, use reduction approach is evidenced in the government's policy document of the time *Tackling Drug Misuse* (HMSO 1985). The document proposed five areas of policy action:

1. reducing supplies from abroad;
2. making enforcement even more effective;
3. maintaining effective deterrents and tight domestic controls;
4. developing prevention;
5. improving treatment and rehabilitation.

The first three are all obviously enforcement led and even the fourth could be seen to refer to increased law enforcement efforts instead of a greater medical involvement. There was very little evidence of any form of co-ordinated or collaborative approach: the police and Customs and Excise continued to enforce the law, whilst the medical profession continued to treat those users who came to their attention. Very little was done in reducing harm to communities or, especially in the case of recreational users, the harm drug users do to themselves. It must be noted that the DoH was beginning to embrace and endorse harm reduction, with harm minimisation policies being launched in drug agencies, as well as the development of needle and syringe exchanges around the country (South 1995: 31). However, much of this had its roots in specific concerns over the transmission of HIV rather than wider concerns over the health and well-being of recreational drug users.

Other measures included the introduction of the Drug Trafficking Offences Act (1986), which provided the police with a substantial increase in power as well as skewing the onus of proof away from accused person in respect of the origins of their assets. As a response to rise in use, and dealing in heroin and cocaine, the government also introduced the 1985 Controlled Drugs (Penalties) Act. As South (1995: 31) comments 'all of this placed the police, customs, courts and prisons at the forefront of control policy and practice'.

Into the 1990s: the rise of joint working and the criminalisation of drug policy?

Three events occurred during the late 1980s and early 1990s each, in its own way, making a significant impact on British illicit drug policy. The first is cultural. It revolves around the dawning of the 'acid house' phenomenon and the emergence of 'clubbing' as a significant development in youth culture. As some of the previous chapters point out, illicit drug use has always been a part of various youth cultures, but the clubbing movement has been particularly synonymous with the use of drugs, even spawning the term 'dance drugs' in reference to ecstasy, amphetamine and LSD. This fuelled the normalisation thesis and has seen a growth in recreational and experimental drug use amongst young people. Moreover, clubbers and experimental drug users are drawn from all sections of society, up to and including offspring from the royal family. This rise in use, coupled with some highly publicised drug-related deaths, led to a rethinking of drug policy (Blackman 2004).

Second, politically, there has been a growing realisation in the UK that unilateral approaches to social problems by various organisations lead to inefficient and ineffective service delivery, creating in their wake a rise in demand for joint working (Leathard 1994). Indeed, this pressure has increased since 1997 and the election of a New Labour government that has consistently championed the 'joined-up' approach to policy making (Micheal 1998). Third, in policy terms, was the growing realisation that there was a link between drug use and some crime, and that drug policy held an important key in the government's ability to begin to reduce the risk that this link posed to society.

Thus drug policy in the last two decades has been based on addressing:

- the normalisation of 'sensible' recreational drug use amongst sections of the population;
- the dominance of multi-agency working as the preferred policy approach;
- the recognition that problematic drug users are often the most persistent offenders, and addressing their drug use can lead to reductions in offending behaviour.

The key to the developments in the 1990s was the publication of *Across the Divide* (Howard *et al.* 1994). This was an independent report commissioned by the Department of Health. It followed a 1991 report (DoH 1991a) that highlighted the problems faced by drug workers in the context of joint working, and the Conservative government's 1992 election promise that drug misuse would be effectively co-ordinated (Conservative Party Election Manifesto 1992). In a nutshell, the report was justified by the changing social and organisational circumstances outlined above, and called for greater levels of co-operation across all agencies involved with illicit drug policy and practice.

By way of response, and in order to fulfil its election promise, the Conservative government set up a new unit in 1994, the Central Drugs Co-ordination Unit (CDCU), tasked with producing a Green Paper, which looked at illicit drug policy. The result was the White Paper *Tackling Drugs Together* (DoH 1995). Interestingly, and the source of some criticism, Scotland and Wales had their own documents produced at roughly the same time, but varying in degrees from their English counterpart (for an overview of this, see Ashton 1994). Space precludes a discussion of the regional documents, thus, this work will concentrate on the English document.

Tackling Drugs Together: a review

Arguably, despite its shortcomings, the document represented a significant shift in policy approach, yet still managed to retain the traditional domination of the law and order, supply reduction discourse. This can be seen in the opening statement where the government promised to 'fully maintain the emphasis on law enforcement and reducing supply'. However, the changing nature of drug policy is visible in the end of the sentence where it identifies the need to recognise 'stronger action on reducing the demand for illegal drugs' (DoH 1995: 1). In many respects, this marked the first central government recognition that drug use amongst the young was endemic and that law and order/supply reduction alone would not 'solve the problem'.

What the document also did was to increase the importance, and broaden the concept of, harm reduction. Witness the following statement of purpose:

To take effective action via law enforcement, accessible treatment and a new emphasis on education and prevention to:

- increase the safety of communities from drug-related crime;
- reduce the acceptability and availability of drugs to young people; and
- reduce the health risks and other damage related to drug misuse.

(DoH 1995: 1)

Implicit in that statement is some recognition that drug misuse has the potential to harm both communities as well as the individual. It allowed the government space in which to develop two distinct, but linked, approaches to the drug problem and problematic drug users: (1) treatment of the individual by welfarist agencies for medical and social problems; (2) treatment of the individual by law and order agencies to relieve the harm drug misusers may do to communities in terms of acquisitive crime.

Three specific policy areas were singled out for special attention: crime, young people and public health. The new policy was to be delivered by 'multi-agency co-ordination, both at local and national levels' (DoH 1995: 1). In terms of structures and resources, the government retained the ACMD, noting the respect with which it was held. The government established a Ministerial Sub-Committee of the Cabinet on the Misuse of Drugs, comprising of ministers from interested departments (DoH 1995: 4). Locally, the government also set up, in 1995, Drug Action Teams (DATs), which are multi-agency forums consisting of 'senior representatives from the police, probation and prison services, local authorities (including education and social services) and health authorities' (DoH 1995: 5). As an acknowledgement of the mixed economy approach to service delivery, the document also encouraged the recruitment of representatives from voluntary sector agencies. The remit of the DATs was to tackle local drug-related issues and problems.

In terms of law and order and supply reduction, the document required all police forces, probation areas and prisons to develop their own drug misuse strategies. Prisons were forced to introduce mandatory testing of prisoners and, from 1996, HM Inspectorate of Constabularies reviewed police force drug strategies. There was a categorical commitment against the legalisation of any controlled drugs.

Young people were the target of efforts designed to provide education and advice, to promote abstinence and resistance. The Home Office Drug Prevention Initiative was expanded in 1995 in order to develop work with young people and their communities. In an effort to demonstrate the importance of education and young people the government provided an extra £5.9 million for training programmes for teachers and support for new and innovative drug education programmes. It also made drug education a part of the national curriculum, although, strangely, under the science and technology heading (SCODA 1998, 1999).

In health terms, the government established a National Drug Help-Line from April 1995 and made a promise to ensure drug misusers had 'easy access' to services. However, the government fell short of an acceptance that illicit drug use may be normalised, and an integral part of sections of British society, by couching harm reduction in the somewhat unrealistic terms of 'drug free states' and declaring that 'abstinence remain[s] the ultimate aim' (DoH 1995: 3).

Tackling Drugs Together provides a number of issues worthy of note. First, it moved the centre of the government's drug policy away from the Home Office and located it within the Cabinet Office. Second, it acted as a catalyst for our current policy explosion in the field of illicit drug policy and practice by identifying and defining illicit drug use as a 'major problem'. Third, it began to create a climate where law and order and medical approaches could be merged, in order to fall in line with the newly expanded concept of harm reduction. Fourth, it placed joint working at the forefront of policy, coercing hitherto isolated agencies into some (at first, tentative) collaboration. Fifth, it gave a tacit and seemingly grudging recognition to the fact that law and order, supply reduction policies were failing, and there needed to be space for education-based demand reduction approaches to tackling illicit drug use.

Reaction to *Tackling Drugs Together* was mixed. In general terms, one of the criticisms was that, in contrast to its Scottish and Welsh counterparts, the English document relegates protecting individual users from harm at the expense of protecting communities from crime (Ashton 1994), thus maintaining the domination of the law and order discourse. More specifically, Roger Howard of SCODA provided a detailed review of the document (Howard 1997: 8–13), giving both positive and negative views.

On the plus side, Howard argues that there are six positive factors: (i) It provides national leadership and co-ordination. Howard notes that the leader of the Ministerial Sub-Committee was the Lord President of the Council, thus negating the powerful influence of departmental needs and influence on policy. (ii) The formation of DATs. This served to cement joint working in areas where it was already established and serves as a good practice model elsewhere. (iii) It gave recognition to the work and strengths of specialist drug service providers. Howard provides examples of good practice in prisons and youth education. (iv) It marks a recognition of the value of a demand reduction paradigm in an hitherto supply reduction dominated area. Howard also comments that an acceptance of the value of demand reduction carries with it a *de facto* support of harm minimisation, fostering a more realistic approach to drug use in England. (v) Additional resources were seen, unsurprisingly, as a positive move. (vi) A more realistic approach to the drug scene was viewed as being positive for public perceptions about the way forward in drug policy, and as a good counter-balance to the more reactionary outpourings of some sections of the press.

On a more negative note, Howard laments the imbalance of resource allocation between, on the one hand, law and supply policies, and on the other, treatment and prevention. He notes that in the year 1993–94 two-thirds of government expenditure went on the former, despite evidence from the US that treatment is effective in reducing criminal behaviour and thus becomes a possible policy tool in reducing drug-related crime. He also takes issue with the manner in which deprivation, dependent drug use and crime is dealt with. He is critical of the manner in which multiple social problems that may have contributed to dependent drug use are ignored by the government. He notes with disapproval that *Tackling Drugs Together* does little to address the inherent problems in community care. Finally, he notes that the new direction in domestic policy is not matched by a rethinking of international policy.

Arguably, the optimum manner in which to view *Tackling Drugs Together* is as laying the foundations and framework for a new approach to drug policy in England. It gave recognition that there was a lack of a coherent drug policy, or for that matter direction, beyond a simplistic reliance on interdiction and prohibition, tactics that were clearly found wanting. In response, the document sets out to make concrete a philosophy and approach that corresponds with illicit drug use in the late twentieth century, and this meant an overhaul of a failing system. As Bean (2002: 55) comments: 'The emphasis in *Tackling Drugs Together* was on reorganising local services'. What the document also did was to provide a green light for innovative and different means of addressing the problems of illicit drug use. In many respects, this view is endorsed by one of the White Paper's architects Stephen Rimmer. Rimmer (1997: 5) states: 'The White Paper is deliberately focused on specific tasks ... [it sets out] an overall statement of purpose and then develop[s] tasks within that framework'.

In terms of our three analytical lenses, *Tackling Drugs Together* still enables the law and order discourse to retain priority, albeit with some challenge. Key here is the moving of control away from the Home Office and into the Cabinet Office. Nevertheless, law and order and supply reduction remains dominant. There is evidence of recognition of the work that can be done by welfarist interventions, in terms of harm reduction on an individual and societal level, with concomitant space being given to demand reduction. Joined-up working was given priority in the policy document. However, referring back to the implementation gap mentioned above, the reality was somewhat different:

> There is a lot spoken about joint commissioning: clearly some agencies ... are used to doing this ... But there doesn't seem to be a particular momentum generated in a lot of DATs to look at pooling resources ... Having worked in a multi-agency forum myself, I know that some of those difficulties require time and patience ...
>
> (Rimmer 1997: 7)

It would appear therefore that the majority of joint working taking place fell into Crawford and Jones' (1996) multi-agency definition, which some have seen as 'mere public relations exercises'.

Enter New Labour: policy from 1998 to 2010

New Labour came to power in 1997 on a wave of public optimism that its election would see major changes in the UK. This belief was fuelled in no small part by New Labour's own rhetoric. Many policy advisors, such as in the case of Frank Field and welfare reform, were given the mandate to 'think the unthinkable' (Toynbee and Walker 2001: 17). However, when it came to illicit drug policy, publicly New Labour demonstrated no signs of newness at all: as Toynbee and Walker (2001: 173) point out, its stance, in public at least, was unequivocal, 'all "drugs" were harmful'. Indeed, MPs Mo Mowlam and Clare Short had to make hasty and embarrassing reversals of statements following their innocuous comments regarding cannabis use. Equally, Jacqui Smith, the then Home Secretary, admitted to cannabis use whilst presiding over a reclassification of the drug that had previously been downgraded to a class C by one of her predecessors, David Blunkett, in 2004. In short, Labour's approach to drug use seems confused and confusing: a closer examination unearths the fact that the approach since 1997 has been to cement and embed the crime reduction aspect of drug policy and ensure the primacy of criminal justice domination of drug policy.

Labour's policy documents: 1998; 2002, 2008

This inability to publicly and overtly tailor policy designed to confront the reality of the situation regarding the use of illicit drugs by large tracts of the population was reflected in New Labour's first drug policy document *Tackling Drugs To Build A Better Britain* (Cabinet Office 1998). Broadly speaking, it resembled the Conservative government's 1995 White Paper. Bean (2002: 56) concurs with this, stating that the document 'largely reiterated the themes of the 1995 document whilst adding performance indicators for drug reduction in the next decade'. Of course, this can be seen as a blanket, general comment regarding New Labour's drug policy. There were clearly differences in the detail, and it is to those this section now turns.

Tackling Drugs To Build A Better Britain begins with New Labour's 'vision'. This aimed to create a 'healthy and confident society, increasingly free from the harm caused by the misuse of drugs'. This was to be achieved by combining enforcement with prevention. In terms of strategy, four specific policy areas were identified:

1. **YOUNG PEOPLE** – to help young people resist drug misuse in order to achieve their full potential in society

2. **COMMUNITIES** – to protect our communities from drug-related anti-social and criminal behaviour
3. **TREATMENT** – to enable people with drug problems to overcome them and live healthy and crime free lives
4. **AVAILABILITY** – to stifle the availability of illegal drugs on our streets.
(Cabinet Office 1998, original emphasis)

This vision was to be achieved within the following structure. Nationally, the government appointed a new anti-drugs co-ordinator, Keith Helliwell, a former chief constable of West Yorkshire. This was generally seen as a positive move, concurring with New Labour's promise to 'think outside the box' – both Helliwell and his deputy, Mike Trace, were seen as people prepared to think radically about drug policy. Helliwell's remit was to head up a new body named the UK Anti-Drugs Strategic Steering Group. This group was comprised of senior government officials, local government representatives, and representatives of independent bodies and voluntary sector agencies.

At government level, the ministerial body responsible for ensuring success was the Ministerial Sub-Committee on Drug Misuse. This was to ensure those individual departments with an interest in illicit drug use contributed to the overall vision and strategy, and, presumably, kept each other informed on developments and best practice. At a local level, DATs remained, being seen as 'the critical link in the chain'. Thus, apart from cosmetic tinkering, it could be suggested that, in policy terms, little had changed from 1995 to 1998.

However, critically, the important point about the 1998 Labour approach lies in its similarity to the Conservative policy: the groundwork and frameworks put in place by the Conservatives were allowed to come to fruition under New Labour. The result has been some interesting developments in both the scope and direction of policy, nationally and locally. Moreover, New Labour appeared to have noted some of the weaknesses inherent in the 1995 document – lack of meaningful multi-agency working, lack of concrete projects – and moved drug policy into a more active, even proactive, realm; a realm that begins to embrace the realities of drug use in the twenty-first century.

2002 – updated drug strategy

Howard Parker (Parker 2006) argues that the 2002 policy was 'discretely launched' and that it signalled a tacit admission that its original attempt to 'tackle drugs' failed, partly because it tried too much too soon. In turn, this led to a major rethink, and the 2002 launch of a much more tightly focused strategy. Ironically, it demonstrated a desire to embed even further one of Tony Blair's insights when he was shadow Home Secretary in 1993 – the drug–crime link.

In short, the 2002 strategy set out to cement a 'tough love' approach that made use of problematic Category 3 users' many contacts with the criminal justice system, be that at the point of arrest or through into prison sentences, to get them into treatment. This was driven by evidence that suggested cost efficiencies gained by using treatment. Gossop *et al.* (2003) noted that the government were keen to point out that research demonstrated for every £1 spent on treatment there was a £3 saving on victim costs and demands on the criminal justice system. Evidence of this was the level of funding that was channelled into the Criminal Justice Intervention Programmes (CJIP), a mechanism through which offenders (read acquisitive prolific offenders using heroin and/or crack) were fast-tracked into treatment programmes. The results of this approach were impressive: by the end of 2004, 54 per cent more users were in treatment (Silverman and Wong 2005).

However, this policy approach was not without its critics. Seddon *et al.* (2008) note that this updated strategy simply reinforced the crime-related nature of British drug policy and, as a result, reduced the capacity for alternative approaches such as a health-led policy structure. That much is true – if there was any doubt before the 2002 updated strategy about the direction of drug policy then the focus on reducing the crime committed by heroin and crack using persistent offenders within the 2002 approach arguably dispersed it once and for all. Nevertheless, in purely pragmatic terms, record numbers of problematic drug users accessed treatment and recorded crime began to fall.

2008: protecting families and communities

In essence the 2008 strategy is simply more of the same in terms of its thrust and direction. The Home Office states that:

> Drug strategy overview
>   The ten-year drug strategy (2008–18) aims to restrict the supply of illegal drugs and reduce the demand for them. It focuses on protecting families and strengthening communities.
>   The four strands of work within the strategy are:
>
> - protecting communities through tackling drug supply, drug-related crime and anti-social behaviour;
> - preventing harm to children, young people and families affected by drug misuse;
> - delivering new approaches to drug treatment and social reintegration;
> - public information campaigns, communications and community engagement.
>
> (Home Office 2008: 2–3)

However, this continuity should not be a surprise as it mirrors (and perhaps further refines) the domination of the criminal justice concerns over all other aspects of British drug policy. This is partly driven by the fact that the cultural factors determining previous policy still exist. Indeed if we return to the three forces that shaped drug policy in the 1990s (outlined above) as drivers of drug policy for the past two decades we can see that, unsurprisingly, once again these are visible in the most recent policy document:

- *The normalisation of sensible recreational drug use amongst sections of the population*

The acceptance of 'normalised' drug use is politically difficult for governments; as it is, drug use remains illegal and any formal recognition that little can be done to prevent either the supply or consumption of drugs for experimental or recreational purposes can be seized on as political impotence: yet it is there in the document. For example, in her opening comments, the then Home Secretary, Jacqui Smith (2008: 4, emphasis added), talks about 'a society free of the problems *caused* by drugs' as opposed to a society free from drugs. Equally, if one examines the PSA targets it is informative to note that the targets do not include young people *using* drugs, rather the success targets focus on those 'young people who *frequently* use illicit drugs' (Home Office 2008: 21, emphasis added).

- *The dominance of multi-agency working as the preferred policy approach*

The multi-agency nature of the delivery of services is embedded into the drug system, to the extent that it almost a given in the documentation. References to it are visible throughout the 2008 document, but as an example on page 31, there is a direct reference to the centrality of joined up working in the five bullet points, which outline the approach to reintegrating drug users into society.

- *The recognition that problematic drug users are often the most persistent offenders, and addressing their drug use can lead to reductions in offending behaviour*

Arguably, it is this policy ambition that dominates the document and is the real policy goal. It is the first in the list of policy priorities and is central to the 'success' or otherwise of the whole approach and it unashamedly builds on 'The previous drug strategy [which] delivered some notable successes in addressing ... drug related offending' (Home Office 2008: 14). In practice this means using the criminal justice system as a vehicle with which to coerce or cajole problematic users who are persistent offenders into treatment, either in the community or within therapeutic communities in the prison system, with the aim of reducing their offending behaviour through a reduction of their drug use.

Current directions in UK drug policy

Taken as a whole the policies outlined above demonstrate the policy dilemmas faced by British governments in the current cultural and political climate. On the one hand, there is the recognition that dependent heavy-end users, who are committing drug driven crime, represent a serious problem both to themselves and their communities. In order to address this problem the government, via a series of criminal justice led schemes, has developed mandated joint working between the health, welfare and law enforcement providers and coerced this problematic group of users into treatment in order to tackle both use and offending behaviour. On the other hand, there is an implicit recognition that recreational use of drugs is widespread, seemingly part of aspects of contemporary British culture and not overly problematic for the majority of recreational users.

As such it is arguable that current policy marks the recognition by the government that not all drug use is 'problematic', and that, in truth, there is very little the government can do to control use or supply. It also signals official recognition as to the distinction between what in Chapter 8 I classed as Category 1 and possibly 2 users, and the more problematic Category 3 user. How, then, does contemporary drug policy look when examined through our three analytical lenses?

First, we could argue that, in terms of domination by the criminal justice discourse, not much has changed. Looking at the key policy initiatives, it is clear that they are criminal justice led and dominated by the needs and requirements of the law and order discourse. Indeed, some have argued that all staff working with problematic drug users, be they health, welfare or justice based, become *de facto* officers of the court as soon as they begin to work within the current framework (Barton and Quinn 2001).

In terms of 'joined-up' working, contemporary policy seems to be faring better, with health, welfare and justice being involved in a number of schemes across the country, accompanied by official recognition that treatment for problematic drug users is at least, if not more, effective, long term, than punishment. However, on a note of caution, it is worthwhile reminding ourselves that joint working in the *inter-agency* sense of the term has had to be mandated in order to become effective, and then only on terms acceptable to the hegemonic discourse of law and order.

Finally, has policy moved away from a law and order, supply reduction approach? This is difficult to answer with any certainty. At one and the same time it is possible to argue that the government has acknowledged it can do little to stem the tide of drugs entering the country. Equally, there is greater weight being given to harm reduction, safe use message in schools and youth groups around the country. Nevertheless, the most recent policy document contains, as part of its vision, a commitment to stifle the availability of drugs on the streets. Perhaps the best way to answer the question, and summarise our current approach, is to suggest that the government seeks to prioritise the control of both the supply and impact on the user, and their communities of 'hard drugs' such as heroin and cocaine, whilst using education to 'deal with' the attendant problems of so-called 'soft' drugs.

Conclusion: a more 'liberal' future?

In the previous edition I asked the same question and suggested that we may well see a hardening of the dichotomy between the problematic 'hard drugs' of heroin and crack cocaine and the 'soft drugs' that are more commonly associated with hedonistic recreational use, with a liberalisation of the laws regarding the latter. I am now not so sure. There are a number of reasons for this doubt.

First, our previous Labour government was seemingly running scared from the middle class media backlash to the downgrading of cannabis, and was apparently more inclined to listen to the outpourings of concern in the middle class (and right wing) tabloids such as the *Daily Mail* and *Daily Express* than its own advisors. This trait was again seen in the rushed banning of mephadrone and led to mass resignations from members of the ACMD in early 2010.

Second, the cultural and political climate has not changed since the inception of this particular policy approach. Indeed, in some instances it is possible to say that culturally there has been a hardening of positions. For example, regardless of the criticisms of the normalisation thesis there can be little argument that it is becoming increasingly difficult to talk about young people's drug use as 'exceptional', as it appears that around half of all young people will at least try a drug, and even amongst those that will not try, the level and sophistication of their knowledge of drugs is unprecedented in recent British social history.

Third, there are pragmatic political reasons for continuing in the current direction. Whilst those who look for reforms of the drug policy see the current approach as 'a crime reduction programme masquerading as treatment' (Kushlick 2006), and others see the over-concentration on problematic users who commit acquisitive crime as skewing the system (Barton 2005), the fact remains that within its own parameters the current approach has been a success, inasmuch as it has engaged with problematic users and enabled them to engage in treatment.

Arguably, this is because the original 1998 policy tried to do far too much. As the previous chapters have shown Britain's 'drug problem' is complex, and I would suggest intractable, if it is viewed in the round. Truly addressing it would involve complex geo-political settlements, a strong international police force, a domestic cultural shift in terms of changing substance use and a re-prioritisation of domestic policy to see health replace criminal justice as the policy driver. Some of those were outside the government's control and some were counter to its beliefs. As a result, the 2002 policy saw a more pragmatic – some would say realistic – approach to the current situation regarding illicit drug use in the UK.

Whither the future with the new coalition government? Arguably, the new government is the first to be populated by the 'normalisation generation' identified in the late 1990s by Parker and colleagues (1998). Many of the cabinet as well as many of the back-bench MPs will have grown up in a cultural environment where drug taking was a feature of their adolescent and young adult lives. Indeed, statistically at least one-third of them will have tried some form of illicit substance. They, more than any previous generation, will know that there is a difference between recreational and problematic use, and that the 'gateway' theory, on which rests the foundation of state paternalism, is flawed for the majority of drug users. Only time will tell if they have the courage to reform a system that, to be frank, is creaking under the strain and does not reflect the lived reality of most drug users.

Suggested further reading

Bean, P. (2010) *Legalising Drugs: debates and dilemmas,* Bristol: Policy Press.
Blackman, S. (2004) *Chilling Out: the cultural politics of substance consumption, youth and drug policy,* Maidenhead: Open University Press.
Hughes, R., Lart, R., & Higate, P. (eds) (2006) *Drugs: policy and politics,* Maidenhead: Open University Press.
Manning, P. (ed.) (2007) *Drugs and Popular Culture: drugs media and identity in contemporary society* Willan: Cullumpton.
Seddon, T., Ralphs, R., & Williams, L. (2008) 'Risk, Security and the Criminalization of British Drug Policy', *British Journal of Criminology,* 48 (6), 818–34.

Questions and areas for reflection

1. The normalisation theory argues that young people are 'drug wise': that is they are aware of the effects and dangers of illicit drug use whether they take them or not. Despite this, the levels of drug use amongst young people remain relatively high. What, if anything, can be done to reduce drug use amongst the young?
2. Other nations (for example the Netherlands) see drug use as a wholly socio-medical problem. Why is drug *use* still viewed as primarily a criminal justice matter in Britain?
3. Identify any restrictions placed on British drug laws by international treaties. What, if any, changes to British drug laws would you support?

10 Comparing British drug policy

Introduction

This concluding chapter once again moves us away from purely Anglo-centric concerns by turning attention to drug policy elsewhere in the developed world. The rationale for this lies in the fact that internationally, just as in domestic policy, there is a recognition that it is impossible to 'go it alone' in dealing with illicit drugs, thus creating a need for international joint working to address the problems caused by a global industry. For example, it is clear that the origins of the raw materials for heroin and cocaine come from Afghanistan and the Andean countries respectively. It should be clear that Britain has some interest in the manner in which those countries 'police' their own drug problem.

Another reason is, as social scientists, we need to expand our horizons and challenge our own ethnocentricity. Giddens (1986: 19) powerfully warns us of the perils of '[T]he tendency to use our own society and culture as a measure to judge all others'. Arguably, Britain is still a long way from winning its own 'war on drugs', yet some British policy-makers seem all too quick to dismiss the actions of others'. Equally, it is important not to overlook the growing influence the European Union has on British policy. In several areas there are strong moves toward harmonisation and integration of policies. For example, Ganghof and Genschel (2007) discuss the harmonisation of taxation policies, and specifically for this work the EMCDDA have documents such as *Decriminalisation in Europe?* (EMCDDA 2001), which examines the possibility of a Europe-wide relaxation of drug laws. That being the case, it is imperative that policy-makers, practitioners and academics become aware of developments elsewhere.

The chapter begins by exploring the usefulness of comparative research, noting the need for some form of comparative framework. Following on from that point, the next two sections explore drug policy in the Netherlands and New Zealand respectively. The chapter, and indeed the book, concludes with a comparison of the factors that influenced drug policy in Britain, the Netherlands and New Zealand, concentrating particularly on the impact society, politics and economics has had on the nature and construction of British illicit drug policy.

The usefulness of comparative research

Comparative research is now an established and important aspect of social science: nearly a decade ago Cochrane (1993: 1) argued that 'it is perhaps no longer necessary to make the case for the comparative approach ... on the contrary, it may be single-country studies that need to be justified'. However, the establishment of comparative research as a central approach to study does not automatically justify its use: undertaking something simply because it is fashionable is often self-defeating. As the same author notes, comparative analysis only becomes really useful if it allows us to examine supranational trends and identify policy specific to individual countries. In that way, we can compare the manner in which different countries deal with similar problems; in our case policy formulation in relation to the use of illicit substances.

What can happen in comparative research is that the researcher, when examining approaches to a social problem elsewhere, begins to look beyond the obvious and delves into a critical examination of history, politics and culture. As a result, these factors are included within the final explanations. On reflection, this is exactly what this and the previous edition of the book has sought to do: look beyond the obvious and attempt to locate the 'drug problem' in a much wider sphere. However, because of the tendency toward ethnocentricity, researchers often fail to give full recognition to a critical examination of their own nation's development, leading to an acceptance of 'traditional' explanations of the state of affairs.

For example, as the previous chapter noted, the feature that is claimed as distinguishing the British approach to illicit drugs from the approach of other punitive regimes, such as the US, is the so-called 'British model'. This claims that British drug policy has an equal space for treatment and law and order. However, as we have seen, the hegemonic discourse in British drug policy has been, and remains, law and order – Britain has had a tendency to punish first and treat later.

Traditionally, the reason for the development of this approach, as spelt out in Chapter 1, is mainly historical and stems from the early Home Office domination of drug policy. This is then added to Britain's ratification of the first, US-led, international treaties that mirrored the emphasis the US placed on prohibition and interdiction over treatment. Seeing this as an encroachment on medical practice, the British medical establishment carved its own niche in drug policy and practice by establishing the right of doctors to treat drug use. Latterly, the adherence to a law and order dominated approach has been explained in terms of the need to reduce supply in order to control use, with equal space given to treat those whose drug use has become problematic.

However, this traditional account ignores several key points. First, the lack of reference to global issues disguises the extent to which the US has sought to influence and dominate a world approach to illicit drugs. The simplistic and moralistic stance that 'luxurious' drug use is wrong, the mantra 'just say no', the continued insistence of linking communism and cocaine, and the certainty of severe punishment for drug offences have been key themes of US drug policy. All have been transported to international treaties, to be embraced to a greater or lesser degree by other nations.

Second, the genesis of the British model reflected a period where there was a distinct lack of a 'drug problem' either for the criminal justice agencies or the health sector. The subsequent rise of recreational drug use amongst the young has not been confined to Britain. Other countries across the globe have witnessed similar trends. The British law and order dominated approach has meant that large numbers of young recreational drug users, whose lives are otherwise law-abiding, have become 'criminals', and many users who do not fit the medical definitions of 'problematic' have been denied treatment and suffered all manners of social exclusion. Yet this does not have to be the case: other European nations have effectively decriminalised the use of some illicit drugs and relied on education and prevention to halt use and demand, viewing drug use as essentially a socio-medical problem. Conversely, as in the case of Sweden, other nations have restricted space in drug policy for medical interventions.

Third, the traditional approach fails to recognise the influence of class, race and gender factors in British drug policy. When Rolleston reported in 1926, the majority of problematic users came from the medical profession, a trend that continued up until the 1950s. Thus, it could be suggested the liberal policies advocated by Rolleston were designed to keep problematic drug use amongst the professional middle classes 'in-house', thereby ensuring that the middle class professional drug user did not suffer the ignominy of being dealt with by the criminal justice system. As drug use increased amongst the (young) working class in the late 1950s and 1960s, the medical profession's claims of ownership of the problem was conspicuous by its absence. Indeed, one could argue that the recent declassification of cannabis in Britain had more to do with the needs of the police than the desire of the medical profession to ensure treatment and education for the masses.

The value of comparative research becomes clear: it allows us to look beyond 'traditional' explanations of events and equips us with the tools to make a critical appraisal of our approach to any number of social problems. In this way, we avoid Giddens' (1986) trap of becoming ethnocentric and can begin to perceive British approaches in a wider context. Paradoxically, comparative research enables us to examine specific policy in more detail. For example, supply reduction techniques that rely on interdiction have been found wanting across all Western nations. Britain has continued with this stance whilst some other European states have seemingly become resigned to the fact that interdiction alone cannot stem either the supply of, or the demand for, illicit drugs. Comparative research may enable us to better understand why this is the case, and what, often hidden, forces lie behind it.

With this in mind, the chapter now turns its attention to the Netherlands. What follows is a concise account of the development of Dutch drug policy. The reader is urged to bear in mind some of the material outlined in Chapter 1, which examines the development of British drug policy and to note some of the degree of similarity that exists between the two nations' 'drug problems'.

Whilst making interesting reading, the purpose of this section of the chapter has been to alert the reader to the fact that, in supranational terms, the 'drug problem' for all Western nations has been the rising numbers of people who are experimenting with illicit drugs, coupled with a rise in problematic drug use in all its forms. However, comparative research enables us to view, not only the actual policies that inform the present day approach, but the background in terms of a framework which includes economics, politics and cultural and social pressures, all of which have figured prominently in developing contemporary policy in the Netherlands and New Zealand. The task for the remaining sections of this book is just that: to attempt to make sense of this, and at the same time engage the reader with the key factors that influence and shape British drug policy in the third millennium.

The development of drug policy in the Netherlands

As was the case in Britain during the nineteenth century, the use of what are now illicit substances for self-medication purposes was the norm rather than the exception in the Netherlands. Kort (1995: 4) informs that by the end of the 1800s, 'a large part of the [Dutch] population had never even visited a physician'. Many of those that self-medicated used opium – or cocaine-based 'quack' remedies – freely available from a variety of outlets. Like Britain, the growing professionalisation of medicine in the 1800s meant there was a sustained attack on the 'quacks' and their patent medicines. This mirrored developments elsewhere in Europe and America, and was justified by the growing science of addiction, particularly related to opium, morphine and cocaine. Unlike the situation in Britain however, Kort (1995) fails to mention any great moral crusade against the 'luxurious' use of substances for recreational purposes.

As Kort (1995 6) notes, the result of this was that, by the end of the nineteenth century, drug use, which just as in the case of Britain had hitherto not been seen as a problem, was redefined by the medical profession as 'problematic', and in need of specialised control for largely the same reasons as in the British experience. However, the parallels with the development of British drug policy do not stop there: like the British, the Dutch had a vested interest in the trade in opium, which had a clear and obvious impact on the manner in which the Dutch state viewed the drug trade.

Again, in a remarkable mirror image of the British experience, concern as to the 'luxurious' use of drugs at home was not shared with a like concern about the luxurious use of drugs in the colonies by the indigenous populations. Kort (1995: 7) views this situation developing from the fact that 'the smoking of opium by the local population [of the colonies] had resulted in huge profits for the Dutch for centuries'. To place this in context, Kort (1995: 7) claims that between 1816 and 1915 profits from opium accounted for 10 per cent of the total income from the Dutch colonies. Moreover, the same author notes that as cocaine grew in popularity, the Dutch traders imported coca bushes from Peru, Columbia and Bolivia and created new coca plantations in Java. These were successful to the point that by 1920 the Dutch had been the world's largest cocaine producer for the previous ten years.

This is seen as a key contributory factor in the reluctance of the Dutch to be any more than unwilling partners in the first series of international treaties in Shanghai in 1909. Given the economic benefits accrued from the drug trade this degree of reluctance on behalf of the Dutch is somewhat understandable. Kort (1995: 10–11) notes that, much to the chagrin of the Americans, the Dutch, Germans and British all failed to see domestic use of drugs as a problem, and gave the impression that there was no pressing need to arrange a further international conference. That notwithstanding, pressure from the US led to the Dutch arranging the world's first international conference on illicit substances, the Hague Opium Convention of 1912. The conference spent most of its time drawing up guidelines for the production and trade in opium and cocaine. In the Netherlands this resulted, eventually, in laying the foundation for the 1919 Opium Act.

Interestingly, Dutch public opinion on drugs in the domestic sphere showed remarkable foresight, given the problems that are now faced by Western nations. Kort (1995: 11) claims that, by the 1920s, 'the majority opinion was that the "war on drugs" … could not be won … ' using law and international treaties. Moreover, the Dutch demonstrated that they were sceptical both about joining the American anti-drug crusade and the feasibility of the American's tactics:

> Several Dutch sources from that period suggest that the illegal drug trade would be difficult to control due to the importance of the financial and economic interests involved in the highly priced, easily concealed drugs … The notion that it was impossible to eliminate international illegal drug smuggling was referred to as the 'American position' – a position which is '(virtually) unenforceable'.
>
> (De Kort and Tan Tong Joe 1929: 13–14 in Kort 1995: 11)

Thus, whilst the Netherlands were signatories of the 1912 Hague Convention, and had their own legislation based on the treaty, enforcing the law was given a low priority. The period between the two world wars saw some prosecution of drug offences, mostly amongst the Chinese community whose method of using opium – smoking – was different from the European norm, and very obviously devoid of any 'medical' connection. Even in those cases however, it appears that the fine was cursory, with mild sentences being the standard. Kort (1995), drawing on the work of Parssinen (1983), likens the illicit drug situation in the Netherlands to that of Britain at the same time: very few addicts, little in the way of a 'problem' and a system policed by both the Justice and Health Departments.

However, mirroring the situation in Britain, the 'drug scene' altered following the Second World War. Initially, there was little in the way of a 'drug problem', although Amsterdam did create a Narcotics Division, following the example of Rotterdam (Kort 1996). In the latter half of that century, developments paralleled Britain: recreational drug use grew amongst the young during the very late 1950s and 1960s. As the drug culture developed, the Dutch Opium Act expanded to keep pace with changes: for example, LSD was included in the Act in 1966. During this period, the Dutch Police and Justice Departments were keen to use the power of the law to clamp down on users and dealers alike. However, despite increasingly severe penalties 'this repressive approach could not prevent the fast increase in the use of marihuana ... ' (Kort 1996: 16). Alongside the use in marihuana there was an increase in the use of heroin, especially amongst the young Dutch population. This led to a more repressive policy that, hitherto (arguably because opium use was more or less restricted to Chinese), had been relatively tolerant to drug use and drug users.

By the end of the 1960s, Dutch drug policy was still closely aligned to Britain. However, the 1970s saw a major change in direction for the Dutch and a departure from the rest of Europe: the *de facto* decriminalisation of marihuana. The foundation for this was twofold. First, the Hulsman Committee issued its report *Options in Drug Policy* (1971). Hulsman, a law professor with strong abolitionist views, was appointed by the state sponsored Institution for Mental Health (Leuw 1996: 28) to review drug policy. The committee took a radical view of illegal drug use, based on the concept of relative risk analysis. Its findings concluded that opiates, barbiturates and amphetamine held potential dangers, but cannabis, relative to other drugs, including tobacco, held little chance of creating dependency. Moreover, Hulsman disregarded the gateway thesis, and held that it was the criminalisation of cannabis that caused a stepping stone effect, not the properties of the drug itself (Leuw 1996: 29).

In sociological terms Hulsman found that cannabis was a subcultural phenomenon. The committee noted that, in a pluriform society such as the Netherlands, space needed to be made for 'alternative' lifestyles, and not all lifestyles needed to conform to the norms of the so-called respectable citizen. Indeed, Hulsman argued that moral rejection, when added to reactionary and repressive control mechanisms, would only serve to marginalise subcultures. Hulsman was particularly specific about overt use of state power in dealing with alternative lifestyles and subcultures: 'The Government should not take a censuring position based on the fact that certain behaviour does not fit into the life concept of those holding state power' (Hulsman Report 1971, in Leuw 1996: 29).

Hulsman used John Stuart Mill's essay 'On Liberty' to defend the philosophical position of minimum state interference in instances where behaviour only had consequences for the individual. It also noted the lack of logic in outlawing one drug (cannabis) when other, legal drugs, caused as much or more harm. Finally, echoing the sentiments of Tan Tong Joe more than 40 years previously, Hulsman observed that recourse to law was unlikely to prevent people using drugs. Moreover, when the law was invoked, it was important that the state recognised and calculated the costs and benefits. As an example Hulsman claimed that over-reliance on the law could lead to the cost of police resources outweighing any benefits accrued in terms of sentences, deviance being amplified, subcultures marginalised and excluded, civil liberties eroded, and respect for the law undermined.

What Hulsman reflected was the moral climate of the Netherlands (and many would argue some sections of most Western societies) at the start of the 1970s. Sagel-Grande (1997: 87) claims that these were, and still are 'sobriety, pragmatism, search for a happy medium, humanity and tolerance of the freely chosen life-style of others'. Hulsman lacked the luxury of being a committee directly appointed by the government – however, the Baan Commission, appointed in 1968, was. Its remit was to re-evaluate the Dutch government's drug policy. Clearly guided by the work of Hulsman, Baan established the philosophical base for contemporary Dutch drug policy. This is:

- a distinction between soft drugs and hard drugs;
- differention between major and minor offences, with possession of soft drugs made a minor offence;
- differention between roles in the drug milieu: between dealers and consumers; between hard drug dealers and soft drug dealers; between national and international dealers;
- a two track approach: medical approach to addicts and users and a law and order, repressive approach to large-scale dealers of hard drugs;
- a central aim of prevention or alleviation of social and individual risks caused by drug use;
- a recognition of the inadequacy of the criminal law with regard to any aspect of the drug problem except trafficking.

(Adapted from Leuw 1996, Sabel-Grande 1997
and Boekhout van Solinge 1999)

This was given a legal basis in 1976 when the Dutch government revised the Opium Act (Boekhout van Solinge 1999: 2). It is important to stress however that the Dutch have not legalised cannabis: 'According to the Opium Act, possession of marijuana for personal use is a crime' (EMCDDA 2001: 5). The revised Act established a number of guiding principles. First, it allowed that drug use should be located firmly in the socio-medical field. Drug problems were to be seen as one of a number of 'normal' social problems, rather than a specific set of problems requiring special treatment. In this way, all forms of drug use and all types of drug users become 'normalised' and not marginalised. This is evidenced by the fact that for drug users punishment is routinely not an option. For example, even possession of small quantities of harder drugs carries with it a low prosecution priority. Moreover, there is an extensive care system with methadone and needle exchanges widely available. As a result, there is a good level of contact between problematic drug users and health agencies, allowing the Dutch to be able to claim that 65 to 85 per cent of addicts are in regular contact with the authorities.

Second, there is recognition in the Netherlands that criminal law should be used as infrequently as possible to address drug problems. Thus, using the police to deal with drug use becomes as unusual as using the police to deal with, for example, unemployment. The policy distinction between soft and hard drugs means that a policy of 'market separation' can be embraced, allowing soft drugs to be bought and used in a marketplace devoid of harder drugs and free from 'criminal elements'. In line with this approach, the Dutch government made possession of up to 30 grams of cannabis a misdemeanour, thereby 'allowing' possession. It also made space for 'house dealers' in youth clubs; a phenomenon that quickly turned into the 'coffee shops' (Boekhout van Solinge 1999: 512).

This situation remained in place until the mid-1990s. Then, in 1995, the Dutch government released a paper entitled 'Drug Policy in the Netherlands: Continuity and Change' (Ministry of Health, Welfare and Sports *et al.* 1995). This made a number of alterations to the Dutch drug policy, including the reduction of the maximum acceptable purchase of cannabis from 30 grams to five, and a crackdown on the importation of cannabis for coffee shops (Boekhout van Solinge 1999). However, whilst this appears to be a tightening of policy and a move away from the liberal base established in 1976, Boekhout van Solinge (1999: 516) argues that the apparent repressive nature of the post-1995 changes obscures an even greater degree of liberalisation and clarification of policy.

For example, he notes that post-1995, Dutch coffee shops can carry larger stocks of the drug than previously, moving from 30 grams of cannabis to 500 grams. Equally, the crackdown on imported cannabis and large-scale domestic production is a clear indication that the Dutch now favour small-scale indigenous cultivation, made increasingly possible by the fact that the post-1995 changes allow for up to five cannabis plants to be cultivated with impunity. The idea is to encourage small-scale producers to stock the coffee shops rather than large importers or large domestic producers. Away from the large cities, the municipalities have the option whether to allow coffee shops: most have allowed them, taking the pragmatic view that cannabis will be used anyway, and opening coffee shops allows safer use in a more controlled and regulated environment, free from criminal influences.

In terms of 'hard drugs' the post-1995 changes to the Netherlands' drug policy have moved to create a higher enforcement priority for hard drugs, especially in the trafficking and production of synthetic drugs, largely as a result of the Netherlands becoming a major producer and exporter of such substances. As far as users of hard drugs are concerned, the focus remains on health intervention above that of the criminal justice system. There have also been experiments with the prescription of heroin, as opposed to methadone, to drug dependent users who are facing real problems in addressing their addiction.

Clearly, the Netherlands' approach to illicit drugs is different from that of Britain, and can be seen to be very much experimental in comparison with other nation states. However, comparative analysis shows that, whilst the Dutch system was different and some would argue, once unique, its uniqueness is disappearing as more and more EU countries seek to embrace a less repressive stance in relation to cannabis. It appears that whilst the supranational trend in Europe is for a rise in illicit drug use, most nation states have begun to move in a similar policy direction. However, it is time to look beyond the narrow confines of Europe, and to examine how drug policy has developed on the other side of the globe, by looking at drug policy in New Zealand.

Drug policy in New Zealand

New Zealand (NZ) presents an interesting comparison to the UK and the Netherlands, inasmuch that whilst its Commonwealth roots means it has a British-inspired system of government, morality and language, its emergence as an independent and confident nation state in its own right means that contemporary New Zealand is a vibrant and multicultural country that recognises and embraces the rights and needs of the indigenous Maori nation and the Pacific islanders. Equally, its geographical position makes it different from Europe. Whilst European states are at the hub of global trade and communications, New Zealand's relative global isolation means that it is a place to specifically go to, rather than a point of transit. Also, NZ has a relatively small population for the size of the country. In terms of locations, around one-third of the total population live in one city, Auckland, with another 10 to 15 per cent respectively living in the two other major urban centres of Wellington and Christchurch. The remainder of the population live in small, sometimes isolated, towns and villages.

This is not the place to provide a detailed history of the development and colonisation of New Zealand. Suffice to say that the Maori peoples were believed to be the first settlers followed by European settlement beginning in the sixteenth century with the Dutch, the French and the British all making attempts to 'own' the country. It was the British who completed the white colonisation of the country, and cemented this in the 1840 Treaty of Waitaingi.

Politically, it is this treaty and the manner in which it regained prominence in the 1970s which makes New Zealand an interesting case. As noted above, its roots are in the British Commonwealth, meaning that many of its political and legal institutions are based on the British system. Also, as was the case in many Commonwealth countries, during the initial colonisation and the subsequent development as a nation state, recognition of the needs and rights of the indigenous peoples were often ignored, or in some cases deliberately suppressed.

However, following a series of events and resurgence in Maori cultural heritage in the 1960s and 1970s that culminated in 1975 with the establishment of the Waitangi Tribunal, gradually Maori rights and recognition of Maori (and latterly Pacific Islander) needs have become mainstreamed into New Zealand policy. As Kingi (2006: 14) notes the original treaty and the work done by subsequent reviews and tribunals have created a political climate that seeks not to erode non-Maori rights, but to promote equality and balance between the many races and cultures that comprise modern New Zealand.

In terms of illicit drug use, as was the case in most other developed-world states, concern about the use of substances increased in the 1980s and 1990s. One example of this would be the first regional report on drug use, published in 1990 and expanded on by Black and Creswell (1991). The findings of the report were sufficiently worrying to see the commissioning of further national surveys on drug use in an attempt by the NZ government to obtain accurate measurements of the extent and nature of drug use.

What it found was that illicit drug use in NZ both mirrored and deviated from European experiences. For example, whilst cannabis was, and is, the most frequently used illicit substance, the 'problem' drugs in NZ are not the same as those in Europe and the US. Wilkins *et al.* (2009) point out: cocaine and heroin are not in common or widespread usage, even amongst regular and/or problematic drug users. This is arguably because of the geographical position of NZ and the difficulties this carries in its wake. Rather, the drug that causes most problems in NZ is methamphetamine (known locally as 'P').

We can use economic and social theories to explain this. In economic terms transportation of goods to NZ is costly due to its geographical isolation. As a result this adds costs to both the consumer and, importantly, the vendor. Equally, in terms of drug smuggling, NZ is not on any major transit routes, meaning that there is a relatively low volume of goods passing through the country waiting in transit to be shipped to other nations. Goods tend to be either waiting to be exported or imported for local use, arguably making it somewhat less difficult for customs officials to check loads for contraband.

Thus, in pure business terms it makes more sense, is more profitable and less risky for the illicit drug business to promote and trade in those substances that can be grown locally (as in the case of cannabis) or manufactured locally (as in the case of P, LSD and ecstasy). Transport costs are lower, there is less risk to the distributor and the relative isolation of some rural areas makes producing these types of drugs relatively risk free.

Socially, the lack of cocaine and heroin use both historically and contemporarily means that there is not an established network of dealers or users. Because of this new entrants into use find it difficult or impossible to learn to use these substances. As Wilkins *et al.* note (2009: 2–3), in NZ '"Homebake" heroin was considered very difficult to obtain and becoming more difficult to obtain' and 'very few … frequent drug users had any experience of cocaine'. Also, the impact of drug use does not fall equally across the population as a whole. As the Ministerial Committee on Drug Policy notes (2007: 19–21): 'Maori suffer disproportionate harm from the use of drugs', and that there is 'growing concern for Pacific communities', with the possibility that 'rates of drug use [amongst Pacific peoples] may continue to increase in the future'.

By the middle of the 1990s it became evident that there was a need for a national policy to 'deal with' drug use and to address the unique set of drug-related problems that NZ had. As a result, the NZ government launched the first *National Drug Policy 1998–2003* (Ministry of Health 1998). Whilst the contents of that policy are important, the focus of the remainder of this section will be on the most recent policy. That said, there are two important points to note concerning the original policy:

1. the NZ government did not differentiate between licit and illicit substances; rather the original policy looked at all forms of drugs be they legal or illegal;
2. the policy itself was based on principles of harm reduction.

Following that, a second *National Drug Policy* was launched in 2007 covering the five year period from 2007 to 2012 (Ministerial Committee on Drug Policy 2007). Like its forerunner, the 2007–12 policy incorporates both legal and illegal, and 'accepts that drug use is primarily a health issue and should therefore be addressed, at least partially, through health-based responses' (Ministerial Committee on Drug Policy 2007: 37).

It also notes that NZ drug policy is founded on harm minimisation principles and recognises that drug use occurs on a continuum of harm and that no single approach will work, rather there is a need for a flexible and inter-sectoral approach to drug use. The overarching goal is to 'prevent, and reduce the health, social and economic harms that are linked to tobacco, alcohol, illegal and other drug use' (Ministerial Committee on Drug Policy 2007: 37).

The policy itself is based on three separate but related sets of strategies, or 'pillars' as they are referred to in the documents. These are:

- supply control – seeking to limit the availability of drugs both legal and illegal;
- demand reduction – seeking to limit the use of drugs by individuals (this also includes the possibility of abstinence);
- problem limitation – seeking to reduce the harm that falls out from existing drug use.

In practice, these pillars translate into policy that in some cases mirrors action that would be familiar to British readers. For example there is an established needle exchange programme; harm reduction programmes for young people; opioid substitution programmes; social marketing and general health education programmes. The important difference is that, unlike in the UK, the NZ government's policy does not distinguish between the harms created by legal or illegal drugs.

As noted, the three pillars of NZ drug policy are not mutually exclusive but rather are seen as a holistic package, which taken together will tackle the problems that drug use, *in all its forms*, presents. Indeed, the NZ drug policy is predicated on an approach that recognises the strengths of each sector in achieving the policy goals – as an obvious example the police and customs are at the forefront of supply control – but also is aware of the need to recognise differences and be flexible enough to accommodate those differences.

Thus, whilst aspects of NZ drug policy are similar to that of the UK, the NZ policy can also be seen to reflect the social, political and economic reality of the country and society it represents. In terms of problem drugs there is a marked difference from Europe inasmuch that cocaine use is relatively rare, as is opioid use. Given the geographical isolation of the country this is not surprising. The main problem seems to come from P which is largely home-produced. As a result, there is, at present, an absence of the acceptance of cocaine use that is established in Europe, largely because it is a difficult drug to obtain. However, the use of methamphetamine, whilst plateauing, remains high, as this drug can be and is produced within NZ borders.

Politically, NZ drug policy reflects the fact that the NZ state recognises Maori and Pacific Islanders as having a different set of problems and needs from the rest of the population. It also recognises that despite legal differences, there are similar sets of harm created by *all* substances and does not differentiate between legal and illegal drugs for policy purposes. This is in stark contrast to the UK, which has separate polices for illicit and licit drugs.

British drug policy

By this stage of the book, it is hoped that the reader has a clear appreciation of the complex nature of illicit drug use, production and policy. As we have seen, there are very few, if any, clear-cut solutions or even agreement as to reasons for the problem in this field. It seems as if every area is contested – there is disagreement as to whether cannabis is a gateway drug; there is vagueness as to the exact nature of the link between drugs and crime; there is confusion as to whether to control supply or use – and so it goes on. Additionally, in many countries there is a huge moral, and therefore political, dimension to illicit drug use and the whole legal and medical approach is wrapped up in a greater and seemingly trans-generational concern about the well-being of young people. As Young (1971) noted more than 30 years ago, it is often not the illicit drug that is the problem, it is the hedonism associated with drug use that leads to moral condemnation.

Clearly, finding a solution to the contemporary 'drug problem' is fraught with difficulties as well as being a product of its own history. The aim here is to make an attempt to navigate through some of the more confusing issues and areas. With that in mind, the first question that needs addressing is to establish whether or not there is an actual 'drug problem'.

The nature of the British 'drug problem'

Vigilant readers will have noticed the almost constant use of inverted commas around the phrase 'drug problem'. It denotes a degree of uncertainty as to the actual problematic nature of drug use. For example, as Chapter 2 noted, our measuring instruments, although improving, provide 'guesstimates' as to the extent of illicit drug use. Self-report data would seemingly indicate that a substantial minority of the British population tries some form of illicit drug at least once, most often in their youth. The same type of data indicates that a smaller proportion continue to use illicit drugs on a semi-regular recreational basis. Over time, such recreational use diminishes across age cohorts, but the trend has been for even greater numbers of the next generation to continue with some form of recreational (illicit) drug use. Finally, there is a small minority within all generations for which drug use becomes problematic in both medical and social terms.

However, does this really constitute a 'drug problem'? True, some of those people with problematic drug use do commit a great deal of crime (Category 3 users outlined and described in Chapter 8), and members of the same category of user do suffer serious legal, social and medical consequences for their actions. However, many of those group were already committing relatively high volumes of crime before their drug use became problematic. Moreover, is the 'problem' here a medical or legal one? For some, especially those Category 1 users, which includes the offspring of royalty and (former) home secretaries, the most 'problematic' aspect of their drug use is the potential for a criminal record and the impact that will have on their own lives. If this is indeed the case, the 'problem' is not a facet of the drug, but is created by social reactions to hedonistic or 'luxurious' use. That being the case, for most users 'the drug problem' could be seen to be a social and political construct, with no medical or legal connotations. That is not to suggest that drug use is unproblematic – it remains the case that use, however infrequent, of any or all illicit drugs (and some legal ones) holds the potential to seriously damage the health of the user, as well as carrying serious social and legal consequences.

The point is that for the majority of users this is palpably not their experienced reality, nor that of their peers. The vast majority of drug users do not commit acquisitive crime in order to feed their drug use, nor do the majority of illicit drug users act as a significant drain on scarce health resources. Moreover, except in a small number of instances there, is little evidence to suggest that recreational use of illicit drugs led inexorably to drug dependency, any more than alcoholism automatically and consistently follows social drinking. This begs the question as to where exactly the 'drug problem' lies and what is its exact nature?

In order to begin to address this question it is necessary to revisit some of the points made in previous chapters, specifically, the impact of economics, politics and socio-cultural factors. It is the contention here that it is a combination of these three pressures that inform and shape drug policy, not just in Britain, but elsewhere. With that in mind, the next section examines the part economic factors play in shaping British drug policy.

Economic pressures

The previous sections of this work established the relationship between economics and illicit drugs in both domestic and international terms. Put bluntly, the illicit drug industry is a huge global phenomenon that produces an annual turnover, which makes that of most licit multinationals look insignificant. It is a major player in international trade and is based on commodities for which there is a seemingly insatiable worldwide demand. Looked at from a business perspective this is startling for a product that, for the most part, cannot be freely advertised, cannot be freely distributed, is relatively difficult to obtain and for which trading in the commodity can cause multiple harms to the consumer and vendor alike. Just as in the case of large, legal multinationals, there is little individual nation states can do to curb the activities of such large and successful enterprises.

Paradoxically, it is the illicit nature of some substances that drives up the prices and levels of profitability in this market. Put simply, the act by nation states of attempting to control the supply of illicit drugs acts to interfere in the market mechanism. The drug producers see interdiction as a factor of production; in turn, this is seen as a 'cost' and factored into the price. In economic terms, the artificial inflating of the price caused by the banning actions of the nation states allows greater profits to be made, and thereby increases the economic power of the large-scale drug dealers. As noted, about 50 per cent of the retail cost of illicit drugs is a direct result of governments attempting to interfere in the market by making these substances illegal. Economic theory tells us that at these levels of profits, new illicit drug entrepreneurs will always be attracted into the business and are quick to replace any dealers who do get caught.

Moreover, and further complicating matters, production of illicit substances has become an integral part of the economy of some developing nations, thereby limiting the range of actions open to the international community. Equally, as the war in Afghanistan has proven once again, one of the potential consequences of action by developed nations in these areas is a change in culture and control, which sometimes leads to increased production of illicit drugs. Thus, in cost/benefit terms, there are real questions to be answered surrounding government actions designed to control the importation of illicit drugs and the effect this has on the market.

What must never be lost sight of is the fact that those nations now reaping economic benefits from the production and distribution of illicit drugs could charge countries such as the Netherlands and Britain with being hypocritical. A convincing case could be made for the claim that the new drug trading nations are simply carrying on a tradition of trading in drugs, pioneered and subsequently refined by these two northern European states. Somewhat ironically, Britain in the third millennium could be seen as akin to Afghanistan's China.

These are the often-quoted macro economic factors. However, there are other micro economic calculations that can be made. According to Kraan (1996), in an examination of the economics of Dutch drug policy, politicians and government organisations in the Netherlands are prone to making explicit cost/benefit analysis of policy implementation. Thus, in deciding the allocation of scarce resources politicians are often forced to consider the benefits of continuing with certain directions in policy, especially if the costs are outweighing the benefits. Here, costs do not always need to be monetary.

For instance, Kraan (1996) examines the costs to the Dutch criminal justice system in policing illicit drug use. He found that seven per cent of the total budget of the Dutch police force was spent on policing drugs. Given the fact that very little of this money will be spent on policing 'soft drugs', it could be argued that this represents a solid investment in an attempt to control 'hard drugs', which the Dutch see as most problematic.

However, what if a similar review was undertaken in Britain? It will be recalled that Chapter 3 noted the vast majority of 'drug crimes' processed by the British criminal justice system centred on simple possession of cannabis. In turn, most of these crimes drew relatively minor sentences of fines or community sentences. Moreover, it appears that large tracts of the British population fail to see cannabis as a major 'problem drug'. It could be suggested that the costs and benefits of a regime aimed at treatment and education would be, in the long run, more successful than the current fire-fighting approach of waiting until some users become problematic and then using the criminal justice system to address the problem.

Arguably, if a British drug policy was structured in pure economic terms, little in the way of law and order-based attention would be paid to relatively unproblematic drugs such as cannabis (and possibly ecstasy and LSD). Moreover, where interventions took place with cannabis, they would be health-based, promoting safe use, harm minimisation approaches. Even in terms of the *users* of hard drugs, law and order would have a restricted role, better to concentrate on the importers and large-scale dealers of these substances. In the changing world of public policy, with its current emphasis on cost-cutting, value for money and measurable outputs, an uneconomic drug policy simply cannot be sustained.

However, whilst the political class can make convincing arguments for a change of drug policy in economic terms, there are also other costs to be considered by politicians: the dual need of being seen to be credible with all sections of the electorate and ensuring respect for the law. This is an often-delicate process in areas where the law is contested, as there will almost always be conflicts of interest, with one group supporting a particular stance and others in opposition. For example, in instances where there is a clear gap between the law, public action and public opinion, the politician risks damaging the often-delicate balance that exists between them and opposing pressure groups.

Sometimes, a situation develops where politicians need to come off the fence and align themselves with one lobby or the other. Failure to judge the public mood correctly holds the potential to 'cost' the politician greatly in terms of credibility and respect for the law. Illicit drugs at the beginning of the twenty-first century is one such area. Unfortunately, whilst politicians may see the economic benefits of a relaxation of drug law relating to so called soft drugs, in moral terms many are hoist by their own petard, unable to move from the entrenched 'all drugs are evil' perspective. This has its roots in the dawn of contemporary drug policy, and it is to this attention now turns.

Moral pressures and state paternalism

As Chapter 1 noted, concerns as to the morality of the working class and young people in particular were central in the formation of British drug policy. Specifically, much of the direction emanated from the Victorian era, where the bourgeois middle class became increasingly worried about the contamination of the 'respectable' poor by the residuum and undesirable elements of society, such as prostitutes. Over time, this form of morality – reflected in the emphasis on middle-class respectability mirrored (and in some instances ridiculed) in contemporary novels by authors such as Dickens and Collins – consciously distanced itself from the more permissive practices of the upper and working classes.

Such a bourgeois view of morality was given even greater credence by the Eugenicist and Darwinian movements of that period, which 'proved' a hierarchy of the classes, the supremacy of European races and the male gender, leading to the promotion of strict controls over the 'feeble-minded' and calls for an eradication of 'bad' character traits of the working classes (Thane 1996: 51). Moreover, this period witnessed the introduction of the age of consent for various sexual acts and a consolidation of heterosexual and homosexual identities (Haste 1993). As the middle class grew, this moral perspective came to be the defining British morality.

As a result, this peculiar perspective on 'right' and 'wrong' imported some anomalies into the emergent moral climate. This can be witnessed elsewhere, away from illicit drugs. For example, a concern with all forms of intoxication is redolent within Victorian morality, but in a quintessential British middle-class approach, different alcoholic intoxicants were treated in different manners – beer was preferred to gin, the latter seen to be more 'evil' and 'corrupting' than the former (Tobias 1972). Much the same point can be made regarding illicit drugs. Laudanum and other opium derivatives, clearly the preference of the working classes, were seemingly singled out as being in need of greater attention than cocaine, which from its introduction into Britain has been associated with creativity – Conan Doyle's character Sherlock Holmes' use of cocaine as a 'mental stimulant' for example – and as a luxurious drug of choice for the rich, the artistic and the chic urban middle classes. Indeed, this continues today: the stimulant effects of cocaine and amphetamine are roughly similar, yet even Robson (1994: 57), in his otherwise excellent book, cannot resist commenting that amphetamine 'lacks the eloquent advocacy of cocaine' and that it is 'a rough and ready drug with a rough and ready clientele'. As we saw above, this is not the case in New Zealand, where methamphetamine use far outweighs cocaine use across all areas of that society.

Over time, and especially since the burgeoning drug culture of the past four decades, middle-class morality has been the dominant factor in British culture, and its concerns have been fuelled every so often by moral panics (Goode and Ben-Yehuda 1994), often surrounding working class youth, violence and/or drug use. Debate about a number of social issues has come to be dominated by these views, aided and abetted by a conservative, mainly right-wing popular press. This, coupled with the growing embourgeoisement of the traditional working class, has seen politicians pander more and more to middle-class values and morality.

In terms of illicit drugs, this has led to the polarisation of views at the expense of reasoned debate. As Goode and Ben-Yehuda (1994: 28) comment, in times of moral panics politicians are most likely to align 'themselves against the devil and on the side of the angels ... what count[s] [is] not the nature of the target but what side they were on and what they were against'. Clearly, over the last four decades British politicians have been against 'drugs', and have been on the side of a variety of anti-drugs 'moral entrepreneurs'.

For example, across the decades we have witnessed panics and concern over cannabis, 'pep-pills', LSD, crack cocaine and heroin. Following the ecstasy related death of Leah Betts, an anti-ecstasy campaign gathered momentum in Britain. Ecstasy became the 'new heroin', the new folk devil: police were instructed to crack down on the sellers of the drug, courts were issuing draconian sentences to those caught and the media stories were such that one could be forgiven in thinking that each and every teenager in the country was taking dangerous amounts of the drug daily. Subsequent research indicates that its use is relatively non-prevalent amongst young drug users (Ramsay and Partridge 1999).

This trend has been repeated recently with the moral panic (and subsequent panicky banning of) the so-called legal high mephedrone. Arguably, it reached its zenith in March 2010 with the death and subsequent media furore over its use of two young men from Linconshire. The results were a hastily, mostly evidence-free, ban on the substance, which resulted in a number of high-profile resignations from the Advisory Council on the Misuse of Drugs and also a highly critical editorial of the whole affair in the *Lancet*. In truth, the two young men had consumed a large amount of alcohol followed by a sedative. There is at present no evidence that either took mephadrone. The whole affair has led the ex-chair of the ACMD to comment that governments should 'have the courage to resist media hysteria and let the truth drive decision making' (Nutt 2010). More tellingly the same author (Nutt 2010: 23) notes that:

> The whole mephadrone debacle illustrates what has been known for many years – there is a real need for a new approach to the drug laws. The 1971 MDA is 40 years old, and in its current classification system is fatally flawed and not fit for purpose. In this new world where drugs may be invented one day and sold over the internet the next, there needs to be a fundamental revision or better still a completely new approach to drug classification.

Alongside this call we have also seen a loosening of concern and attitudes toward illicit drug use and users. Many people in the public eye are open and honest about their drug use and this seems to have no impact on their lives or social standing: witness the former Home Secretary Jacqui Smith's admission of cannabis use. This gradual loosening of the moral stranglehold over the tone of the debate, and the direction of drug policy in Britain, is an emergent feature of the early twenty-first century. One can only suppose at reasons for this. Arguably, it is part of a shifting of social and cultural values that has its roots in the 'Swinging Sixties'.

The generation that holds the power in Britain are all 'post-Sixties' children, and have lived through a period where drug use has moved from a marginal activity to somewhere near normalised behaviour in sections of society. Across all forms of social behaviour – sexuality, promiscuity, marital status, pornography and others – the Victorian-based value system is under challenge as people either reject its strictures or, more likely, are honest about their actions. Political rhetoric and action needs to reflect this change in attitude in order to remain credible. Equally, with large tracts of the population breaking drug laws relating to cannabis on a regular basis respect for the law is under challenge, as it has become increasingly difficult to defend what many see as an unjust or unenforceable law.

Political pressure

As the previous two sections have highlighted, politics and politicians play a leading role in the construction of British drug policy, and also have a significant influence in defining and redefining the problematic nature of illicit drug use. Building on the points made above relating to morality, shifts in policy are difficult for politicians as they demonstrate weaknesses and fallibility in previous policy directions. The relaxation of drug laws, often made for very good reasons, can be seen to be an admission of having lost the 'war', and as a last-ditch attempt to salvage a decent peace.

Politicians are also under pressure themselves from a variety of sources. Above, it was noted that Europe-wide there is a trend toward a relaxation of drug laws. This in itself is an overt and obvious political pressure. However, there may be less obvious political pressures: that of the disengagement of the young from politics. One of the reasons being furthered on this subject is the irrelevance of politics to the lifestyle of the young, and the distance between them and politicians. Showing an awareness of issues – including the (contested) normalisation of illicit drugs within the culture of the young – may be one tactic in the re-engagement process.

Politicians are also under pressure from agencies and organisations charged with implementing policies. This is clearly the case with cannabis. The medical profession is keen to use the drug for medicinal purposes. From a critical perspective, we could argue that it is a case of history repeating itself. Just as the medics were unwilling to allow widespread self-medication of opiates in the 1800s, they are now keen to 'own', and thus stop self-medication, of cannabis in the year 2011. The willingness and desire for this to happen on the part of the medics has caused the politicians to allow trials, which seemingly will lead to the prescription of cannabis for medicinal purposes.

Finally, they are also under pressure from each other. Gauging swings in public opinion is a key skill, and failure to do so can lead to calls of 'being out of touch'. It may be there is a big enough groundswell of opinion toward the re-classification of certain substances that opposition to the movement becomes politically damaging. That is a price few politicians are prepared to pay. In many ways, all drug policy since DORA, and before, could be subjected to the same examination and, arguably, the conclusion would be the same. What is interesting is that virtually the same set of pressures – economic, moral and political – that led to the criminalisation of drug use in the first instance could eventually lead to a change in approach.

In many respects, this is little different from elsewhere in the world. As demonstrated, the current drug policies of both the Netherlands and New Zealand are aimed at addressing a growth in the use of illicit drugs. Each nation state has developed a policy that reflects, not just their respective cultures, but also the economic and political climate as well. What we have in Europe is the supranational trend of a surge in the use of recreational drugs. In most countries there appears to be a pragmatic move toward the liberalisation of 'soft' drugs, a division in the market between soft and hard drugs and a move toward treatment and harm reduction policies, especially in terms of the user.

Final thoughts

It has been the intention of the book to enable the reader to understand that illicit drug use and the state's response to it is a complicated, multi-faceted phenomenon, free from clear-cut answers. Hopefully, by now it will be clear that the weekend cannabis user settling down with their spliff after work on

Friday evening, or a Saturday night clubber feeling the first rush of cocaine prior to leaving home, are the final link in a process that, amongst many other things, has its roots in the last century; has taxed the resources of a number of nation states; is part of a global industry almost without parallel; and represents an ongoing battle between the needs of law and order and the needs of health agencies.

The subtitle of the book, *use and control,* sums up the problem in a nutshell. Use, I believe, will always be a part of society: people have seemingly always used mind-altering substances and show no desire to stop. The problem comes in attempts to control, or at least supervise use, arguably a necessary but incredibly difficult task. As we have seen, it requires an almost impossible combination of national and international policy, political will, a shared perspective on morality, and a conducive set of economic circumstances to even begin to control the production, distribution and consumption of drugs. In an uncertain future there is arguably just one certainty – dealing with the use of illicit drugs will be near the forefront of developments in all aspects of social policy.

Bibliography

Advisory Council on the Misuse of Drugs (ACMD) (1982) *Treatment and Rehabilitation*, London: HMSO.

——(1984) *Prevention*, London: HMSO.

——(1988) *Aids and Drug Misuse* (Part One), London: HMSO.

——(1989) *Aids and Drug Misuse* (Part Two), London: HMSO.

——(1995) *Volatile Substance Abuse: Report by the Advisory Council on the Misuse of Drugs*, London: Home Office.

Afghan-Web (2009) Afghan child mortality linked to uneducated mothers, online available http://www.afghan-web.com/health/#motherandchild (accessed 30 August 2010).

Amnesty International Report (1999) *Afghanistan*, New York: Amnesty International.

Anderson. T. L. (2008) Introduction, in Anderson, T. (ed.) *Neither villain nor victim: empowerment and agency among women substance abusers*, New Brunswick, NJ: Rutgers University Press.

Anglin, M. & Hser, Y. (1990) Legal coercion and drug abuse treatment: research findings and policy implications, in Inciardi, J. (ed.). *Handbook of drug control in the United States*, Westport, CT: Greenwood.

Ashton, M. (1994) New drug strategies for England and Scotland, *Druglink*, November/December.

Ashworth, A. (1998) *The Criminal Process: an evaluative study* (2nd edition), Oxford: Oxford University Press.

Bailey, M.D. (2003) *Battling Demons: Witchcraft, heresy and reform in the late Middle-Ages*, University Park, PA: Pennsylvania State University Press.

Bal, M. & Bryson, N. (1991) Semiotics and art history, *Art Bulletin* 73, 174–208.

Balding, J. (1999) *Young People in 1998*, Exeter: Schools Health Education Unit.

Barber, J.G. (1995) *Social Work with Addictions*, Basingstoke: Macmillan.

Barclay, G.C., Tavares, C. & Prout, A. (1995) *Information on the Criminal Justice System 3*, London: Home Office.

Barton, A. (1999) Sentenced to Treatment? Criminal justice orders and the health service, *Critical Social Policy*, 19(4), 463–83.

——(1999) Breaking the crime/drugs cycle: the birth of a new approach? *Howard Journal*, 38 (2), 144–57.

——(2000) A tale of two projects: the growth and development of two neigbourhood watch schemes in South Wales, *Crime Prevention and Community Safety: an International Journal*, 2 (3), 7–16.

——(2001) Devising substance use education programmes for parents: a case study from Wales, *Health Education,* 101 (6), 274–82.

——(2005) *An Evaluation of the Persistent Offenders Unit*, Plymouth: University of Plymouth.

Barton, A. & Quinn, C. (2001) The Supremacy of Joined Up Working: A Pandora's Box for Organisational Identity? *Public Policy and Administration*, 16 (2), 49–62.

——(2002) Risk Management of Groups or Respect for Individuals? Issues for information sharing and confidentiality in Drug Treatment and Testing Orders, *Drugs: education, prevention, policy*, 9 (1), 35–43.

BBC (2001) *Pain drove me to pot*, http.//www.bbc.co.uk (accessed 19 December 2001).

Bean, P. (1994) The Drug Takers 1920–70, in Coomber, R. (ed.) *Drugs and Drug Use in Society: A Critical Reader*, Greenwich: Greenwich University Press.

——(2002) *Drugs and Crime*, Cullumpton: Willan Publishing.

——(2004) *Drugs and Crime*, (2nd edition) Cullumpton: Willan Publishing.

——(2010) *Legalising Drugs: debates and dilemmas*, Bristol: Policy Press.

Benavie, A. (2009) *Drugs: America's holy war*, London: Routledge.

Bennett, T. & Sibbett, R. (2000) Drug use amongst arrestees, *Home Office Research Findings 19*, London: Home Office.

Bennett, T. & Holloway, K. (2005) *Understanding Drugs, Alcohol and Crime*, Maidenhead: Open University Press.

Berridge, V. (1978) Victorian Opium Eating: Response to opiate use in nineteenth century England, *Victorian Studies*, Summer 1978, 437–61.

——(1989) Historical Issues, in MacGregor, S. (ed.) *Drugs and British Society: Responses to a social problem in the eighties*, London: Routledge.

Berridge, V. & Edwards, G. (1981) *Opium and the People*, London: Allen Lane.

Black, S. and Creswell, S. (1991) *Drugs in NZ – A survey*, Auckland: APHRU Auckland University.

Blackman, S. (2004) *Chilling Out: the cultural politics of substance consumption, youth and drug policy*, Maidenhead: Open University Press.

Blagg, H., Sampson, A., Pearson, G., Smith, D. & Stubbs, P. (1988) Inter-agency co-operation: Rhetoric and reality, in Hope, T. & Shaw, M. (eds) *Communities and Crime Reduction*, London: HMSO.

Boekhout van Solinge, T. (1999) Dutch Drug Policy in a European Context, *Journal of Drug Issues*, 29 (3), 511–28.

Bourdieu, P. (1984) *Distinction: A social critique of the judgement of taste*, Cambridge, MA: Harvard University Press.

British Medical Association (BMA) (1997) *The Misuse of Drugs*, Amsterdam: Harwood.

Brittain, J.J. (2010) *Revolutionary Social Change in Columbia: the origin and direction of FARC-EP*, New York: Pluto Press.

Bruun, K., Pan, L. & Rexed, I. (1975) *The Gentlemen's Club: International Control of Drugs and Alcohol*, Chicago: University of Chicago Press.

Burke, R. (1996) *The History of Child Protection in Britain: A Theoretical Reformulation* (Crime, Order and Policing, Occasional Paper no. 9), Leicester: The Scarman Centre for the Study of Public Order.

Bush, G. (1989) Speech to Congress, in Hoffman, D., Proposal is Marked Shift from Border Interdiction, *Washington Post*, 27 May.

Cabinet Office (1998) *Tackling Drugs to Build a Better Britain*, London: HMSO.

Caulkins, J.P. & Reuter, P. (1998) What price data tells us about drug markets, *Journal of Drugs Issues*, 3, 593–612.

Caulkins, J.P., Johnson, B., Taylor, A. and Taylor, L. (1999) What drug dealers tell us about their costs of doing business, *Journal of Drug Issues*, 29 (2), 323–40.

Central Intelligence Agency (2009) *World Factbook*, online available http://cia.gov/library/publications/the-world-factbook/index.html (accessed 6 July 2010).

Chaiken J. and Chaiken, M. (1991) Drugs and predatory crime, in Tonry, M. and Wilson, J. (eds) *Drugs and Crime: Crime justice, Volume 13*, Chicago: Chicago University Press.

Chasteen, J.C. (2001) *Born in Blood and Fire: A concise history of Latin America*, W.W. Norton: New York.

Chernick, M.W. (1996) *Testimony to the US Congress House Committee on International Relations*, 114 Congress, 2nd Session, Washington, DC: US GPO.

Chesneaux, J., Bastid, M. & Bergere, M-C. (1976) *China from the Opium Wars to the 1911 Revolution*, New York: Pantheon.

Chivite-Matthews, N., Richardson, A., O'Shea, J., Becker, J., Owen, N., Roe, S. & Condon, J. (2005) *Drug Misuse Declared: Findings from the 2003/04 British Crime Survey England and Wales*, London: Home Office Statistical Bulletin.

Cicourel, A. (1964) *Methods and Measurement in Sociology*, London: Macmillan.

Cicourel, A. & Kitsuse, J. (1963) *The Education Decision-Makers*, New York: Bobbs-Merril.

Cleveland Police (2000) *Drugs*, paper supplied to the Chairman and Members of the Cleveland Police Authority, 10 December 1999, www.drugtext.org/reports/ukpol/clp1.htm (accessed 24 May 2000).

Cochrane, A. (1993) Comparative Approaches to Social Policy, in Cochrane, A. and Clarke, J. (eds) *Comparing Welfare States: Britain in an International Context*, London: Sage.

Coid, J, Carvell, A., Kittler, Z., Healy, A. and Henderson, J. (2001) *Opiates, Criminal Behaviour and Methadone Treatment*, London: Home Office.

Colebatch, H.K. (1998) *Policy*, Buckingham: Open University Press.

Coleman, V. (1985) *The Story of Medicine*, London: Jill Norman.

Conservative Party Election Manifesto (1992) *The Best Future for Britain*, London: Conservative Central Office.

Consroe, P., Musty, R., Rein, J., Tillery, W. and Pertwee, R. . [F3](1997) The Perceived Effects of Smoked Cannabis on Patients with MS, *European Neurology*, 38, 44–48.

Cooper, N. (2002) State collapse as business: the role of conflict trade and the emerging control agenda, *Development and Change*, 33 (5), 935–55.

Corkery, J.M. (2001) *Drug seizures and Offender Statistics, United Kingdom 1999*, Home Office Statistical Bulletin, 5/01, London: Home Office.

Courtwright, D.T. (2001) *Forces of Habit: drugs and the making of the modern world*, Cambridge, MA: Harvard University Press.

Courtwright, D.T. (2002) *Forces of Habit: drugs and the making of the modern world*, Cambridge, MA: Harvard University Press.

Crawford, A. & Jones, M. (1996) Kirkholt Revisited: Some reflections of the transferability of crime prevention initiatives, *Howard Journal*, 35 (1), 21–39.

Crawshaw, P. (2001) Negotiating Space, *Youth and Policy*, 74, 59–72.

Davidson, N. & Sturgeon-Adams, L. (1997) Participatory drug profiling: Developing a Police Contribution to Tackling Drugs Together, paper presented to *British Criminology Conference*, Belfast.

Davis, D. (2008) Comments to the floor of the House of Commons, in *Hansard*, 9 June.

Department of Health (DoH) (1991a) *Co-ordinating drug services: the role of regional and district drug advisory committees*, London: Department of Health.

——(1991b) *Drug Misuse and Dependence: Guidelines on Clinical Management*, London: HMSO.

——(1995) *Tackling Drugs Together*, London: Department of Health.

Departmental Committee on Morphine and Heroin Addiction (1926) The Rolleston Report, London: HMSO.

Department of Health (1999) *Drug Misuse and Dependence: Guidelines on Clinical Management*, London: Department of Health.

——(2000) *Statistics from the Regional Drug Misuse Databases for the six months ending March 2000* (Bulletin 2000/31), London: HMSO.

——(2005) *United Kingdom Drug Situation 2005 edition*, (Report to the EMCDDA) London: DoH.

——(2007) *Drug misuse and dependence: UK Guidelines on Clinical Management*, London: DoH.

——(2009) *Statistics from the National Drug Treatment Monitoring System (NTDMS) 1 April 2008– 31 March 2009*, London: DoH.

Department of Health and Social Security (DHSS) (1976) *Prevention and Health: Everybody's Business*, London: DHSS.

——(1982) *Treatment and Rehabilitation*, London: HMSO.

——(1984) *Guidelines of Good Clinical Practice in the Treatment of Drug Misuse*, London: HMSO.

DeQuincey, T. (1822) *Confessions of an Opium Eater*, Harmondsworth: Penguin Classics.

Dorn, N. & South, N. (1994) The power behind practice: drug control and harm minimization in inter-agency and criminal law contexts, in Strang, J. & Gossop, M. (eds) *Heroin Addiction and Drug Policy: The British System*, Oxford: Oxford University Press.

Downes, D. (1977) The drug addict as folk devil, in Rock, P. (ed.) *Drugs and Politics*, New Brunswick, NJ: Transaction Books.

Doyal, L. & Pennell, I. (1979) *The Political Economy of Health*, London: Pluto Press.

Drug Prevention Advisory Service (DPAS) (2001) *Let's Get Real: Communicating with the public about drugs*, London: Home Office.

DrugScope (2000) *UK Drug Situation 2000: The UK report to the European Monitoring Centre for Drugs and Drug Addiction (EMCDDA)*, London: DrugScope.

Duin, N. & Sutcliffe, J. (1992) *A History of Medicine*, London: Simon and Schuster.

Dyer, C. (2002) *Making a living in the Middle Ages: the people of Britain 850–1520*, New Haven, CT: Yale University Press.

Edmunds, M., May, T. & Hough, M. (1998) Drugs Interventions and the Criminal Justice System, paper presented to *Evaluating effectiveness: Drugs prevention Research Conference*, Liverpool.

Edmunds, M., Hough, M., Turnbull, P.J. & May, T. (1999) *Doing Justice to Treatment: referring Offenders to Drug Services*, London: DPAS paper 2.

Edwards, G. (1981) The Background, in Edwards, G. & Busch, C. (eds.) *Drug Problems in Britain: A Review of Ten Years*, London: Academic Press.

Escohotado, E. (1999) *A Brief History of Drugs: from the stone age to the stoned age*, Rochester, VT: Park Street Press.

Escribano, M. (2003) Militarism and Globalization: Conference Synopsis , in Fisher, W.F. and Ponniah, T. (eds) *Another World is Possible: popular alternatives to gloabalization at the World Social Forum*, London: Zed, 296–308.

Ettore, E. (2007) Women, drugs and popular culture, in Manning, P. (ed.) *Drugs and popular culture: drugs, media and identity in contemporary society*, Cullumpton: Willan.

——(2008) Seeing women, power, and drugs through the lens of empowerment, in Anderson, T. (ed.) *Neither villain nor victim: empowerment and agency among women substance abusers*, New Brunswick, NJ: Rutgers University Press.

European Monitoring Centre for Drugs and Drug Addiction (EMCDDA) (2001) *Decriminalisation in Europe?* EMCDDA: Brussels

——(2009) *2009 Annual Report on the state of the drug problem in Europe*, www.emcdda.europa.eu/ publications/annual-report/2009 (accessed 12 January 2010).

Felson, M. (2002) *Crimes of Everyday Life* (3rd edition), London: Sage.

Flint, C. (2006) *Introduction to Geopolitics*, London: Routledge.

Fraser, D. (1984) *The Evolution of the Welfare State* (2nd edition), Basingstoke: Macmillan.

Fraser, P. & Sneddon, T. (2002) *Relearning old lessons*, *Criminal Justice Matters*, Spring 2002, 47, 22–23.

Fraser, S. & Valentine, K. (2005) Gendered Ethnographies: Researching drugs, violence and gender in New York, *Australian Feminist Studies*, 20 (46), 121–24.

Fuller, N. (1990) *Fundamental Economics*, Sevenoaks: Tudor Publishing.

Gamble, A. (1981) *An Introduction to Modern Social and Political Thought*, London: Macmillan.

——(1986) *Britain in Decline* (2nd edition), London: Macmillan.

Ganghof, S. & Genschel, P. (2007) *Taxation and Democracy in the EU*, Cologne: Max Plank Institute for the Study of Societies.

Garland, D. (1996) The Limits of the Sovereign State: Strategies of Crime Control in Contemporary Society, *British Journal of Criminology*, 36 (4), 445–71.

George, V. & Wilding, P. (1992) *Ideology and Social Welfare* (2nd edition), London: Routledge.

Gerada, C. & Farrell, M. (1998) Shared Care, in Robertson, R. (ed.) *Management of Drug Users in the Community: a practical handbook*, London: Arnold.

Giddens, A. (1986) *Sociology: a brief but critical introduction*, Cambridge: Polity Press.

Gilleard, F., Higgs, P., Hyde, M., Wiggins, R., and Blane, D. (2005) Class, Cohort, and Consumption: The British Experience of the Third Age, *Journals of Gerontology Series B: Psychological Sciences and Social Sciences*, 60, 305–10.

Gilman, M. (1999) Beyond Opiates … and into the '90s, in Coomber, R. (ed.) *Drugs and Drug Use in Society: A Critical Reader*, Greenwich: Greenwich University Press.

Gladstone, D. (1995) The Welfare State and the State of Welfare, in Gladstone, D. (ed.) *British Social Welfare: Past, present and future*, London: UCL Press.

Goddard, E. & Higgins, V. (1999a) *Smoking, drinking and drug use among young teenagers in 1998: Volume 1: England*, London: HMSO.

——(1999b) *Smoking, drinking and drug use among young teenagers in 1998: Volume 2: Scotland*, London: HMSO.

Goode, E. and Ben-Yehuda, N. (1994) *Moral Panics: The social Construction of Deviance*, Oxford: Blackwell.

Gossop, M. & Grant, M. (1990) *Preventing and Controlling drug Abuse*, Geneva: WHO.

Gossop, M., Marsden, J., Stewart, D. and Kidd, T. (2003) The national treatment outcome research study (NTROS): 4–5 year follow up results, *Addiction*, 98, 291–303.

Grapendal, M. (1992) Drugs and crime in an accommodating social context: the situation in Amsterdam, *Contemporary Drug Problems*, Summer, 303–26.

Grilly, D.M. (1998) *Drugs and Human Behaviour*, Boston, MA: Allyn and Bacon.

GW Pharmaceuticals (2001) *Home Page and related links*, www.gwpharm.com (accessed 19 December 2001).

Hallett, C. & Birchall, (1992) *Co-ordination and Child Protection: A Review of the Literature*, London: HMSO.

Halpert, B. (1982) Antecedents, in Rogers, D.L. & Whetten, D.A. (eds) *Inter-organisational co-ordination: Theory, Research and Implementation*, Boise, IA: Iowa State University Press.

Ham, C. (1992) *Health Policy in Britain: The politics and organisation of the National Health Service* (3rd edition), London: Macmillan.

Hammersley, R., Forsyth, A., Morrison, B. & Davis, J.B. (1989) The relationship between crime and opiod use, *British Journal of Addiction*, 84 (9) 1029–43.

Hammersley, R., Forsyth, A. & Lavelle, T. (1990) The criminality of new drug users in Glasgow, *British Journal of Addiction*, 85 (12), 1583–94.

Harding, G. (1998) Pathologising the Soul: The Construction of a 19th Century Analysis of Opiate Addiction, in Coomber, R. (ed.) *The Control of Drugs and Drug Users: Reason or Reaction?* Amsterdam: Harwood.

Hardy, T. (1880) *The Trumpet Major*, Harmondsworth: Penguin Classics.

Harrison, P. (1985) *Inside the Inner City*, Harmondsworth: Penguin.

Harvey, J. (1998) *Intermediate Economics*, London: Blackwell.

Haste, H. (1993) *The Sexual Metaphor*, London: Harvester Wheatsheaf.

Hay, G. (1998) Estimating the prevelance of substance misuse, in Bloor, M. and Woods, F. (eds) *Addictions and problem drug use: issues in behaviour, policy and practice*, Research Highlights, Social Work 33, London: Jessica Kingsley Publishers.

Hay, G., Gannon, M., MacDougall, J., Millar, T., Eastwood, C. and McKeganey, N. (2006) Local and National Estimates of Opiate and/or Crack Cocaine Use, in Singleton, N., Murray, R. and Tinsley, L (eds) *Measuring Different Aspects of Problem Drug Use: Methodological Developments*, London: Home Office.

Health Education Authority (1995) *D-mag*, London: ISDD.

Health Prevention Agency (HPA) (2009) *Shooting up: infections among injecting drug users in the United Kingdom 2008*, London: HPA.

Heuston, J., McNeill, A., McVey, D. & McLean, D. (1996) *Drug Realities: National Drugs Campaign Survey (Summary of Key Findings)*, London: Health Education Authority.

Hill, M. (1997) *The Policy Process in the Modern State* (3rd Edition), Hemel Hempstead: Prentice Hall.

HMSO (1985) *Tackling Drug Misuse*, London: HMSO.

Hobsbawm, E. (1969) *Industry and Empire*, Harmondsworth: Penguin.

Hollis, T. (2008) Think tank: Fight smart in the war on drugs: A chief constable calls for a fresh strategy, *Sunday Times*, 3 August.

Holloway, S.W.F. (1995) The regulation of the supply of drugs in Britain before 1868, in Porter, R. and Teich, M. (eds) *Drugs and Narcotics in History*, Cambridge: Cambridge University Press.

Holmes, J.S. & Gutierrez de Pineres, S.A. (2006) The Illegal drug industry, violence and the Columbian economy: a departmental analysis, *Latin American Politics and Society*, 25 (1), 157–84.

Home Office (1997) *Drug Treatment and Testing orders: Background Issues for Consultation*, London: Home Office.

——(2001) *The United Kingdom Anti-Drugs Co-ordinators Report 2000–01*, London: Home Office.

——(2007a) *The Illicit drug trade in the United Kingdom* (2nd edition), London: Home Office.

——(2008a) *Drug Misue Declared: Findings from the 2007/08 British Crime Survey (England and Wales)*, London: Home Office.

——(2008b) *Drugs: protecting families and communities: the 2008 drug strategy*, London: Home Office.

——(2009) *Drug Misue Declared: Findings from the 2008/09 British Crime Survey (England and Wales)*, London: Home Office.

Hooker, P. (1996) *Chinese Cultural Studies – Opium Wars*, www.accc6.its.brooklyn.cuny.edu (accessed 21 March 2001).

Hopkins, N. (2001) Police extend softly-softly pilot scheme on cannabis possession, *The Guardian*, 29 December.

Hough, M. (1996) *Drugs misuse and the criminal justice system: a review of the literature*, London: Home Office.

Howard, R. (1997) The Service Provider's Perspective, in Braggins, J. (ed.) *Tackling Drugs Together: One Year On*, London: ISTD.

Howard, R., Beadle, P. & Maitland, J. (1994) *Across the Divide: Building Community Partnerships to tackle Drug Misuse*, a report to the Department of Health, London: Department of Health.

Howarth, G. (1999) A view from Government, in Marlow, A. & Pearson, G. (eds) *Young People, Drugs and Community Safety*, Lyme Regis: Russell House Publishing.

Hudson, B. (1987) Collaboration in Social Welfare: a framework for analysis, *Policy and Politics*, 15 (3), 175–82.

Hughes, R., Lart, R., & Higate, P. (eds) (2006) *Drugs: policy and politics*, Maidenhead: Open University Press.

Hughes, R. & Anthony, N. (2006) Drugs, Crime and Criminal Justice, in Hughes, R., Lart, R., & Higate, P. (eds.) *Drugs: policy and politics*, Maidenhead: Open University Press.

Hutchinson, J. (2001) *The role of doctors in treating drug dependency*, unpublished papers, Glamorgan: University of Glamorgan.

Hylton, F. (2006) *Evil hour in Columbia*, Verso: New York.

Institute for Study of Drug Dependency (ISDD) (1995) *Drug misuse in Britain*, ISDD: London.

Institute for the Study of Drug Dependency (1995) *Drug Misuse in Britain*, London: ISDD.

James, A. & Raine, J. (1998) *The new politics of criminal justice*, Longman: London.

Johnston, P. & Moore, M. (2007) Jacqui Smith admits to smoking cannabis, in *The Daily Telegraph*, 19 July.

Jones, L.J. (1994) *The Social Context of Health and Health Work*, London: Macmillan.

Joseph Rowntree Foundation (2005) *Understanding drug selling in local communities*, Findings November, York: Joseph Rowntree Foundation.

Kaal, H. (1998) Do trends in criminal justice statistics reflect changing attitudes in the English criminal justice system toward drug offences? paper presented to *The 9th International Conference on the Reduction of Drug Related Harm*, Sao Paulo, Brazil, 15–19 March 1998.

Kahn, S. (2001) Mothers March To Clean Up Needle City, in *The Observer*, 8 April.

Kaplan, J. (1983) *The hardest drug: Heroin and Public Policy*, Chicago: University of Chicago Press.

Karstedt, S. & Farrall, G. (2006) The Moral Economy of Everyday Crime, *The British Journal of Criminology*, 46 (6), 1011–36.

Kemshall, H. (2002) *Risk, social policy and welfare*, Milton-Keynes: Open University Press.

Khan, K. (2006) Race, Politics and drugs, in Hughes, R., Lart, R. & Higate, P., *Drugs: policy and politics*, Maidenhead: Open University Press.

Kidd, B.A. & Sykes, R.A.D. (1999) UK Policy, in Stark, C., Kidd, B.A., & Sykes, R.A.D. (eds) *Illegal Drug Use in the United Kingdom: Prevention, Treatment and Enforcement*, Aldershot: Ashgate.

Kingi, Te. K. R. (2006) *The Treaty of Waitaingi and Maori health*, paper presented to Te Mata o te Tau Lecture series 2 March 2006.

Kleiman, M.A.R. & Young, R.M. (1995) The factors of production in retail drug dealing, *Urban Affairs Review*, 30 (5) 731–48.

Kohn, M. (1992) *Dope Girls: The Birth of the British Drug Underground*, London: Lawrence and Wishart.

Kort, M de (1995) *Tussen Patient, en Delinquent. Geschiedenis van het Netherlandse Drugsbeleid*, Veloren: Hilversum.

——(1996) A short history of drugs in the Netherlands, in Leuw, E. and Haen Marshall, I. (eds) *Between Prohibition and Legalization: the Dutch Experiment in Drug Policy*, London: Sage.

Kraan, D.J. (1996) An economical view on Dutch drug policy in Leuw, E. and Haen Marshall, I. (eds) *Between Prohibition and Legalization: the Dutch Experiment in Drug Policy*, London: Sage.

Kraul, C. (2006) US indicts Columbian guerrillas, online available http://latimes.co./news/nationworld/world (accessed 23 September 2009).

Kushlick, D. (2006) Clarke clings to the grand illusion of prohibition, *Guardian*, 24 January.

Kushner. A. B. (2009) The truth About Plan Columbia, in *Newsweek,* 12 January.

Labrousse, A. (2005) The FARC and the Taliban's connections to drugs, *Journal of Drug Issues*, 35 (1), 169–84.

Lawrence, C. (1994) *Medicine and the Making of Modern Britain 1700–1920*, London: Routledge.

Leathard, A. (ed.) (1994) *Going Inter-Professional: Working Together for Health and Welfare*, London: Routledge.

——(2000) *Health Care Provision: Past, Present and into the 21st Century* (2nd edition), Cheltenham: Stanley Thornes.

Leech, K. (1991) The Junkies' Doctors and the London Drug Scene in the 1960s: Some Remembered Fragments, in Whynes, D. & Bean P. (eds) *Policing and Prescribing*, London: Macmillan.

LeGrand, C. (2003) The Columbian Crisis in historical perspective, *Canadian Journal of Latin American and Caribbean Studies*, 28, 165–209.

Leitner, M., Shapland, J. & Wiles, P. (1993) *Drugs Use and Prevention: The Views and Habits of the General Public*, London: HMSO.

Leng, R., Taylor, R. & Wasik, M. (1998) *Blackstone's Guide To The Crime & Disorder Act 1998*, London: Blackstone Press.

Leuw, E. (1996) Initial Construction and Development of the Official Dutch Drug Policy, in Leuw, E. and Haen Marshall, I. (eds) *Between Prohibition and Legalization: the Dutch Experiment in Drug Policy*, London: Sage.

Levi, M. (2006) The media construction of financial white collar crimes, *The British of Criminology*, 46 (6), 1037–57.

Lewis, R. (1994) Flexible hierarchies and dynamic disorder – the trading and distribution of illicit heroin in Britain and Europe 1970–1990, in Strang, J. & Gossop, M. (eds.) *Heroin Addiction and Drug Policy: The British System*, Oxford: Oxford University Press.

Lifeline (1993) *A Trip Around Manchester With Peanut Pete*, Manchester: Lifeline.

——(1994) *Claire and Jose Get Off Their Cake*, Manchester: Lifeline.

Livingstone, G. (2003) *Inside Columbia: Drugs, democracy and war*, London: Latin American Bureau.

London, M., O'Regan, T., Aust, P. & Stockford, A. (1990) Poppy tea drinking in East Anglia, in *British Journal of Addiction*, 85 (10), 1345–47.

Lowes, P.D. (1966) *The Genesis of International Narcotics Control*, Geneva: Libraire Droz.

Macdonald, D. (2007) *Drugs in Afghanistan: opium, outlaws and scorpion tales*, London: Pluto Press.

Maher, L (1996) Hidden in the light: occupational norms among crack using, street level sex workers, *Journal of Drug Issues*, 26 (1), 143–73.

Manning, P. (ed.) (2007) *Drugs and Popular Culture: drugs media and identity in contemporary society* [F14], Willan: Cullumpton.

Marks, P. *et al.* (1973) Public attitudes to drug taking: short report on work carried out by the OPCS for the Home Office, unpublished.

Martin. E., & Symansky, S. (2009) Macroeconomic impact of the drug economy and counter narcotics efforts, in Buddenberg, D & Byrd, W.A. (eds) *Afghanistan Drug Industry: structure, functioning, dynamics and implications for counter narcotic policy*, www.unodc.org/paf/afg/publications/afghanistan_drug_industry_pdf (accessed 21 January 2009).

Matthews, R. (1995) Dealing with Drugs: A New Philosophy? in Martin, C. (ed.) *Dealing with Drugs: A New Philosophy?* Report of a conference organised by the Institute for the Study and Treatment of Delinquency, 1 March, London: ISTD.

May, T. (1997) *Social Research: Issues, Methods and Process* (2nd edition), Maidenhead: Open University Press.

May, T. & Hough, M. (2004) Drug Markets and Distribution Systems, in *Addiction, Research and Theory*, 12 (6), 549–63.

Mayhew, P. (2000) Research the State of Crime, in King, R.D. & Wincup, E. (eds) *Doing Research on Crime and Justice*, Oxford: Oxford University Press.

Mawby, R. I. & Walklate, S. (1994) *Critical Victimology*, London: Sage.

McDermott, P. (1998) Contemporary Drug Taking Problems, in Robertson, R. (ed.) *Management of Drug Users in the Community: a practical handbook*, London: Arnold.

McKeganey, N.P., Bloor, M., Robertson, M. (2003) *What happens to drug users in Scotland eight months after they contact drug services?* Glasgow: Centre for Drug Misuse Research.

McLeod, I. (1999) *Legal Theory*, Macmillan: London.

McSweeney, T., Turnbull, P.J. & Hough, M. (2008) *Tackling Drug markets and Distribution Networks in the UK: a review of the recent literature*, London: UK Drugs Policy Commission.

Medina, C. G. (1991) *Bolivia y sus presidents*, Producciones Hepta: La Paz, Bolivia.

Michael, A. (1998) *Keynote Speech to the Social Policy/Criminal Justice: Compatible or in Conflict Conference*, Cardiff, May.

Midwinter, E. (1994) *The Development of Social Welfare in Britain*, Maidenhead: Open University Press.

Miller, I. (2001) Customs let cannabis smugglers walk free, *The Daily Mirror*, 31 May.

Ministerial Committee on Drug Policy (2007) *National Drug Policy 2007 to 2012*, Wellington: Ministry of Health.

Ministry of Health, Welfare and Sports (1995[F16]) *Drug Policy in the Netherlands: Continuity and Change*, The Hague: Netherlands.

Ministry of Health (1998) *National Drug Policy 1998–2003*, Wellington: Ministry of Health.

Ministry of Justice (2008) *Sentencing Statistics 2007*, London: Ministry of Justice.

MORI (1998) *Modern Britain* Survey, conducted for *Independent on Sunday*.

Morrison, S. (1997) The dynamics of future drug production: future sources and threats, *Crime, Law and Social Change*, 27, 121–38.

Mott, J. (1994) Notification and the Home Office, in Strang, J. & Gossop, M. (eds) *Heroin Addiction and Drug Policy: The British System*, Oxford: Oxford University Press.

Mott, J. & Bean, P. (1998) The Development of Drug Control in Britain, in Coomber, R. (ed.) *The Control of Drugs and Drug Users: Reason or Reaction?* Amsterdam: Harwood.

Mott, J. & Mirllees-Black, C. (1993) Self-Reported Drug Misuse In England And Wales: Main Findings From The 1992 British Crime Survey, in *Home Office Research And Statistics Department, Research Findings no 7*, London: Home Office.

Navarro, V. (1979) *Medicine under Capitalism*, London: Croom Helm.

Neale, J. (2006) Social Exclusion, Drugs and policy, in Hughes, R., Lart, R. & Higate, P., *Drugs: policy and politics*, Maidenhead: Open University Press.

Newburn, T. & Elliott, J. (1999) *Risk and Responses: Drug Prevention and Youth Justice*, London: DPAS Report 3 DPAS.

Nixon, R. (1971) Message to Congress, in *New York Times*, 15 July 1971.

Nutt, D. (2010) Mephadrone: classifying legal highs, *The Guardian*, 1 March.

Office of National Drug Control Policy (ONDCP) (1997) *Pulse Check: National trends in Drug Abuse*, Washington, DC: ONDCP.

Office of National Statistics (ONS) (2009)[F19] *United Kingdom Health Statistics 2009*, London: ONS.

O'Tuathail, G. (1996) *Critical Geopolitics*, Minneapolis, MN: University of Minnesota Press.

Pallister, D., Brodzinsky, S. & Bowcott, I. (2003) Secret aid poured into the Columbian drug war, *Guardian*, 9 July.

Parker, H. (2006) Keeping the lid on: policing drug related crime, *Criminal Justice Matters*, 63, Spring, 6–8.

Parker, H., Aldridge, J & Measham, F. (1998) *Illegal leisure: the normalization of adolescent recreational drug use*, London: Routledge.

Parker, H., Measham, F. & Aldridge, J. (1995) *Drugs Futures: Changing Patterns of Drug Use Amongst English Youth*, London: Institute for the Study of Drug Dependency.

Parker, H, Williams, L & Aldridge, J. (2002) The Normalization of 'sensible' recreational drug use: further evidence from the North West Longitudinal Study, *Sociology*, 36 (4), 213–33.

Parry, B. (2008) *Amazon*, London: Micheal Joseph.

Parssinen, T.M. (1983) *Secret Passions, Secret remedies: Narcotic Drugs in British Society 1820–1830*, Manchester: Manchester University Press.

Partridge, S. (1999) *Drug Misuse Declared results from the 1998 British Crime Survey*, London: Home Office.

Pearson, G. (1999) Drug Policy Dilemmas: Partnership, Social Exclusion, and Targeting Resources, in Marlow, A. & Pearson, G. (eds) *Young People, Drugs and Community Safety*, Lyme Regis: Russell House Publishing.

Peceny, M. & Durnan (2006) The FARC's best friend: US anti-drug policies and the deepening of Columbia's civil wars in the 1990s, in *Latin American Politics and Society*, 48 (2), 95–116.

Plymouth Evening Herald (2001) *100,000 reasons why we must rid Plymouth of drugs*, 23 July.

Pomeranz, K. & Topik, S. (2006) *World That Trade Created: Society, Culture, and the World Economy, 1400 to the Present*, New York: M.E. Sharpe.

Porter, R., & Teich, M. (eds) (1995) *Drugs and Narcotics in History*, Cambridge: Cambridge University Press.

Preston, A. (1992) *The Methadone Handbook*, Dorset: Andrew Preston in association with CADAS, West Dorset Mental Health Trust.

Quinney, R. (1970) *The Social Reality of Crime*, Boston: Little Brown.

Ramsay, M. & Percy, A. (1996) *Drug Misuse Declared: Results of the 1994 British Crime Survey*, London: Home Office.

Ramsay, M. & Spiller, J. (1997) *Drug Misuse Declared: Results of the 1996 British Crime Survey*, London: Home Office.

Rayner, G. (2010) Edlington attacks: Battle rages over 'Broken Britain', *The Daily Telegraph*, 22 January.

Read, A. (1995) Why Prescribe? The philosophy behind good practice, *Release*, 8, 1–3.

Reagan, R. (1982) Remarks on Signing Executive Order 12368, Concerning Federal Drug Abuse Policy Functions, 24 June.

Reiner, R. (2000) *The Politics of the Police* (3rd edition), Oxford: Oxford University Press.

——(2002) Media Made Criminality: The representations of crime in the mass media, in Maguire, M., Morgan, R. & Reiner, R. (eds.) *The Oxford Handbook of Criminology* (3rd edition), Oxford: Oxford University Press.

Renzetti, C.M. (2008) Forward, in Anderson, T. (ed.) *Neither villain nor victim: empowerment and agency among women substance abusers*, New Brunswick, NJ: Rutgers University Press.

Revolutionary Association of the Women of Afghanistan (RAWA) (2009) *RAWA: the voice of the voiceless*, Pasadena, CA: Afghan Women's Mission.

Richani, N. (2002) *Systems of violence: the political economy of war and peace*, New York: Columbia State University of New York Press.

Rimmer, S. (1997) Tackling Drugs Together: An Overview, in Braggins, J. (ed.) *Tackling Drugs Together: One Year On*, London: ISDD.

Robertson, I. (1975) Personal communication to Berridge, V. in Victorian Opium Eating: Response to opiate use in nineteenth century England, in *Victorian Studies*, Summer 1978, 437–61.

Robertson, R. (2000) New British guidelines on the clinical management of drug misuse and dependence, *Addiction*, 95 (3), 325–26.

Robins, L. (1973) *The Vietnam Drug User Returns*, Washington, DC: US Government Printing Office.

Robson, P. (1994) *Forbidden Drugs: understanding drugs and why people take them*, Oxford: Oxford University Press.

Rose, G. (1993) *Feminism and Geography: the limits of geographical Knowledge*, Oxford: Polity Press.

Runciman, B. (1999) *Drugs and the Law: Report Of The Independent Inquiry Into The Misuse Of Drugs Act 1971*, London: Police Foundation.

Sabel-Grande, I. (1997) Drug Policy in the Netherlands: continuity and change, in Braggins, J. (ed.) *Tackling Drugs Together: one year on*, London: ISTD.

Sage, C. (1991) The discourse on drugs in the Americas, *Bulletin of Latin America Research*, 10 (3), 325–32.

Sangster, D., Shiner, M., Sheikh, N. & Patel, K. (2002) *Delivering Drug Services to Black and Ethnic Minority Communities*, London: Home Office.

Scarborough, J. (1995) The opium poppy in Hellenic and Roman medicine, in Porter, R., and Teich, M. (eds) *Drugs and Narcotics in History*, Cambridge: Cambridge University Press.

Seddon, T., Ralphs, R. & Williams, L. (2008) Risk, Security and the Criminalization of British Drug Policy, *British Journal of Criminology*, 48 (6), 818–34.

Self, W. (1992) Drug dealer by appointment to HM Government, *The Observer*, 13 September.

Shapiro, H. (1999) Dances with Drugs, in South, N. (ed.) *Drugs: Culture, Controls and Everyday Life*, London: Sage.

Silverman, L.P. & Spurill, N.L. (1977) Urban Crime and the price of heroin, *Journal of Urban Economics*, 4, 80–103.

Silverman, K. & Wong, C.J. (2005) A web-based theraputic workplace for the treatment of drug addiction and chronic unemployment, *Behaviour modification*, 29 (2), 417–63.

Singleton, N., Murray, R. & Tinsley, L. (eds) [F22](2006) Measuring different aspects of problem drug use: methodological developments (2nd edition), Home Office online report, 16 June, www.homeoffice.gov.uk/rds/pdfs06/rdsolr1606.pdf (accessed 12 January 2009).

Smith, K. (2008) *Seizures of drugs in England and Wales*, London: Home Office, www.nta.nhs.uk [F24] (accessed 23 September 2009).

South, N. (1995) Innovation and Consolidation: New and Old Directions in Current Drug Control Policy, in Martin, C. (ed.) *Dealing with Drugs: A New Philosophy?* Report of a conference organised by the Institute for the Study and Treatment of Delinquency, 1 March, London: ISTD.

——(1997) Drugs: Use, Crime and Control, in Maguire, M., Morgan, R. & Reiner, R. (eds) *The Oxford Handbook of Criminology* (2nd edition), Oxford: Clarendon Press.

South, N. & Teeman, D. (1999) Young People, Drugs and Community Life: Messages from the Research, in Marlow, A. & Pearson, G. (eds) *Young People, Drugs and Community Safety*, Lyme Regis: Russell House Publishing.

Standing Conference on Drug Abuse (SCODA) (1998) *The Right Choice: Guidance on selecting drug education materials for schools*, London: SCODA.

Standing Conference on Drug Abuse (SCODA) (1999) *The Right Approach: Quality standards in drug education*, London: SCODA.

Stearn, P.N. (1975) *European Society in Upheaval: Social History Since 1750* (2nd edition), London: Macmillan.

Stimpson, G. (1987) The War on Heroin, in Dorn, N. & South, N. (eds) *A Land fit for Heroin: Drug Policies, Prevention and Practice*, London: Macmillan.

Strang, J. & Gossop, M. (1994) The 'British System': visionary anticipation or masterly inactivity? in Strang, J. & Gossop, M. (eds) *Heroin Addiction and Drug Policy: The British System*, Oxford: Oxford University Press.

Strang, J., Griffiths, P., Powis, B. & Gossop, M. (1994) [F25]First Use of Heroin: changes in the route of administration over time, *British Medical Journal*, 304, 1222–23.

Strang, J., Ruben, S., Farrell, M. & Gossop, M. (1994) Prescribing heroin and other injectable drugs, in Strang, J. & Gossop, M. (eds) *Heroin Addiction and Drug Policy: The British System*, Oxford: Oxford University Press.

Sutherland, E. & Cressey, D. (1970) *Principles of Criminology*, New York: Reynolds.

Sutton, S. & Maynard, A. (1993) Are drug policies based on "fake" statistics? Addiction, 88 (4), 455–58.

Taylor, A. (1993) *Women Drug users: An ethnography of a female injecting community*, Oxford: Oxford University Press.

Taylor, A.J.P. (1992) *English History 1914–1945*, Oxford: Oxford University Press.

Thane, P. (1996) *Foundations of the Welfare State*, London: Longman.

The Sun (2006) Kate: My lines for Pete, 22 September.

Thurlow, R. (1994) *The Secret State: British internal security in the Twentieth Century*, Oxford: Blackwell.

Tobias, G. (1972) *Victorian Life: The Changing nature of City Living*, London: Edward Arnold.

Toynbee, P. & Walker, D. (2001) *Did Things Get Better? An Audit of Labour's Successes and Failures*, Harmondsworth: Penguin.

Travis, A. (2001) Up in Smoke, *Guardian*, Society Section, 12 December.

Trebach, A. (1982) *The Heroin Solution*, New Haven, CT: Yale University Press.

Turk, A.T. (1969) *Criminality and Legal Order*, London: Rand McNally.

United Kingdom Drug Policy Commission (2008) *Supporting the supporters: families of drug misusers*, www.ukdpc.org.uk/reports.shtml[F26] (accessed 03 July 2010).

United Nations International Drug Control Programme (UNDCP) (1996) *Economic and Social Consequences of Illicit Drug Abuse and Trafficking*, Geneva: United Nations.

——(2001) *Global Illicit Drug Trends*, Geneva: United Nations.

United Nations Office on Drugs and Crime (UNODC) (2008a) Is poverty driving the Afghan opium boom? Discussion Paper, New York: UNODC.

——(2008b) *Coca cultivation in the Andean region: a survey of Bolivia Columbia and Peru*, Geneva: UN.

——(2009) *World Drug Report*, New York: UN.

van-Ree, E. (2002) Drugs, the democratic civilising process and the consumer society, *International Journal of Drug Policy,* 13, 349–53.

Wagstaff, A. (1989) Economic aspects of illicit drug markets and enforcement policies, *British Journal of Addiction*, 84, 1173–82.

Walker, W.O. (1991) *Opium and Foreign Policy: The Anglo-American Search for Order in Asia, 1912–1954*, London: Chapel Hill.

Wallace, G. & Eastham, G. (1994) *A survey of drug use and offending in Plymouth*, Plymouth: Harbour Centre.

Warner, K.E. (1993) Legalizing drugs: lessons from (and about) economics, in Bayer, R. & Oppenhiemer, G.M. (eds) *Confronting drugs policy: Illicit drugs in a free society*, Cambridge: Cambridge University Press.

Wasik, M., Gibbons, T. & Redmayne, M. (1999) *Criminal Justice: text and Materials*, London: Longman.

Wasserman, H. (2006) *Paul's Pot-Bust Shocker Makes Him A Jailhouse Rocker*, www.taima.org/en/hemplib3.htm#mccartney (accessed 14 November 2006).

Watson, J.E. (1984) *Medical–Surgical Nursing and Related Physiology*, London: Saunders.

Weatherburn, D. & Lind, B. (1997) The impact of law enforcement on a heroin market, *Addiction*, 92 (5), 557–69.

Weber, M. (1976) *The Protestant Ethic and the Spirit of Capitalism*, London: Allen and Unwin.

Weiss, J. (1981) Substance vs. symbol in administrative reform: the case of human services coordination, *Policy Analysis*, 7 (1), 21–45.

Weldes, J. (1999) *Constructing National Interests: The United States and the Cuban Missile Crisis*, Minneapolis, MN: University of Minnesota Press.

Welsh Drug and Alcohol Unit (1998) *A Strategic Prevention Action Plan for Drugs and Alcohol in Wales*, Cardiff: Welsh Office.

Westermeyer, R.W. (1998) *Reducing Harm: A Very Good Idea*, www.cts.com/crash/habsmrt/harm.html (accessed 17 December 1998).

Whetten, D.A. (1981) Interorganisational relations: a review of the field, *Journal of Higher Education*, 52 (1), 1–28.

Whitaker, A. & McLeod, J. (1998) Care in the Community, in Robertson, R. (ed.) *Management of Drug Users in the Community: a practical handbook*, London: Arnold.

Wilde, O. (1986) *The Portrait of Dorian Gray*, London: Marshall Cavendish.

Wilkins, C., Griffiths, R. & Sweetsur, P. (2009) *Recent trends in Illegal Drug Use in New Zealand, 2006–2008: findings from the 2006, 2007 and 2008 Illicit Drug Monitoring System (IDMS)*, Auckland: Massey University CSHORE.

Williams, S. & Milani, C. (1999) The Globalization of the drug trade, *Sources (111)*, Paris: UNESCO.

Young, J. (1971) *The Drug Takers: The social meaning of drug use*, London: Paladin.

Index